Pathology of the Elites

PATHOLOGY OF THE ELITES

How the Arrogant Classes
Plan to Run Your Life

MICHAEL KNOX BERAN

Ivan R. Dee
CHICAGO 2010

www.ivanrdee.com

Most of the contents of this book appeared originally in *City Journal*,
published by the Manhattan Institute, and in the *National Review*.

Library of Congress Cataloging-in-Publication Data:
Beran, Michael Knox.
  Pathology of the elites : how the arrogant classes plan to run your life /
Michael Knox Beran.
     p. cm.
  Includes bibliographical references and index.
  ISBN 978-1-56663-874-6 (cloth : alk. paper)
  1. Elite (Social sciences)—United States. 2. Liberalism—United States.
3. United States—Social conditions—21st century. 4. United States—Politics
and government—21st century. I. Title.
  HN90.E4B47 2010
  320.510973—dc22   2010015699

To Mary

O, what a world of profit and delight,
Of power, of honour, of omnipotence . . .

—Marlowe, *The Tragical History of Doctor Faustus*

Contents

Preface

*I*n 1950 Lionel Trilling, the Columbia teacher and critic, published *The Liberal Imagination.* The book, though it made Trilling a liberal saint, is very far from being a celebration of modern liberalism. It is a criticism of modern liberalism's dependence on what might be called the social imagination—the imagination that seeks not merely to understand society but even to save it. "Some paradox of our nature leads us," Trilling wrote, "when once we have made our fellow men the objects of our enlightened interest, to go on to make them objects of our pity, then of our wisdom, ultimately of our coercion. It is to prevent this corruption, the most ironic and tragic that man knows, that we stand in need of the moral realism which is the product of the free play of the moral imagination."

This book is a study of how easily an enlightened pity can be made to serve the ends of an enlightened coercion. It is a study of the evil to which Trilling drew attention when he pointed to the "dangers which lie in our most generous wishes." This is an evil of which we are, too often, very little conscious, for it is characteristic of the modern mind, Trilling said, that when it covets power it cannot admit that it covets power. It is animated by a will that "masks itself in virtue, making itself appear harmless." This is the modern will, which "hates itself and finds its manifestations guilty and is able to exist only if it operates in the name of virtue."

The guilty "will" Trilling described is apt to cover itself, he believed, in a philosophy of social altruism. This philosophy is now the preferred costume of power—the mantle of benevolence that conceals the imagination of dominion. The "ultimate threat to human freedom," Trilling wrote in a sympathetic account of the thought of George Orwell, might well come from a "massive development of the social idealism of our democratic culture."*

This social idealism is the more effective a disguise precisely because it demands, of its practitioners, a show of virtue: it enjoins a spirit of sacrifice, even of self-denial, which is meant to be an evidence of its purity. Thus Felix Djerjinski, who was to direct Lenin's Cheka, took it upon himself, when he was a prisoner under the tsarist regime, to clean the prison latrines. I know very well how limited, in the nineteenth century, was the share of power actually obtained by those who embraced the social imagination. But in

---

*John Stuart Mill foresaw the same possibility. "Almost all the projects of the social reformers in these days," he wrote in 1855, "are really *liberticide*—Comte particularly so." Comte, he said, sought with his "social system" to establish "a despotism of society over the individual, surpassing anything contemplated in the political ideal of the most rigid disciplinarian among the ancient philosophers." There was, Mill believed, a place for the social expert; but Comte "exaggerated this line of thought into a practical system," and "lived to carry out these doctrines to their extremest consequences, by planning, in his last work, *Système de Politique Positive*, the completest system of spiritual and temporal despotism which ever yet emanated from a human brain, unless possibly that of Ignatius Loyola: a system by which the yoke of general opinion, wielded by an organized body of spiritual teachers and rulers, would be made supreme over every action, and as far as is in human possibility, every thought, of every member of the community, as well as in the things which regard only himself, as in those which concern the interests of others." Comte's work "leaves an irresistible conviction that any beliefs concurred in by the community generally, may be brought to bear upon the whole conduct and lives of its individual members, with an energy and potency truly alarming to think of. The book stands as a monumental warning to thinkers on society and politics, of what happens when once men lose sight in their speculations, of the value of Liberty and Individuality." It should be noted that Mill was at other times sympathetic to Comte.

the twentieth century fidelity to the social imagination has been one of the surest passports to authority. The social mandarins, Trilling observed, sit in the cabinet now; they are on their way to Downing Street. Yet so successful has their deception—their *self-deception*—been that they have only the slightest conception of the truth of their own motives. Even now, when they dominate the cultural heights, they are conscious only of a magnificent generosity of intention. This is the pathology of the elites.

Everyone, Trilling believed, wants power; and the concealment of this desire is certainly nothing new. Tiberius, Tacitus says, "valued himself more for his art of dissimulation, than for all his other talents." Yet if everyone wants power, not everyone has at his disposal the means with which at once to glory in such power as he obtains, and at the same time to suppose (even in the deepest privacy of his heart) that he is not glorying in that power at all—*he is doing good.* The social imagination—this is Trilling's point—is such a means.

Edmund Wilson once observed that the "sincere reactionaries" from Dr. Johnson to Dostoevsky are beset by a "vision of human sin." The radical, by contrast—the progressive reformer—is either "free from a sense of guilt" or has "evolved a psychological mechanism which enables him to turn moral judgments against himself into moral judgments against society." The social imagination supplies the reformer with such a psychological machinery. It is precisely because Dostoevsky's Grand Inquisitor has abjured an older faith and has developed a social imagination that he is able to wield power as masterfully as he does, and as cruelly. So at any rate Trilling's fellow New York intellectual, Hannah Arendt, believed. It is by no means certain that she put the case too strongly when she said that the social imagination might yet "reduce man as a whole, in all his activities, to the level of a conditioned and behaving animal."

＿＿

Balzac in his novels shows that all of us who live in the modern world must in some measure develop a social imagination. In *Le Père Goriot*, Rastignac, confronting for the first time the complexities of Paris, finds that he must develop new ways of seeing, thinking, and feeling if he is to make sense of the new world he has entered. "Passing through one initiation after another," Balzac says of Rastignac, "he gradually loses his greenness, and in the end he achieves some perception of how human beings are packed in strata, layer above layer, in the framework of society." He develops, in other words, a social imagination.

The question is one of degree. Trilling himself praised the social imagination; it had its place in our comprehension of "social actuality." The social imagination was for Trilling, as it was also for Balzac, a prism that both reveals and distorts. Within certain limits it is useful. Relied on too implicitly, it becomes a substitute for other, in some circumstances more valuable, ways of understanding the world. When you affix a social or social-scientific label to a person ("bourgeois," "anal-retentive," "extrovert") or classify him according to his social provenance ("working class," "Ivy League," "inner city," "WASP," "Jew"), you have, very often, the illusion that you have plucked out the heart of his mystery and know the essential thing about him. It is a dangerous conceit. As soon as you have reduced a person to a type, you have begun to forget that he is a human being. In his 1947 novel *The Middle of the Journey*, Trilling makes Gifford Maxim, a character modeled on his Columbia

schoolmate Whittaker Chambers, disparage the myopia of those
who have cultivated the social vision too intensely: "social causes,
environment, education—do you think they really make a differ-
ence between one human soul and another?"*

The difficulty in our time is that those who have cultivated
the social imagination most passionately have not limited themselves to the elucidation of social facts. They have judged moral
facts in the light of social theories; they have applied the devices of
the social imagination in domains that were once the province of
what Trilling (following Edmund Burke) called the moral imagination. In using the latest social technic to remodel the curriculum
of schools, to rewrite clauses of the Constitution, to refashion the
operation of charity, and to revise the history of liberty in order to
discredit her heroes, members of our modern power classes have
weakened practices and customs that have over the centuries been
nourished by the moral imagination, and that are very likely essential to its continued vitality. Not least, the social techniques have
given the coup de grâce to the oldest civic and communal tradition
of the West, that of the agora, which was at once a repository of

*In his essay "Art and Neurosis" in *The Liberal Imagination*, Trilling pointed to the
limitations of such social-scientific terms as "neurosis" and "neurotic" when they are
used to understand particular human beings. "In the case of Henry James," he writes,
"the reference to the neurosis of his personal life does indeed tell us something about the
latent intention of his work and thus about the reason for some large part of its interest
for us. But if genius and its sources are what we are dealing with, we must observe that
the reference to neurosis tells us nothing about James's passion, energy, and devotion,
nothing about his architectonic skill, nothing about the other themes that were important
to him and which are not connected with his unconscious concern with castration [the
supposed source of his neurotic qualities]. . . . Let us grant for the sake of argument that
the literary genius, as distinguished from other men, is the victim of a 'mutilation' and
that his fantasies are neurotic. It does not then follow as the inevitable next step that his
ability to express these fantasies and to impress us with them is neurotic, for that ability
is what we mean by his genius. Anyone might be as injured as Henry James was, and
even respond within himself to the injury as James is said to have done, and yet not have
his literary power."

practical moral know-how and the source of a pastoral care superior to that of the remedial bureaucracies of the social state. (See the essay "Revenge of the Castle People: Reflections on the Death of the Agora" in this volume.)

It is characteristic of the more ardent champions of the social imagination that they seek to dominate not merely the economy of a nation but its culture as well. Where they succeed in dominating the economy, the result is fewer material goods; where they succeed in dominating the culture, the result is fewer cultural goods. If, in our day, the social evangels have very often been defeated in the economic sphere, they have had more success in the sphere of culture, particularly in those departments of culture concerned with the grooming and nurturing of the young, and with the maintenance of the institutions of local civic life.

The result has been the culture struggle of the last few decades. The culture wars are not an expression of populist share-the-wealth envy, the desire of contemporary Jack Cades to plunder the better-off classes that the gutters might "run nothing but claret wine." Nor are they an expression of the resentment that stupid people sometimes feel toward the more intelligent or the more highly educated, the perversity that prompts the Yahoo, in Swift's book, to trample down the oats and grasses of the Houyhnhnm, who is his superior in wisdom and virtue. The current cultural battles are better understood as an expression of popular frustration with a dwindling supply of moral and cultural goods. The social state has banished a variety of these goods from places (such as public schools) where they once traded briskly. Education in the West has traditionally been the process by which grown-ups civilize the young by introducing them to their civilization's moral and cultural heritage. America's public schools have to a great extent abdicated this role; traditional methods of cultural initiation have been replaced by vapid forms of "social" study. Modern social education, the critic Paul Goodman observed, is founded on the belief that children are "human social animals" who must be "socialized" and "adjusted to the social group." This emphasis on the socialization of the young has led to the deposition of the moral and cultural elements in education. As a result, public schools grow ever more culturally vacuous and ever less capable of engaging what Trilling called the "deep places" of the imagination.

Ordinary people are apt to resent members of what might be called the elite classes,* not merely because they associate these classes with the development and imposition of the new social techniques but also because members of these classes are much less likely to suffer from the resulting cultural privations. This is particularly true where schools are concerned. Nowhere perhaps is the disparity between elite America and average America greater than in the matter of education. The elite classes avoid the cultural problem by sending their children to private elementary and secondary schools, where traditions of culture with their roots in the grammar and Latin schools of Europe are still to some extent carried on. In Manhattan, professors at Columbia and NYU do not usually send their children to public schools; they send them to Brearley or St. Bernard's or the Lycée Français. Wall Street bankers and Washington power brokers are more likely to send their children to schools like Sidwell Friends, or to Andover or St. Paul's, than to the local government-run institution. Ordinary

---

*No simple definition of the term "elite" is likely to prove satisfactory; one can say only that upbringing, education, income, and success in a particular profession play a part in its composition. T. S. Eliot, in *Notes Towards the Definition of Culture*, distinguishes between the concept of elites and that of classes: he describes elites as groups composed of "superior individuals" skilled in such things as government, administration, art, science, or philosophy. The pathologies I am concerned to isolate are more characteristic of some sections of our contemporary elite than others.

people can't afford to do that; they must either put up with the social curriculum or home-school their children.

The scarcity of cultural goods under a social regime reinforces the power of the mandarins who manage it. The social techniques have, I try to show in this book, less power to nurture well-rounded, self-reliant citizens than the older traditions they have superseded. A less self-reliant citizenry needs more assistance, and the need for more assistance justifies yet more state intervention. The social state grows apace, as does the power of the managers who have their fingers on the levers of the machine.* My object, in putting together these essays, is to draw attention to what is being lost as a result of the revolution.

---

*Overall government spending in the United States, which accounted for less than 7 percent of the gross domestic product in 1903, was estimated in 2009 to account for nearly 43 percent of GDP.

Pathology of the Elites

Elements That Are Wanted:
Lionel Trilling's Critique
of Vulgar Progressivism

"*H*e gave liberalism a good name," *Newsweek* said in a recent tribute to Lionel Trilling. Certainly it is true that in *The Liberal Imagination* Trilling consigned, or seemed to consign, American conservatism to the ash-pit of ideas. The conservative impulse in America, he wrote, expressed itself not "in ideas but only in action or in irritable mental gestures which seek to resemble ideas." But *The Liberal Imagination* was neither an indictment of conservatism nor a panegyric upon liberalism. In it Trilling attempted to show that the human mind is too complex, too various, too lively in its sense of "contingency and possibility" to prosper where it is subject to the organizing and directing impulses of even the most accomplished practitioners of social technique.

Trilling questioned the faith in social regulation that descends from the nineteenth-century social philosophers, the belief (expressed in the 1940s by a writer in the journal *Science*) that "if by employing the methods of science, men can come to understand and control the atom, there is a reasonable likelihood that they can in the same way learn and control human group behaviour." But his criticism of the social element in modern liberalism has never gotten the attention it deserves. Critics have dismissed the central argument of *The Liberal Imagination* as a relic of a particular moment in history, long since passed, when many American liberals were enchanted with Stalin and Soviet communism. "*The Liberal Imagination*," Louis Menand writes, is "a Cold War book." "In many ways," Morris Dickstein says, "the book is a belated obituary" for attitudes that were already defunct in mid-twentieth-century America. Trilling was flogging the "dead horse" of liberalism's romance with Stalin—a romance that had largely collapsed with the closing of the Iron Curtain in 1946, if not with the Nazi-Soviet nonaggression pact of 1939.

The easiest way to avoid taking a thinker seriously is to date him. Trilling was criticizing the influence of the Stalinist left on American liberalism; the Stalinist left is dead; ergo Trilling's book is an antique. But *The Liberal Imagination* was always something more than an attack on the assumptions and complacencies of the Stalinist left. It was also a prophetic meditation on the consequences of an overreliance on the social imagination, which was coming to usurp, Trilling believed, the kingdom of what he called the "moral imagination."

<hr>

The place to begin is the fourth essay in *The Liberal Imagination*, Trilling's reading of Henry James's 1886 novel *The Princess Casamassima*. In it Trilling fingers a line of nineteenth-century novels "defined as a group by the character and circumstance of their heroes . . . Stendhal's *The Red and the Black*, Balzac's *Père Goriot* and *Lost Illusions*, Dickens's *Great Expectations*, Flaubert's *Sentimental Education*." The typical hero of these novels is a character Trilling calls the "Young Man from the Provinces," the romantic adventurer who sets out to conquer the metropolis, to master Paris or London or New York.

The young man from the provinces is a creature of his age, one in which the West made the transition from community to society. In his 1887 book *Community and Society*, the German thinker Ferdinand Tönnies distinguished between community, a place in which people "remain essentially united in spite of all separating factors," and society, a place in which "they are essentially separated in spite of all uniting factors." The provincial towns in which Trilling's young heroes grow up are examples of community: they are small, and the people in them know one another. The metropolis the young men set out to conquer is an example of society: in the big city one knows very little of most of the people one encounters, and one is bound to be indifferent to most of them. In *Lost Illusions*, Balzac describes the shock Lucien de Rubempré experiences when he first encounters this indifference. In provincial Angoulême even those who despised him "took him for a human being." In Paris "he did not even exist for Madame d'Espard," a great hostess whom he sought to impress.

In his 1972 book *Sincerity and Authenticity*, Trilling said that the emergence of society required "something like a mutation in human nature." The young provincial who, like Rastignac in *Le Père Goriot*, confronts its complexities for the first time must develop new ways of seeing, thinking, and feeling. He must, that is, develop a social imagination.

~

The journey of the young man from the provinces absorbed Trilling precisely because it was his own. He conceived his own journey in Balzacian terms, and in his day the psychological distance between Queens, where he was born in 1905, and Manhattan, where he made his reputation, was almost certainly as great as that between Paris and a provincial center like Angoulême in Balzac's time. Trilling made the leap in 1921. The sixteen-year-old bridge-and-tunnel kid from Queens went to Columbia, where he gained a national reputation as a critic and intellectual. But he paid a price for his mastery, as Balzac's provincial *ingénu* invariably does. "I have one of the great reputations in the academic world," Trilling wrote in his journal in 1948. "This thought makes me retch."

Balzac says of his provincial heroes that they have the "lofty souls of poets." The ultimate object of the young man from the provinces, Trilling thought, is to be a "hero of civilization." But the young man's imagination is corrupted by the social sensibility he cultivates during his metropolitan ascent, and his career as a rule ends tragically. Continuously judging people in terms of their social attributes and social utility—the power they possess to advance his career in society—the young man either becomes estranged from the human heart or is destroyed in the effort to break free of the arts he has practiced in order to succeed. Balzac typically phrases the dénouement in moral terms: the young man has sold his soul. Lucien de Rubempré hangs himself in prison; Raphaël de Valentin perishes of the dark bargain he has made in the name of success. Rastignac, it is true, eventually becomes a peer of France and acquires an immense fortune; but morally he is a ruin, one of those cosmopolite debauchees "grown old in the knowledge of Parisian depravity, all clever in one or another way, equally corrupt, equally corrupting, all pledged to insatiable ambitions."

Trilling developed his critique of the limits of social perception in several of the essays in *The Liberal Imagination*. Liberals who studied social facts and pathologies were convinced that they could, through the "organization" and "rational direction of human life," solve social problems. Organization, Trilling said, led to "agencies and bureaus and technicians." These, he conceded, had their place in the liberal scheme, but they were at the same time responsible for the drift of liberalism "toward a denial of the emotions and the imagination."

As evidence of this coarsening of the liberal sensibility he pointed to liberal thinkers who, like the critic Vernon L. Parrington, had begun to classify not only people but works of art in the light of their creators' social attributes and their sense of "social responsibility." These thinkers, Trilling said, supposed that Henry James would have been a better novelist if his books had been "pleas for co-operatives, labor unions, better housing, and more equitable taxation." They disdained Hawthorne because he had little sympathy for social reformers "eager to pull down the old temples to make room for nobler." The deficiencies of liberal literary criticism might seem a comparatively trivial matter, but to Trilling they were of the greatest importance, for it is art, he believed, that enables a people to do justice to the complexity of "the sentiments and the imagination." It was therefore an ominous sign that liberals should have begun to turn away from that complexity in order to assert their social values.

The deeper problem, for Trilling, was that the social values were themselves dubious. Although he did not apply the term "social" to them, the ideals he attributed to the liberal "educated class" of his day were evidently products of the progressive social imagination. In his essay "The Function of the Little Magazine," the fifth essay in *The Liberal Imagination*, he summarized the liberal-social breviary: "a ready if mild suspiciousness of the profit motive, a belief in progress, science, social legislation, planning, and international cooperation, perhaps especially where Russia is in question." Trilling said that these ideals did "great credit" to those who held them. But his praise was the disingenuous mask of his aversion. There was "no connection between the political ideals of our educated class," he said, "and the deep places of the imagination." There was rather a "fatal separation." Trilling leaves the reader to draw the unstated conclusion. If the social vision has so little insight into the "deep places of the imagination," how can the social reformer pose as a savior of humanity?

꙳

Even where Trilling appears to honor the social imagination, he often expresses a subtle antipathy to it. Sociologists like David Riesman, he said, were able to tell him more about society than those writers who employed more traditional literary methods. Few novelists writing after World War II, Trilling wrote, "have added anything genuinely new to our knowledge of American life. But the sociologists have, and Mr. Riesman, writing with a sense of social actuality which Scott Fitzgerald might have envied, does literature a service by suggesting to the novelists that there are wonderfully arable social fields for them to till."

Riesman, however, was not a typical sociologist. He had been trained not in the social sciences but in the law, and his 1950 book *The Lonely Crowd* was the work of a sociologist in revolt against the social-scientific idea of man. Auguste Comte, the father of social science, deplored the "revolt of the individual against the species." Riesman deplored the submergence of the individual in the species. In *The Lonely Crowd* he lamented the rise of the "other-directed" man, the conformist who all too easily fitted his nature into a prefabricated social mold. Social reformers, it is true, were not themselves responsible for the mass of influences that combined to favor the progress of "other-direction" in the modern world, but neither were their techniques calculated to further individual initiative and the free development of human personality, or what Riesman called "inner-direction."

⌒

Trilling was unnerved not only by the shallowness of the social imagination but also by the moral corruption it fosters when it is conceived as an instrument of social progress. The young man from the provinces, as he figures in the novels of Balzac, puts the social imagination to a frankly cynical use: he uses it to rise into a higher social class and make his mark on the world. Balzac did not live to witness the further evolution of the social imagination—its conversion, during the course of the nineteenth century, into a gospel of social hope in which the higher social classes would be leveled in the name of social justice. It was this conversion, together with its attendant moral ambiguities, that drew Trilling to *The Princess Casamassima*.

Hyacinth Robinson, the hero of James's novel, is for Trilling another young man from the provinces: the "province from which he comes," Trilling writes, "is a city slum." James's hero is initially a social reformer, and in London he accepts a commission in a secret revolutionary cadre. But in Venice he has a change of heart. James traces the conversion he experiences in "a little *campo* opposite to a small old church." Hyacinth's eyes are opened to a range of feelings, values, and aspirations that lie outside the social imagination. James lays it on with a trowel: the polished Venetian stones; the cracked marble; the ancient fountain to which the Venetian girls, with their copper water jars, come to draw their water; the faded magenta divan on which Hyacinth reclines, smoking cigarettes and reading Leopardi as hot light streams through the chinks of the shutters.

Hyacinth experiences not death in Venice but rebirth. He finds himself nauseated by the social imagination, the "dry statistical and scientific air" which, even before he came to Venice, cost him an effort to breathe. He no longer cares for the "demoralizing" business of contriving "a fresh deal" for the "social pack." James chose his adjectives with care: the social imagination is for him "demoralizing" because it undermines the older traditions of moral and artistic culture, which he figuratively identifies with the Venetian *campo*, with its rich concentration of civilized forms. Hyacinth has awakened to the splendor of this inheritance. He has been led by his "imagination into quite another train"; has had a "revelation of the exquisite"; has tasted "the fruits of the creative spirit" of old Europe, which for both James and Trilling was closely related to its moral spirit. When Hyacinth returns to England he refuses to act on the commission that the social vanguard (the "People Higher Up," the elite of the social revolution) have given him. Originally "torn between his desire for social justice" and his fear lest the pursuit of it destroy "the civilization of Europe," Hyacinth turns his back on the "social forces" of the day.

This repudiation of the social ideal, Trilling observed, angered critics of the novel who had been schooled in a "vulgar and facile progressivism." Hyacinth's rejection of the social imagination was for these critics evidence of James's "impotence in matters sociological." But Trilling himself applauded James's resolution of the story.

The extravagance of Trilling's praise of *The Princess Casamassima* is revealing precisely because the novel is not really such a good one. Trilling himself concedes the implausibility of Hyacinth's career, which undercuts the Jamesian fantasy. It is evident that the critic has brought to his reading of the book a quantity of private passion sufficiently strong to compensate for its weaknesses. One source of this overreading was the politics of the 1940s. Trilling's essay is among other things a defense of his own repudiation of the social imagination of the Communist party. Just as James's Hyacinth turns against the social revolutionists of the 1880s, so Trilling and his wife, Diana, who were fellow travelers in the early 1930s, turned against the social revolutionists of their own time.

But it would be wrong to read Trilling's essay simply as an exercise in Cold War controversy. His larger point is that those who cultivate the "facile sociological" point of view are incapable of comprehending a character like Hyacinth. If, to reverse Shakespeare's formula, the study of society takes a "precious seeing" from the eye, such study, valuable though it is in the elucidation of social facts, undermines qualities of vision that do justice to human beings in all their arbitrariness, their idiosyncratic originality: just the part of them the social classifier, statistician, and reformer does not reach. The artist, by contrast, can do a more complete justice to human personality; and Trilling finds it telling that Hyacinth, a bookbinder by trade, has by the end of the novel "become aware of his desire no longer to bind books but to write them."

Hyacinth's decision to reject the social in favor of the artistic might seem merely whimsical, but it did not seem so to Trilling, who looked upon the artist as the explicator and defender of the "emotions and the imagination," and who maintained that in our time the "most effective agent of the moral imagination has been the novel." The social managers, by contrast, were consciously or unconsciously hostile to art. In an unfinished novel posthumously published in 2008 under the title *The Journey Abandoned,*

Trilling makes Harold Outram, whom he called the "socially aware" character in the book, argue that art is incompatible with social progress. Outram praises Soviet Russia, where the social imagination has been carried farthest:

> Sooner or later we will understand that Russia is our future and our hope. And Russia has produced not one single notable work of art. Oh, don't jump to what you think is the defense, don't tell me that time will produce masterpieces. . . . In nearly twenty years, out of those millions of people, not one young man has forced his way forward with his creative talent. . . . And the fact is that Russia is right. Literature—art—it was a phase of man's development and Russia is showing the way to the new phase. And you know as well as I do that the arts cannot survive. . . . Russia has perceived before any of us that the arts, about which we are so politically sentimental, are one of the great barriers in the way of human freedom and decency.

Those who, like Trilling's Outram, conceive progress as the equitable reorganization, by the state and a socially trained elite, of the interests of various social classes are virtually bound to regard art as an obstacle, for except in its more primitive forms (the ideological novel, for example), art is impatient of the type and alive to the pathos of the particular. "The lively sense of contingency and possibility," Trilling said, "and of those exceptions to the rule which may be the beginning of the end of the rule—this sense does not suit well with the impulse to organization."

If the social imagination knows only the law of the group and the reality of the type, art asserts the truth of the individual and the value of the exceptional. Yet under the influence of the social imagination, Trilling believed, art was losing its eccentric character. Liberal critics, he observed, preferred as a rule such a mediocre artist as Dreiser to one who, like James, did not traffic in the social commonplaces of the day. The liberal critics, Trilling wrote, were always putting James

> to the ultimate question: of what use, of what actual political use, are his gifts and their intention? Granted that James was devoted to an extraordinary moral perceptiveness, granted too that moral perceptiveness has something to do with politics and the social life, of what possible practical value in our world of impending disaster can James's work be? And James's style, his characters, his subjects, and even his own social origin and the manner of his personal life are adduced [by liberal critics] to show that his work cannot endure the question.

To James "no quarter" was "given by American criticism in its political and liberal aspect." But "in the same degree that liberal criticism is moved by political considerations to treat James with severity," it treated Dreiser

> with the most sympathetic indulgence. Dreiser's literary faults, it gives us to understand, are essentially social and political virtues. ... [W]hen Dreiser thinks stupidly, it is because he has the slow stubbornness of a peasant; when he writes badly, it is because he is impatient with the sterile literary gentility of the bourgeoisie. It is as if wit, and flexibility of mind, and perception, and knowl-edge were to be equated with aristocracy and political reaction, while dullness and stupidity must naturally suggest a virtuous democracy.

The apologists for the social dispensation, Trilling believed, had no room in their millennium for the "electric qualities of the mind," for the "superbness and arbitrariness which often marks great spirits." It was as though what James called the "richest and noblest" expressions of the soul represented a kind of social deviancy, an anomalousness retrograde and unforgivable.

~~

Nowhere was the poverty of the social reformer's conception of the mind more evident than in his shallow understanding of his own motives and desires. He had not cultivated those faculties of imagination without which, Trilling said, "the mind cannot work and *cannot properly conceive itself.*"

In *The Middle of the Journey*, Trilling has Gifford Maxim unmask the "hope of power" that has driven the prophets of "society and social justice and sociology" to promulgate their social ethos. Trilling found the same "hope of power" in Paul Muniment, the social guru-on-the-make whom James sketched in *The Princess Casamassima*, and in Muniment's fellow reformer, the princess herself. In Muniment, Trilling observed, "a genuine idealism coexists with a secret desire for personal power." He is the "idealist who takes license from his ideals for the unrestrained exercise of power."

Yet so slenderly do Muniment and the princess know themselves that they fail to recognize their own instinct to coerce; they suppose that because they are (in their own conceit) saviors of the people, their impulses are wholly pure. The princess, Trilling argues, "is the very embodiment of the modern will which masks itself in virtue, making itself appear harmless, the will that hates itself and finds its manifestations guilty and is able to exist only if it operates in the name of virtue."

It was not simply that liberalism, where it has come under the influence of the social imagination, strives for an unattainable perfection—makes "its alliances only when it thinks it catches the scent of Utopia in parties and government, the odor of sanctity in men." The visionary liberal, Trilling implied, has erected a Utopia in his own heart. In believing his motives to be pure, he aspires to something "more than human." It was this mantle of perfected virtue—one that conceals the imagination of gross dominion—that Trilling dreaded as a thing corrupt in itself and dangerous to others. When he attributed to George Orwell the belief that the "ultimate threat to human freedom" might well come from a "massive development of the social idealism of our democratic culture," he was speaking as much for himself as he was for Orwell.

⌁

Trilling himself was conscious of his own mixed motives. Two years after he questioned, in *The Liberal Imagination*, the social reformer's love of power, he continued to be enthralled by the vision of mastery, the drive to penetrate some facet of the vast social mystery and use the knowledge to make a mark on society. In the summer of 1952 Norman Podhoretz, whom Trilling thought the most brilliant of his Columbia students, visited him in Westport, Connecticut. Trilling startled the young man—so Podhoretz later recalled—"by asking what kind of power I was after." Podhoretz "piously replied that I had no interest in power at all." "Don't be silly," Trilling said, "everyone wants power."

In *Le Père Goriot*, Rastignac takes as his own the credo of Vautrin, the metropolitan Mephistopheles who has mastered the social *mystères* of Paris. "Vautrin is right," Rastignac exclaims, "success is virtue!" It is curious to find Trilling, in his relations with Podhoretz, playing the part of the Vautrin-like tempter, the facilitator of young ambition. Success is virtue. Or is it? When, more than a decade later, Podhoretz showed Trilling the manuscript of his book *Making It*, in which he described his own journey from provincial obscurity in Brooklyn to success in Manhattan, he found his mentor unsympathetic. Trilling urged Podhoretz either to soften the tone of the book or to abandon it altogether.

Was he questioning the desire for mastery, or was he merely pointing, from the point of view of prudence, to the consequences of confessing one's desire for it too openly? (Yet *Making It* is not a celebration of success, or at any rate is not an unqualified one: it is both a classic autobiographical study and a penetrating analysis of the taboos that hedge the subject of success in America.) Whatever his ultimate view of success, Trilling was conscious of the moral stakes, and with a remarkable humility he criticized the manner in which he himself played the game. In the preface to *The Journey Abandoned* he describes how Harold Outram, who is "brilliantly established in the world" through "some compromise with his best talents," is instrumental in the corruption of the brilliant young Vincent Hammell, the provincial naif in the tale. The older man is caught precisely, Trilling said, "by the boy's possibility of duplicating his career, thereby justifying his falsifications."

If there is an element of autobiography in Trilling's depiction of Outram, there is even more in his picture of Vincent Hammell. Trilling shows Hammell ritually placing three books—Flaubert's *Sentimental Education*, Balzac's *Père Goriot*, and Stendhal's *The Red and the Black*—on the chest of drawers in his room to remind him "of the several fates which might destroy a young man," particularly one who, like Hammell, has set out to conquer large worlds, to make his mark on society. Trilling left the novel unfinished; we do not know how Vincent's career would have ended. That Trilling took an equivocal view of his own achievement is suggested by the startling confession in *Sincerity and Authenticity,* which appeared three years before his death, in 1975, from pancreatic cancer. In it he implied that society had overmastered him and those like him, and had made them (in his words) "ashamed of our lives."

~

If Trilling's work has a place in the history of Cold War controversy, its importance extends beyond it. Its value lies in its insistence that the social imagination must always be subservient to the moral imagination. "It is probable," Trilling wrote in *The Liberal Imagination,* "that at this time we are about to make great changes in our social system. The world is ripe for such changes and if they are not made in the direction of greater social liberality, the direction forward, they will almost of necessity be made in the direction backward, of a terrible social niggardliness. We all know which of those directions we want. But it is not enough to want it, not even enough to work for it—we must want it and work for it with intelligence." The last words, "with intelligence," may be translated, roughly but accurately, from the Trilling vernacular as "in the light of the moral imagination."

David Hume once warned of the "grave philosophic Endeavour after Perfection" which strikes "at all the most endearing Sentiments of the Heart." He counseled against reforms that would depart "too far from the received Maxims of Conduct and Behaviour, by a refin'd Search after Happiness or Perfection." Trilling was himself skeptical of the endeavor after secular perfection characteristic of the social reformers of his day. He was not, however, unwilling to be guided by thinkers who defended "the received Maxims of Conduct and Behaviour." In "Elements That Are Wanted," an essay he published in *Partisan Review* in

1940, Trilling looked to T. S. Eliot for inspiration and quoted Matthew Arnold with approval. Criticism, Arnold said in an essay in *The National Review* in November 1864, "must be apt to study and praise elements that for the fulness of spiritual perfection are wanted, even though they belong to a power which in the practical sphere may be maleficent."* "The audacity of this proposal," Getrude Himmelfarb writes in her book *The Moral Imagination*,

> is hard to recapture now: first, the implication that there were elements that were wanted in his own intellectual circle; then, that these elements were wanted "for the fullness of spiritual perfection"; and finally, most provocatively, that these elements might be found in a thinker like Eliot, whose ideas could well be maleficent in the practical sphere. Yet it was precisely in the practical sphere—not as a poet but as a political thinker—that Trilling went on to commend Eliot to readers of *Partisan Review*.

Himmelfarb argues persuasively that Trilling wrote from the point of view of the moralist. Certainly it is in his capacity as a moralist that he speaks most powerfully to us today. He looked upon the moral imagination as a kind of personal inquisition, one in which a man's conscience is made to sit in judgment on itself. In doing so he showed that the moral imagination is something more than the contrivance of fantasy Edmund Burke took it to be, though an element of fantasy will of course always figure wherever the imaginative faculties are engaged.† If the moral imagination is

---

*Arnold reprinted the essay, "The Function of Criticism at the Present Time," in *Essays in Criticism* (London: Macmillan, 1865).

†In a famous passage in *Reflections on the Revolution in France*, Burke described the moral imagination as a drapery that concealed the naked passions of men:

> All the pleasing illusions which made power gentle and obedience liberal, which harmonized the different shades of life, and which, by bland assimilation, incorporated into politics the sentiments which beautify and soften private society,

a hatchery of illusion, it is also, Trilling believed, an instrument of *dis*illusion: it enables a person to penetrate the pious fictions of his egotism. Surely he was right to suppose that we need such a discipline of "moral realism." The only hope man has of becoming actually good, he seems to have thought, is to recognize that he is in some ways really and incorrigibly bad.

Art and literature were for Trilling essential adjuncts of the moral imagination because they helped the mind to strip away its pretenses and confront the vileness of its suppressed aspirations: the novel in particular, he believed, through its power of "involving" the reader "in the moral life," forced "him to put his own motives under examination." *Madame Bovary, A Room with a View, The Wings of the Dove*—each forced the reader to scrutinize his shibboleths. Yet schools are ever less faithful to the liberal humanist conviction that the close study of classic texts has a part to play in awakening the moral imagination. The social administrators who exert a large influence over the curriculum of public schools naturally look with complacency on the virtual abolition, in the classroom, of the older literary and artistic culture, which has long appeared to the social mandarinate to be an obstacle that stands in the way of the ambition to remake human personality along social lines.*

If the teacher has forsaken his role as a transmitter of moral culture, so too has the artist. The Greeks, the classical scholar Werner Jaeger wrote, "always felt that a poet was in the broadest

---

are to be dissolved by this new conquering empire of light and reason. All the decent drapery of life is to be rudely torn off. All the superadded ideas, furnished from the wardrobe of a moral imagination, which the heart owns and the understanding ratifies as necessary to cover the defects of our naked, shivering nature, and to raise it to dignity in our own estimation, are to be exploded as a ridiculous, absurd, and antiquated fashion.

*One of the earliest reformers, d'Alembert, expressed "the wish that all record whatever of past events could be blotted out."

and deepest sense the educator of his people. Homer was only the noblest example, as it were the classic instance, of that general conception. We should be wrong not to take it seriously, to limit our understanding of Greek poetry by substituting for that ideal the modern belief in art for art's sake. . . . In early Greek thought there was no separation between ethics and aesthetics." Artists in the past were not ashamed to be agents of the moral imagination, but those who possess a creative sensibility today are more likely to pride themselves on their estrangement from the moral life of their fellow men. They obtain their effects by deliberately and cynically, if often rather skillfully, shocking the sensibilities and repudiating the pieties of others.

The artist has become, indeed, an ally of social reformers who, jealous perhaps of a rival power, seek to diminish the role of art in the everyday life of the people. The social managers reward the artist just insofar as he produces art that is facile, oversimple, and negligible in its spiritual depth and moral comprehension. For years the National Endowment for the Arts perpetuated the Romantic stereotype of the artist as alienated freak, a jaded *déca-dent* whose highest aspiration is to provoke (in T. S. Eliot's phrase) "one more quiver and giggle of art debauch." As long as his art was virtually a parody of Max Nordau's thesis that the modern artist is a degenerate who feeds on his own degeneracy, the NEA was willing to keep him in funds; the bureaucrats had no interest in sponsoring art that revealed a deeper apprehension of what Trilling called the "variousness, possibility, complexity, and difficulty" of the human condition.

How far the outré artists of the present have forgotten the higher responsibilities of their calling is evident in Trilling's description of Henry James's sense of artistic vocation. Far from disdaining, or regarding with a sneering and cynical condescension, even the most morally wretched of his characters, James made them real precisely by loving them, even as he acknowledged their faults. His moral insight into his creations arose, Trilling said, not "from any analytical intelligence as we usually conceive it but from love." His "special moral quality," "his particular gift of human understanding," was for Trilling the "expression, not of intellect, nor even, as we sometimes now think, of will, but of love."

There is doubtless a certain naïveté in Trilling's belief that "the moral intelligence of art" can by itself do very much to mitigate the egotism of man's "conscious will." Matthew Arnold, the subject of Trilling's first book, believed that poetry is "the interpretress of the moral world." T. S. Eliot said that Arnold was apt to confuse "poetry and morals in the attempt to find a substitute for religious faith." In portraying the novel as the arbiter of the moral world, Trilling was carrying on the work of the moralizing Victorians— Arnold, Leslie Stephen, and George Eliot among them—who in their different ways sought a secular substitute for spiritual traditions which seemed to them to have lost not only their intrinsic plausibility but also much of their moral sanction. But in an age of electronic pleasures and literary degeneracy Trilling's faith in the moral efficacy of the novel may be simply too bookish, too remote from the way we live now, to be an adequate foundation for moral culture.

The weakness of Trilling's remedy has its origin in his own experience. In his essay on *The Princess Casamassima* Trilling observed that the young man from the provinces must abjure his native provincial tradition and find a new and more urbane one. In his own journey to the metropolis, Trilling found a substitute for forsaken provinciality in the tradition of the Victorian and Edwardian moralists: if, as he said, Stendhal's Julien Sorel is the spiritual son of Napoleon, he was himself the foster child of Arnold, James, and E. M. Forster, men to whom he was closer, in style and spirit, than he was to the liberals of his own generation.

Trilling derived much illumination from his foster fathers, but however great the moral light a purely intellectual and literary relation may give, such a communion will probably always be in some measure artificial if it is remote from living people and a living culture, one in which art cooperates with tradition to refine moral sensibility. Morals are intimately related to *mores*, to manners and customs, to the immemorial habits of decency inculcated by the traditions of particular communities. Trilling perceived the weakening of the moral sense that has taken place with the growth of the social imagination, that disintegrator of tradition; he saw that where the moral imagination is not regularly and habitually cultivated it becomes difficult even for the best-intentioned to resist the allure of a narrow and obtuse self-righteousness. He was wrong only in supposing that literature can be a sufficient hedge against the forces of disintegration he dreaded.

The Secret Heresies of Isaiah Berlin

*S*ir Isaiah (pronounced aye-ZYE-ah) Berlin, who died in 1997 at eighty-eight, was one of the last century's notable talkers. "One was startled from the beginning," Arthur Schlesinger said, "by the glittering rush of words and wit, the dazzling command of ideas, the graceful and unforced erudition, the penetrating assessments of personalities, the passion for music, the talent for merriment and, most remarkable of all, the generosity of spirit that led him to treat all of us as his intellectual equals. He had the exciting quality of *intensifying* life so that one perceived more and thought more and understood more."

Such exuberance opened doors. A refugee from the Russian Revolution, the eleven-year-old "Shaya" arrived in England, in February 1921, speaking scarcely a word of English. Eleven years later he was elected a fellow of All Souls College, Oxford, one of the choicer intellectual sanctuaries in the realm. He had, his biographer Michael Ignatieff writes, "been plucked from donnish obscurity and elected to what was then the most select club in English life, a college where Cabinet ministers, editors of *The Times* and the leading intellectual figures of his day mingled on equal terms." All Souls has long sought to promote scholarship by relieving its scholars of the burden of teaching; the college admits no undergraduates. Yet even after he was installed in this citadel of scholarly luxury, Berlin continued to be better known as a talker than as a writer and thinker. When, in 1957, he received his knighthood from the queen, a friend, contemplating the slenderness of his œuvre, said that it must have been bestowed in recognition of his services to conversation.

Margaret Thatcher used to chide Berlin for his idleness. "Whenever they met," Ignatieff wrote, "she would ask him what he was working on and when he replied not very much, she would shake her finger at him in mock reproach: 'You must work, Isaiah, you must work.' 'Yes, madam,' he would dutifully reply." Yet he was less of a dilettante than he seemed. When, in the 1970s, Oxford University Press began reissuing essays that Berlin had published over the years in sometimes obscure venues, it became clear that the man who always called himself a reluctant writer had managed, almost unwittingly, to shed light on the ways in which people come to devote themselves to a principle, an ideal, a moral vision of life, as well as to propound a theory that undermined the whole notion of living a life illuminated by the moral imagination. A puzzle, evidently—though not a purely academic one: Berlin's thinking had consequences beyond the cloisters of Oxford, not all of them benign.

Berlin's essay "Winston Churchill in 1940" is perhaps his best-known study of how a man cultivates a moral imagination. Berlin begins by painting the age of "bitter disillusion" that followed World War I, when Lytton Strachey, Bertrand Russell, and much of the rest of Bloomsbury set out to expose the hollowness, the "false splendours," of the moral ideals of the preceding generations. Churchill was himself an object of their ridicule. His rhetoric, the scoffers said, was "false" because it was "artificial," the product of an anachronistic view of the world, a series of risible clichés ("King and Country," the "Righteous Cause" of liberty), so much "tinsel and hollow pasteboard."

Berlin allowed that there might have been an element of self-deception in Churchill's "grand style," but it was, he believed, a "necessary illusion." Such an imagination as Churchill's, Berlin said, "fuses hitherto isolated beliefs, insights, mental habits, into strongly unified systems. These, if they are filled with sufficient energy and force of will—and, it may be added, fantasy, which is less frightened by the facts and creates ideal models in terms of which the facts are ordered in the mind—sometimes transform the outlook of an entire people and generation."

Churchill, in other words, had a highly developed moral imagination, the kind of imagination which, Gertrude Himmelfarb has written, "penetrates all aspects of life—mind, literature, politics, social affairs, and, of course, personal conduct." It was precisely this sort of imagination that enabled Churchill to perceive the evils of National Socialism much earlier than did most of his contemporaries, and to feel the implications of these evils so deeply. His imagination was, Berlin said, "heroic, highly coloured, sometimes over-simple and even naïve." But it was never false; it was always a "genuine vision," however much it differed from the less inspired perception of those around him. Berlin noted how Churchill, commenting on a 1940 Foreign Office draft, said that its ideas seemed to him "to err in trying to be too clever, to enter into refinements of policy unsuited to the tragic simplicity and grandeur of the times and the issues at stake." Churchill "created a heroic mood and turned the fortunes of the Battle of Britain," Berlin argued, "not by catching the mood of his surroundings . . . but by being

stubbornly impervious to it." He "idealised" his fellow citizens
"with such intensity that in the end they approached his ideal and
began to see themselves as he saw them."

"Winston Churchill in 1940" revealed Berlin's ability to enter
into the mind of another and understand the sources of its moral
and imaginative power. This faculty—his hero, the Neapolitan
sage Giambattista Vico, called it *fantasia*, a "depth of imaginative
insight that characterises gifted novelists"—was Berlin's greatest
strength. He brought the buried mental processes to life by means
of psychological insight, intellectual empathy, and literary skill.
His studies of Leo Tolstoy and Benjamin Disraeli, Moses Hess and
Chaim Weizmann, Boris Pasternak and Anna Akhmatova, are in
the tradition not of such twentieth-century psychologists as Lytton
Strachey, who sought to strip their subjects of their moral dignity,
but of the literary essayists of the nineteenth century. "Winston
Churchill in 1940" is closer to Macaulay's essays on the Pitts or
Mill's essay on Coleridge than it is to Strachey's *Eminent Victorians* or his *Queen Victoria*. Berlin, like Strachey, was a belated mandarin, and there is a touch of the baroque in the elaboration of his
prose, in the accumulation of his clauses. His style enabled him, as
he held his jewels up to the light, to capture the various glints and
flashes. This was the method of Strachey; but the effect of Berlin's
essays is quite different: it is to add to the moral luster of his subjects, not, as Strachey's writings so often do, to take away from it.

How disappointing then, beside these *moralia*, are Berlin's osten-
sibly more ambitious essays on liberty and pluralism. Take "Two
Concepts of Liberty," Berlin's 1958 inaugural lecture as Chichele
Professor of Social and Political Theory at Oxford. Many in the

audience inclined to a donnish Menshevism, and Berlin, who was not a Marxist himself, was wary. His lecture was not precisely the "ringing manifesto" for "individual freedom" that some have claimed it to be. He was searching—cautiously—for a way to prevent liberal purists in the tradition of "Jefferson, Burke, Paine, Mill" (he called this, with a touch of academic pomposity, the tradition of "negative" liberty) from coming to blows with advocates of what he called "positive" liberty.

With much huffing and puffing Berlin demonstrated that the advocate of "positive" liberty believes that human beings, if they are to achieve true freedom, must be liberated (by force if necessary) from the restraints of their lower selves. "Positive" liberty has appeared in many guises, but Berlin was most concerned with the variety that in the twentieth century piled up so many corpses, the social philosophy that descends from Hegel and Marx. He believed that it was folly for liberals, in their struggle with the proselytes of the "positive" liberty of the social imagination, to insist, as Churchill did in his struggle with National Socialism, that their own "negative" liberty was a "sacred, untouchable value." They must learn the virtues of accommodation. A "practical compromise," Berlin said, "has to be found."

In fact the "practical compromise"—the welfare state—had already been found, and Berlin endorsed it enthusiastically. He "applauded the way the postwar welfare state expanded the freedoms of the less well-off," Alan Ryan wrote. He "believed in the welfare state," Ignatieff says. In a 1955 essay on Franklin Roosevelt in the *Atlantic Monthly*, Berlin argued that FDR had "strengthened democracy everywhere" by demonstrating that it was possible to reconcile "social justice" with "individual liberty." When Friedrich Hayek raised doubts on this score in books like *The Road to Serfdom*, Berlin was dismissive. It was precisely in order to justify the new social regime, and at the same time to preserve "a measure of 'negative' liberty," that Berlin set forth, after much beating around various learned bushes, his theory of the "pluralism of values."

In George Orwell's *Animal Farm*, unscrupulous pigs are the agents of evil. In the pluralist mythology of Berlin, the hedgehog is the villain. Unlike the fox, who, the Greek poet Archilochus said, "knows many things," the hedgehog knows "one big thing." For Berlin, it is man's hedgehoglike pursuit of "one big thing"—a "good," a "value," a "Platonic ideal"—that is continually getting him into trouble. This contempt for the hedgehog Berlin expressed most memorably in the lecture "The Pursuit of the Ideal," which he delivered upon accepting the Agnelli Prize in 1988. Gathered in the Turin opera house (where the orchestra played selections from Beethoven and Tchaikovsky) were many notables; Fiat heir Giovanni Agnelli amused Berlin by saying that he would relieve the tedium of the proceedings by revolving in his mind images of the beautiful women he had known—an undertaking, he boasted, that might easily consume an hour. The lecture Berlin delivered, after the last strains of the *Emperor* concerto faded away, was at once his pluralist testament and his intellectual autobiography— the most candid of his essays, his account of how his own pursuit of the ideal led him to recognize that the unequivocal exaltation of *any* ideal is a form of "self-induced myopia."

"Happy are those," he proclaimed, "who live under a [hedge-hog-inspired] discipline which they accept without question, who freely obey the orders of leaders, spiritual or temporal, whose word is fully accepted as unbreakable law; or those who have, by their own methods, arrived at clear and unshakeable convictions about what to do and what to be that brook no possible doubt. I can only say that those who rest on such comfortable beds of dogma are victims of self-induced myopia, blinkers that may make for contentment, but not for understanding of what it is to be human."

⌁

Although Berlin's pluralist writings are not free from ambiguity, two things are reasonably clear. First, his approach to moral ideals and principles resembled Giovanni Agnelli's approach to women. In a universe abounding in attractive goods, one must glory in diversity and resist the singularity of the hedgehog, who attaches too much value to particular manifestations of beauty and virtue. Whether Platonist or Christian, socialist or liberal, the hedgehog has purchased peace of mind by surrendering to some (perhaps virtuous) lie.

Second, Berlin's pluralist universe is like a fable of Borges, a puzzle that admits of no solution; its goods form no harmonious pattern, no "perfect whole." They "clash" and cancel one another out. "Both liberty and equality are among the primary goals pursued by human beings through many centuries," he argued,

> but total liberty for the wolves is death to the lambs, total liberty of the powerful, the gifted, is not compatible with the rights to a decent existence of the weak and the less gifted. . . . Equality may demand the restraint of the liberty of those who wish to dominate; liberty—without some modicum of which there is no choice and therefore no possibility of remaining human as we understand the word—may have to be curtailed in order to make room for social welfare, to feed the hungry, to clothe the naked, to shelter the homeless, to leave room for the liberty of others, to allow justice or fairness to be exercised. . . . Some among the

Great Goods cannot live together. . . . We are doomed to choose, and every choice may entail an irreparable loss.

In the Berlinian mythology, the weak soul seeks refuge from the *Sturm und Drang* of colliding moralities: he attempts, like the hedgehog, to escape the danger by rolling himself into a ball. But he does this at the expense of his humanity, for "collisions of values are the essence of what we are," both collectively, as peoples and nations, and as individuals.

Berlin conceded that individuals and nations must sometimes follow the hedgehog: they must choose particular moral goods and reject others. No person or nation can encompass every good, and not all goods are compatible. The number of values one can embrace, Berlin said, "is finite—let us say 74, or perhaps 122, or 26, but finite, whatever it may be." We are "doomed to choose," and every choice is potentially tragic, because it entails a retreat from the humanity of doubt and because it may involve the renunciation of other, equally valuable but antithetical goods. In embracing the good of national security, for example, a nation may be forced to curtail personal liberty. An individual, "in order to create a masterpiece," Berlin wrote, may "lead a life which plunges his family into misery."

꞊

The weakness of Berlin's picture begins with the abstraction in which he presented the dilemma that chiefly perplexed him—the collision of liberty (the touchstone of the old-fashioned liberal imagination of the nineteenth century) and the ideals of the social imagination (the touchstone of the modern creed of social justice). This concrete historical crisis Berlin painted in a language shot through with metaphysical ambiguity. His portrait of man as a Chooser of Values is a philosopher's ghost much like Rousseau's Natural Man or the Economic Man of the classical economists. The Chooser of Values is helpless in the face of clashing ideals because he comes to his choices, as no actual human being ever does, morally naked. The actual human being brings to his choices a moral history, a pattern of impressions and experiences, of sentiments and ideals, that have been conditioned by customs and manners, by religion or vestiges of religious devotion, by the insights of poets and teachers and artists, by traditions that have endured precisely because they express a truth of human nature.* In working up his picture of the anxiety of the Chooser of Values in the face of competing ideals, Berlin lost sight of the fact that the actual human being comes to his choices furnished with what Edmund Burke called "the wardrobe of a moral imagination," one that, even in its dressed-down forms, makes some choices almost impossible and others all but inevitable.

Just as misleading is the paper dilemma Berlin conjures with his metaphysical oppositions between "total liberty" and "a decent existence," between submissive "sheep" and "those who wish to dominate." This is an odd way to describe the conflict between the socialist and (classical) liberal ideals that Berlin sought to compromise. His "total liberty for the wolves" is a contrived nightmare in which Bronze Age beasts sprung from the pages of Nietzsche have been converted to the laissez-faire tenets of the Manchester

---

*Coleridge, Mill wrote, "considered the long or extensive prevalence of any opinion as a presumption that it was not altogether a fallacy. . . . The long duration of a belief, he thought, is at least proof positive of an adaption in it to some portion or other of the human mind; and if, digging down to the root, we do not find, as is generally the case, some truth, we shall find some natural want or requirement of human nature which the doctrine in question is fitted to satisfy."

School. Odd, too, that Berlin should have made free-market liberalism the bloody, wolflike creed, when anyone who undertook to count the bodies would doubtless give that palm to the social-justice communitarians.

Yet however distorted his description of the alternatives the West confronts, it enabled Berlin to portray the value-pluralist welfare state as all that stands between reasonable, pluralistic foxes and fanatic, monomaniacal hedgehogs on both the right (who worship the idol of free enterprise) and the left (who worship the idol of the social state).*

This split-the-difference philosophy Berlin dressed up in language of tragedy, of "doom" and "irreparable loss." But the morbidity is manufactured and, moreover, false to Berlin's own essentially happy temperament. "I live much more on the surface than people suppose," he told Ignatieff. "My life is the opposite of my views. . . . I believe all choice is painful, not that choice is painful to me."

In his effort to make value-pluralism into something more than an *ad hoc* theory capable of meeting the demands of a particular historical moment (the twentieth-century collision of Marx and Madison) and of justifying a particular political settlement (the welfare state), Berlin attempted to endow it, too, with the prestige of universality. Individual liberty and social justice, he argued, are not the only irreconcilable ideals that force us to make tragic

*Joshua Cherniss finds fault with conservative critics of Berlin who fail to appreciate the amount of moral conviction that underlay his "critique of fanaticism." To counter their criticisms he gives the reader a Berlin who heroically resisted the rising tide of moral fanaticism in the West: "he recognized that it would be a hollow victory if, in fighting Communism, the Western democracies became as intolerant, dogmatic, and single-minded as their opponents." This seems to me an odd way of defending Berlin's historical significance, for the spirit of intolerance in the Western democracies at no time even remotely approached that of the Communist nations, where the reigning orthodoxies were enforced by the secret police and the threat of the Gulag.

choices. He pointed to the incompatible aspirations of different civilizations and their rival conceptions of human potential. If I would be Pericles, I cannot be St. Bernard. If I would be Rockefeller, I cannot be Rashi. In dwelling on these antagonistic ideals, Berlin only grudgingly conceded that they are in some measure factitious, and that "there is a great deal of broad agreement among people in different societies over long stretches of time about what is right and wrong, good and evil."*

⌒

The emotions underlying Berlin's picture of the Chooser of Values—the love of foxlike compromises, the horror of the hedgehog's unitary moral imagination—grew in part out of his own experience. As a Jew born in the Baltic, raised in England, and educated at Oxford, Berlin inhabited multiple and incongruous homes—comfortably, but with always a trace of unease. He felt himself fully a Jew and had no desire to belong to what he called the "Order of Trembling Amateur Gentiles," yet he was cut off from certain aspects of Jewish culture and was himself an amateur in the spiritual traditions of his people. His relations with his father, a timber merchant, were marked in later years by a strain of mutual incomprehension.

---

*There is, moreover, an inherent contradiction in Berlin's belief that pluralism, "with the measure of 'negative' liberty it entails," is a "truer and more humane ideal than the goals of those who seek in the great, disciplined, authoritarian structures the ideal of 'positive' [freedom]." For if, as Berlin maintains, pluralism is itself a moral ideal—the "ideal of freedom to choose ends without claiming eternal validity for them"—it must, under pluralist theory, take its place among a host of other, many of them antithetical ideals; its upholders cannot claim for it a special validity or apprehension of truth. Under Berlin's theory a pluralist society is a contradiction in terms: its very existence privileges one ideal—the pluralist one—over other, very different ideals, and so commits the sin of hedgehogism the true pluralist ought always to avoid. The defender of a pluralist society has no right, under pluralist theory, to deny the right of others to overturn the pluralist state; to do so would be to demonstrate the sort of certitude that good pluralists must always lament.

"As for the Jews," Berlin told Felix Frankfurter after a visit to Palestine in 1934, "they are most odd and fascinating, and I felt equally uneasy with them and away from them, like relations one hasn't seen for thirty years or something, to whom one knows one is, even feels, related, but whom one doesn't really know."

He was an Englishman, Sir Isaiah Berlin, O.M., Oxford don, pillar of the realm, at home in the Georgian splendor of Headington House, his Oxford residence, and in his rooms in London's Albany, where Byron and Macaulay once had digs; but however high he rose, he knew that, like Disraeli before him, he would always be an exotic in that Anglo-Saxon kingdom. Nor did he find the Christian traditions that were once central to British culture sympathetic. (Visiting a Shinto shrine, Berlin declared that he could worship "any god except the Christian God.") His life was an exercise in "incommensurable values."

Berlin hesitated to commit himself beyond his initial attachments to his family, to an abridged version of his hereditary tradition, to Oxford, and to England—bonds formed before he was twenty. For years he lived the celibate life of an old-fashioned don. He enjoyed vicarious glimpses into other people's lives—he was devoted to gossip and socialized, Columbia's Steven Marcus said, "to the point of addiction"—but for a long time he suffered no one to come too close. Eros he submitted to late, at forty-one, when, according to Ignatieff, he began "adult sexual life." Six years later he married. He developed an intense loyalty to Zionism and later to Israel, but he politely turned away when Chaim Weizmann urged him to make *aliyah* and thereby avoid the fate of Justice Frankfurter, who, Weizmann complained to Berlin, "sits there among those Gentiles, seven days a week. How can he? What is he doing?"

Yet it was not Berlin's wariness of attachment alone that led him to dwell so lugubriously on all that one loses in committing oneself to an ideal, and to pass rapidly over all that one gains. There is another reason why he made Keats's "negative capability" (a man's capacity to be "in uncertainties, mysteries, doubts," to feel there "is nothing stable in the world. . . . Uproar's your only music") the master principle of pluralism. Berlin had, as a boy living in St. Petersburg, watched a collision of ideals degenerate into bloodshed. He had seen a tsarist policeman, in the last paroxysm of fear, hurried toward his death, and he had been present when the Cheka raided his family home. Later, after he emigrated to England, he learned that his uncle had been tortured by Stalin's agents. The boy who had seen the Russian Revolution with his own eyes was all his life to worry that the smallest surrender of the humility of doubt, the slightest acquiescence in the arrogance of certitude, could put a man on the road to hedgehogism, which was for Berlin "almost always the road to inhumanity."*

---

*Although the hedgehog-inspired terror that Berlin encountered as a boy in Russia was inspired by a particular form of the social imagination, he maintained that any system of dogma and orthodoxy may foster in a man the self-righteousness that leads him consciously and deliberately to inflict on others intolerable pain. It is certainly true that, if Felix Djerjinski was a cruel man, so also were many of the Catholic inquisitors, as indeed were the Protestant spymasters of Elizabeth I. Yet a distinction might nevertheless be drawn. Unlike creeds that derive from the social imagination, the older and enduring moral and spiritual traditions of the West have highly developed protocols of self-examination. These are intended to make a person conscious of his own capacity for evil, and to oblige him to contemplate, as the saint in S. Y. Agnon's *The Bridal Canopy* does, his own contemptibleness: "When my host offers me a bed, I repeat the Hear O Israel and cover my face with shame. Lord of the Universe, how many men are there in the world whose very fingernails are worth more than all my body, and yet they're left without food or lodging or couch, while I lie abed on pillows and cushions." Such a discipline of humility cannot, of course, wholly prevent offenses, which "must needs come." Still, these protocols, so intimately connected with the traditions of the moral imagination of the West, are superior to such safeguards as the social imagination has evolved. It is curious that Berlin himself, who in spite of his gifts was not in the least an arrogant man— was in many ways an endearingly modest one—could never bring himself to believe that those moral traditions which inculcate such modesty and humility are more valuable, and more deserving of our approbation, than those which excite only pride, or the condescending pity which is indistinguishable from the love of power.

The world has changed since Berlin, taking up his Oxford professorship, declared that value-pluralism might yet save humanity from its "craving" for the "certainties of childhood" and the "absolute values" of the "primitive past." But for many progressives it is still 1958 and value-pluralism a useful means of curbing "negative" liberty. Berlin's theory, devised in the Sputnik era to justify a welfare state that has since been partially dismantled in the United States, has become entrenched in modern liberalism and has weakened society's defenses against the very kinds of moral and political tragedy Berlin himself dreaded.

The most obvious casualty of contemporary value-pluralism is the pluralism it superseded, the pluralism of John Locke and James Madison. The older pluralism was in part procedural; it emerged in the aftermath of the Reformation, when the West puzzled over how to keep people of different religions from killing one another. Locke's answer was to tolerate different religious beliefs, a then-novel idea enshrined in the Toleration Act, a pillar of the Whig settlement worked out after England's Glorious Revolution in 1688. During the drafting and ratification of the American Constitution a century later, James Madison elaborated a more sophisticated theory of pluralism. A nation's interests and factions could be made, by an ingenious constitutional machinery, to check and balance one another. Edmund Burke and Alexis de Tocqueville, studying France's revolution, saw another justification for pluralism. The various groups—the little platoons—that make up civil society act collectively as a salutary check on the power of an aggrandizing government and are for that reason a valuable element in the state.

Old-fashioned pluralists sought to protect dissenters, minorities, and unpopular points of view. They never attempted to discredit the traditional moral ideals of the majority. On the contrary, they believed that these had a part to play in the maintenance of a free society. "Paradoxical as it may appear," Hayek wrote in defense of the older pluralism, "it is probably true that a successful free society will always in a large measure be a tradition-bound society." By contrast, modern value-pluralism has prompted the state to accord second-class status to traditional and popular forms of moral belief as part of its effort to promote the value-pluralist ideal of diversity. In the 1970s and 1980s the Supreme Court began invoking a version of value-pluralism in deciding cases having to do with religious freedom, freedom of speech, and "alternative lifestyles." Under the new standard, the values of minority groups that embody an *épater les bourgeois* spirit must be not simply tolerated but accorded a privileged status, for such contrarian opinions counteract the influence of the dominant hedgehogs. By the same token, a moral system that commands the *assent* of a large body of citizens is under the new pluralist standard suspect; however tolerant it appears, such a creed may lead to tyranny.

The double standard is apparent in the 1996 *Romer* v. *Evans* case, in which the Court struck down an amendment to Colorado's constitution that prohibited the creation of special rights (beyond those which all citizens enjoy) for homosexuals. In his dissent in *Romer*, Justice Scalia argued that the Court, forsaking its role as neutral umpire in a pluralist society, had chosen "to take sides" in a "culture war" and impose upon the nation values "favored by the elite class from which the Members of this institution [the Court itself] are selected." The old standard of "equal protection of the laws" was being superseded, Scalia maintained, by a "novel and extravagant constitutional doctrine" of "*preferential* treatment under the laws" for views at odds with "traditional American values."

Under the new pluralist standard it is lawful to burn an American flag on the town hall steps, for flag burning is respectable in the eyes only of a small number of citizens, while it is unlawful for a local school board to reserve a moment for silent prayer in a public school. School prayer does not, even remotely, amount to a constitutionally prohibited "establishment" of religion,* but it stands for a sentiment embraced by a majority of Americans and is for that reason, under a value-pluralist analysis, a potential threat to the republic. Value-pluralism, as applied by the courts, has ceased to be a machinery of impartial arbitration and has become what Berlin never intended it to be: a dogmatic, discriminating creed in its own right, one that reflexively delegitimates beliefs that have shaped the moral imagination of the West. We may, as Justice Sandra Day O'Connor has stated, "live in a pluralistic society," but for the value-pluralist, some values are more equal than others.

～

The effect of value-pluralism on the welfare state has been perhaps even more demoralizing than its effect on the courts. Berlin believed that the welfare state was the one system capable of mediating between the incompatible ideals of individual liberty and social justice. His hope lay in the welfare state's bureaucratic blandness. Welfare-state liberals traced their inspiration to the technocratic reformers of the early twentieth century who were convinced that the progress of society depended on the administrative élan of a "specialized class" (the young Walter Lippmann's phrase) of experts and social engineers armed with the insights

---

*Yale Law School's Stephen L. Carter has argued, in *The Culture of Disbelief*, that "ordained moments of silence to begin the school day probably do not violate the Establishment Clause."

of social science and clinical psychology. Berlin, with his humanist inclinations, could not personally have found this technocratic
utopianism appealing; but as he aged he came to insist on the virtues of blandness. The very dullness of the welfare state's credo,
he seems to have thought, was a recommendation. The stolidity of
the bureaucracy would forestall the impulse to extremism or revolution, whether on the left or the right.

If the welfare state was useful to value-pluralism, value-pluralism was as useful to the welfare state. In the 1940s and 1950s the
faith in scientific planning that had originally inspired welfare-
state liberals began to fade. In *The End of Reform*, Alan Brinkley
observed that during the last years of FDR's presidency many
New Dealers became disenchanted with the "statist planning"
that had once been their hope. In the postwar years it became
evident that the rule of the experts had produced not Herbert
Croly's New Republic or Graham Wallas's Great Society but
the spiritual poverty of the welfare office, with its whiff of Lysol
and futility. Value-pluralism supplied welfare-state liberals with a
fresh justification for what remained of their progressive dream—
their antipathy to the middle-class conventions that stifle, to the
Pleistocene morality that prevailed before the advent of the social
worker, the guidance counselor, and the clinical psychologist. In
the 1960s value-pluralist liberals began to use welfare-state programs to cut the tie between mainstream behavioral norms (such
as hard work and self-discipline) and the material rewards of a
good life; the elite "Haves," Myron Magnet has argued, sought to
liberate the "Have-Nots" from the traditional restraints of morality and seemly conduct. When, in the 1980s, Margaret Thatcher
advocated a moral counterrevolution—a return to "Victorian virtues"—value-pluralists committed to a morally neutral welfare
state denounced her.

Corrosive, too, has been the influence of value-pluralism in schools. One of the fruits of Berlin's philosophy is multicultural-ism, whose defenders have used the Berlinian notion of a universe of "incommensurable values" to extirpate the weed of "Eurocen-tric" or "dead white male" civilization. For the multiculturalist, all values are equal except those of the West. This is a radical-chic version of the Oxford skepticism that underlay Berlin's own value-pluralism ("nothing new or true,—and no matter," as Emerson characterized it). Although Berlin was wary of the multicultural movement, its apologists justifiably regard him as a patron saint: they are faithful to the central aspiration of the value-pluralist phi-losophy, a world in which no principle is taken too seriously. Ber-lin always maintained that value-pluralism "is not relativism." But his multicultural heirs might be forgiven for supposing that one of his objects was to make it harder for people to say that some ideals are true and others false, some good and others evil.

Toward the end of "The Pursuit of the Ideal," Berlin apologized for the absence, in his philosophy, of a visionary gleam—a flash of poetry, of intellectual splendor, the very qualities he associated with the moral imaginations of Churchill and Disraeli. Value-pluralism was, he conceded, a "little dull as a solution," a "very flat answer, not the kind of thing that the idealistic young would wish, if need be, to fight and suffer for, in the cause of a new and nobler society."

To be sure, the great difficulty with pluralism, in both its old (Madisonian) and new (Berlinian) incarnations, is that it offers the heart so little. The old pluralism is pragmatic, procedural, a machinery for impartial arbitration. The new value-pluralism is

avowedly hostile to the old inspirational traditions. Both plural-
isms appeal rather more to reason than to the imagination; they
share what John Stuart Mill and Lionel Trilling diagnosed as liberalism's greatest weakness: its tendency to "envisage the world"
in a "prosaic" way.

Value-pluralism—praised by its present-day apologists, in
their curious jargon, as a theory that fosters a "zone within which
individuals will freely associate to pursue shared purposes and
express distinctive identities, creating a dense network of human
connections called civil society"—is undoubtedly a formula for the
pasteurization of the human spirit. Berlin himself seems at times to
have found it a great bore; he never bothered even to paper over the
overt ambiguities, to endow the thing with a merely verbal coherence, or to make it the subject of the Big Book that he was expected
to write but never did. Like the aficionado, the passionate amateur
who puts more zeal into his hobby than his day job, Berlin devoted
many hours to the investigation of philosophies that possessed all
the inspiring qualities value-pluralism did not. In his book *The
Magus of the North* he described the German mystic Johann Georg
Hamann's critique of the French Enlightenment in terms reminis-
cent of Lionel Trilling's critique of the social imagination of modern liberalism. Hamann, Berlin wrote, despised the ideals of such
enlightened reformers as Helvétius: they did "not delve into the
depths and splendours of the ravaged human soul. . . . In a world
built by Helvétius there would be no colour, no novelty, no thun-
der or lightning, no agony or transfiguration."

Berlin's best work concerns the insights into the human condition of thinkers who would have scorned the ideals of value-
pluralism and the social imagination; he wrote little on liberal-social
minds (as distinct from liberal-social theories): there is an essay on
Mill, a piece of puffery about FDR, a eulogy of Felix Frankfurter, not

much more. The social imagination of modern liberalism seems not to have interested him very much.

Yet the Catholic reactionary Joseph de Maistre captivated him. Maistre occupies a special place in Berlin's imagination, akin to that which Samuel Taylor Coleridge filled in the thought of John Stuart Mill. Although he recoiled from Coleridge's conclusions, Mill profited from his encounter with a philosopher who "saw so much farther into the complexities of the human intellect and human feelings" than social utilitarians like Jeremy Bentham. Berlin similarly drew back from Maistre's "violent" mind, but he found him "bolder, more interesting, more original" than any political thinker of his age, including Burke. Maistre, in Berlin's account, is "penetrating and remarkably modern," "vigorous, brilliant, original and amusing," a "ferocious critic," "icy, smooth, clear." His thought is "dry light against the flickering flame," conveyed in language that rises to "classical dignity and beauty." His insights are "passionate but lucid," "bold and penetrating," "exceedingly pungent," "unique" in their "grasp," similar to but "far more powerful" than Burke's. Beside Maistre, Rousseau and Hugo are "turbid" and "gushing," Flaubert "an imperfectly drained marsh."

Maistre's genius, for Berlin, "consists in the depth and accuracy of his insight into the darker, less regarded, but decisive factors in social and political behaviour." Maistre was "an original thinker, swimming against the current of his time, determined to explode the most sacrosanct platitudes and pious formulas of his liberal contemporaries." Maistre conducted his attack on the philosophy of enlightened pity "with much exaggeration and perverse delight," yet also "with some truth," for the Savoyard thinker perceived, as the reformers did not, "the persistence and extent of irrational instinct, the power of faith, the force of blind tradition." Maistre showed "the willful ignorance about their human material of the progressives—the idealistic social scientists, the bold political and economic planners, the passionate believers in technocracy." Maistre understood, as the progressives did not, "the impalpable strands which hold societies together and give them their strength." He knew, as they did not, that "societies have a general soul, a true moral unity, by which they are shaped" and that a government, if it is to retain its hold on its citizens, must have "its dogmas, its mysteries, its priests."

Maistre appealed to Berlin precisely because he delved, as the modern social reformer does not, into the "unexplained and unexplainable depths." He felt, as they did not feel, the "dark unanalysable . . . poetry of the world." He fathomed, as the seekers of the social millennium never could, man's infinite capacity for self-destruction, apparent at once in his desire to exalt and to abase himself, to suffer, to prostrate himself before a superior power. For all Maistre's "paradoxes" and "descents into sheer counter-revolutionary absurdity," he was able, Berlin contended, to look unflinchingly at what "humane and optimistic persons tend not to want to see," and for this reason he was often "a better guide to human conduct" than the starry-eyed reformers: "at any rate [he] can provide a sharp, by no means useless, antidote to their often over-simple, superficial and, more than once, disastrous remedies."

Particularly valuable, Berlin believed, were Maistre's insights into the moral vocabulary of civilizations, the "accumulated wealth of meaning" with which the "mere passage of time enriches an old language, endowing it with all the fine, mysterious properties of an ancient, enduring institution." For Maistre, "thought is language," and language "enshrines the oldest historical memories of a people or a church." Maistre understood that the literature of a civilization contains an inheritance of knowledge deeper than the reach of mere philosophy, particularly Enlightenment philosophy. "Since words are the repository of the thought and feeling and view of themselves and of the external world of our ancestors, they embody also their conscious and unconscious wisdom, derived from God to form experience," Berlin wrote in his précis of Maistre. "Hence ancient and traditional texts, especially those contained in sacred books which express the immemorial wisdom of the race, modified and enriched by the impact of events, are so many valuable quarries whence expert knowledge, zeal and patience may extract much hidden gold." To cast aside this moral poetry was, for Maistre, "suicidal lunacy." Yet this is precisely what reformers were continually doing. The reformer "annihilates" the "virtue" of the old texts and "dehydrates them of their significance," leaving what is "profound and fertile" in them to evaporate.[*]

If Berlin found much truth in Maistre's critique of liberalism, he was careful to keep the Savoyard at arm's length. It was almost as though he could not bring himself to admit the effect Maistre produced on him. Instead he attempted, in a perfunctory and unconvincing way, to connect the "dark" philosopher to "the paranoiac world of modern Fascism." But Maistre's insights into history, suffering, and "the expiation of sin" find few echoes in the rhetoric of totalitarianism. The Maistre Berlin gives us—"consumed by the sense of original sin," fearful lest men, in their "self-destructive stupidity," fall yet again into "the bottomless abyss of anarchy and the destruction of all values"—is less an embryo Nazi than a prophet warning against those weaknesses in human nature

---

*Berlin affected to find in Maistre's literary conservatism a foreshadowing of modern totalitarian rule, and he drew a connection between Maistre's thought and the Newspeak imposed by the elite in George Orwell's *1984*. It seems to me, however, that Big Brother was doing just what Maistre counseled *against*: the totalitarian rulers in *1984* sought to abolish the old language, with all its precious deposits of civilization, and to replace it with a new, shallow, and brutal language devised by the state.

that make a regime like Hitler's possible. Nor did Berlin explain why this staunchly Catholic philosopher and ultramontane champion of the pope—a man who felt himself to be "the last defender of a civilization that was perishing"—ought to be considered the begetter of Goebbels and Mussolini. Berlin's hastily sketched contention that "modern totalitarian systems . . . combine the outlooks of Voltaire and Maistre" rings hollow; it is his tribute to Maistre's profundity that rings true.

—

Berlin portrayed himself as a value-pluralist, yet his essays on value-pluralism—"Two Concepts of Liberty," "Political Ideas in the Twentieth Century," "Does Political Theory Still Exist?"—contain what is surely his weakest writing. They are shapeless monsters filled with labored sentences and tortuous digressions. His essays on romantic conservatives, by contrast, are alive with the exuberance of discovery. This chasm at the heart of his work—the divide between decent (but uninspiring) value-pluralism and exhilarating (but dangerous) moral idealism—he seems not consciously to have perceived; certainly he never pretended to have bridged it.

But there are clues. In his essay on Mill, Berlin described how that divided philosopher rebelled against liberal utilitarianism—the Mill family business—to pursue a deeper culture of the mind. Mill's "unceasing revolt against his father's outlook and ideals," Berlin wrote, was the "greater for being subterranean and unacknowledged." The same can be said of Berlin's own subterranean revolt against what is unintelligent in the social imagination of so many modern reformers. In his work on romantic anti-reformers Berlin wrote sympathetically of all that is lacking in the social imagination: an awareness of the evil that is found even in the

well-intentioned heart, an acknowledgment of the moral significance of poetry and religion, an engagement with the ancient traditions of the moral imagination.

Berlin never brought these heresies into the open; he seems not
to have had the courage of his convictions—indeed, he expended
much energy in explaining why one ought *not* to have the courage
of one's convictions. Yet he remains, in spite of this unconscious
cowardice, an appealing figure. He possesses the power of his
discrepancies, the inward antagonisms that give distinction to his
writing and (we are told and can well believe) contributed to the
splendor of his conversation. The different personas emerged, one
after another, in the flood of talk for which he was celebrated. At
one moment he was the Jewish *chacham*, the scholar of gifts from
whom great things were expected, expectations that proved to be
a burden. Now again he was the convivial Oxford don, delighting
in high-table tittle-tattle about the great world. Next he was the
acutely perceptive Russian psychologist, possessed of an insight
into the soul that enabled him to function at All Souls as a churchless abbé, a father confessor to the confused young scholars who
came to him looking for a wise man.

At other times he was himself the searcher, pursuing, like Pierre
in *War and Peace*, a solution to the enigma of life. His quest was
more methodical than most. Berlin's writings are a catalog, at times
a laundry list, of the various answers that philosophers have proposed, not only the great figures but also the more obscure sages—
Campanella and Nicholas of Cusa, Festugière and Mandelberg-
Posadovsky, ghostly intelligences roused by Berlin from their
slumber in dusty libraries. The cacophony of competing solutions is painful: Berlin spoke a "Babel of voices," a "monstrous
muddle," and the reader of his essays feels at times as though he

has entered the philosophical Hell of Milton, where the demonic sages "reason'd high,"

And found no end, in wandring mazes lost. . . .
Vain wisdom all, and false philosophie.

Where so many others had failed to find a persuasive Answer, it was, Berlin concluded, futile to make yet another attempt, to add another flawed theory to philosophy's ash heap. And so he proclaimed his anti-Answer—value-pluralism, his theory that there is no Answer.

This was, finally, a nihilist philosophy; but it was not Berlin's whole philosophy, and it was unfaithful to what is most perceptive in his writings. His critique of the poverty of the social imagination is surely the buried gem of his intellectual art. Yet Berlin showed no inclination to bring the muddy diamond to the surface; it would have made him enemies; and to be a prophet without invitations could only be, for a man constituted as he was, inordinately painful. Value-pluralism, by contrast, was a philosophical calling card on which he could dine out; it made him a celebrity philosopher, a yogi to the postwar Anglo-American political establishment. Supple, plastic, flexible, Berlin's Chooser of Values was congenial to the spirit of an age in which the West lost confidence in its traditions and sought a precarious refuge in accommodation, in moral détente, in the ethically elastic. Berlin rushed from Rothschild house parties at Waddesdon to the parties of Joe Alsop in Georgetown; he tutored the Kennedys in the White House, then went off with the Arthur Schlesingers and the Walter Lippmanns to the Plaza in New York, where Truman Capote was tossing his garter to Kay Graham.

Like his establishment patrons, Berlin feared extremism on the left, yet he was not a sufficiently confident apostle of liberty to dismiss the social imagination altogether. Rather than swim "against the current," he crafted an apologia for the welfare state and seemed to slight the moral imagination—an admittedly imperfect defense against fanaticism, but the best we have. He attempted to throw over his papier-mâché philosophy the veil of the tragic, but he is least plausible when he poses as a tragic sage. How could one immersed in *lacrimae rerum* have steeled himself to so many dinner parties? Yet in his most perceptive moments he was better than this, was a man who kept, however shyly, a better faith.

The Trivialization of Emerson:
How the Philosopher of Self-Reliance
Became a Prophet of Self-Esteem

> Man has one foot in the finite and the other
> in the infinite.
>
> —L'Abbé Lamennais

*T*he bicentennial of Ralph Waldo Emerson in 2003 was a melancholy occasion. Although a few of Emerson's verses are still read and one or two of his essays still cherished, he has been largely forsaken by the common reader. "My whole philosophy—which is very real—teaches acquiescence and optimism," he told Thomas Carlyle in 1841. This optimism, it is true, failed him more often than is commonly supposed; it was hard won; yet even so it did his reputation no good. After his death it became the philosophical fashion to flaunt one's despair; in so dark a critical universe, he could not hope for a hearing. Henry James said of Emerson that he lacked a sense of "the evil and sin of the world"; T. S. Eliot dismissed his essays as "an encumbrance."

Yet nothing Emerson's detractors have said against him has done as much to blight his memory as the homage paid to him by his friends. Ever since John Dewey, in his 1916 book *Democracy and Education*, drew on Emerson's thought in his efforts to reform American schools, the philosopher of self-reliance has come to figure, in the American imagination, as a prophet of the flimsier forms of self-esteem.

Emerson's ghost is implicated in a mass of unintelligent policy; but Emerson himself is necessary to any renovation we can conceive. He is America's primal essayist, the vindicator of its naive optimism, yet he is also the thinker who showed the "American Adam" how the new American culture, the culture of the last-reached sunset lands of the West, could be at least the equal of the culture of the old civilizations of the dawn and of the East. He did this by adapting, to American conditions, methods of opening minds derived from the earliest days of the West, from the morning of the Greeks and the Jews—methods which until not so very long ago had an important place in American schoolrooms.

⌒

He was born in 1803, the descendant of a line of Protestant divines. His early life was troubled: a few days before his eighth birthday his father died of stomach cancer; two of his brothers were tubercular. His own health was delicate. "I am not sick," he said at twenty-four, "I am not well; but luke-sick."

His characteristic habits of introspection appeared early. Like Wordsworth, he was a child of Calvinism, with its traditions of self-interrogation, and of Romanticism, with its burden of morbid self-consciousness. At eighteen he undertook, in his journal, to assay the "history" of his "heart." "A blank, my lord," the young Harvard student wrote. "I have not the kind affections of a pigeon. Ungenerous and selfish, cautious and cold, I yet wish to be romantic; have not sufficient feeling to speak a natural, hearty welcome to a friend or stranger. . . . There is not in the whole wide Universe of God (my relations to Himself I do not understand) one being to whom I am attached with warm and entire devotion . . . a true picture of a barren and desolate soul."

He spent many hours hiding out in the woods. "I deliberately shut up my books in a cloudy July noon," he confided to his journal in 1828, "put on my old clothes and old hat and slink away to the whortleberry bushes and slip with the greatest satisfaction into a little cowpath where I am sure I can defy observation. . . . I seldom enjoy hours as I do these. I remember them in winter; I expect them in spring." On a fine night, the twenty-three-year-old Emerson said, "the stars shed down their severe influences on me, and I feel a joy in my solitude that the merriment of vulgar society can never communicate." In his rambles he attempted to decipher the inarticulate language he overheard in the woods—a phenomenon common enough at that time in young people who had fed on such mystics as Emanuel Swedenborg, Jakob Boehme, and Wordsworth himself, and who, like them, sought to read in nature's mystic book.

꿈

Emerson's father had been pastor of Boston's First Church, and after completing his studies at Harvard Divinity School Emerson himself became junior pastor of the Second Church. In the same year he married Ellen Tucker. The pulpit he occupied was one in which Increase Mather and Cotton Mather had, more than a century before, asserted the godly rule of the Congregational clergy.

By Emerson's time, however, New England Calvinism had lost the greatest part of its spiritual authority. Worshipers no longer wanted to be told that they were sinners in the hands of an angry God. Churches like the Second Church, which had once been Puritan strongholds, came to be dominated by Unitarians, reformers who sought to purge Protestantism of its Calvinist dogmas.

Although he began his career as a Unitarian, Emerson soon became convinced that the reformers, in liberalizing Christianity, had impoverished it. Unitarianism, he said, was a "corpse-cold" creed: Luther "would cut his hand off sooner than write his theses against the Pope, if he suspected that he was bringing on with all his might the pale negations of Boston Unitarianism." Just as he began to waver in his calling, his wife died of consumption. "My angel is gone to heaven this morning," he wrote, "& I am alone in the world & strangely happy." A month after her death he wrote in his journal, "I visited Ellen's tomb and opened the coffin."

In the course of the next year, Emerson resigned his pulpit and boarded a merchant ship for Europe. There he attempted to repair what he called the miserable debility in which his wife's death "has left my soul." When, after meeting his literary heroes, Wordsworth, Coleridge, and Carlyle, he returned to America, he found that the spiritual preoccupations of New England in its "sabbath morning" had given way to the broad daylight of the Yankee afternoon, bright with the lust for accumulation. Two of his brothers, William and Edward, embraced the new dispensation; abjuring the pious traditions of the Emersons, they studied law—William on Wall Street, Edward on State Street under the supervision of Daniel Webster. Emerson himself, however, possessed too abundantly the spiritual qualities radical Protestants spoke of as constituting an interior "light" to content himself with a stool in a counting house. Like Carlyle—another nineteenth-

century secular preacher—Emerson was deeply rooted in the old
Protestant culture, and he was not without sympathy for the "rig-
orous, scowling, ascetic creed" of the Puritans. He was, moreover,
as intensely preoccupied with the state of his soul as any Calvinist.
Krishna in the *Bhagavadgītā*—a text that deeply influenced him—
believed that a man could "rise from his animal ancestry to the
divine ideal." He could become one of "God's tools," a channel
"of his love and purpose." The more radical Protestants, forever
searching their Bibles and scrawling in their self-inquisitive jour-
nals, similarly believed that in the intensity of inward contempla-
tion a man could find within himself not only sin but also the light
of God. This idea of an intuitive apprehension of divinity within
left its mark on the future author of "Self-Reliance." The essay is
the font of what is most nourishing in Emerson's thought, and also
what is most poisonous in it, for in it he counseled his readers not
to be "ashamed of that divine idea which each of us represents."

Emerson's hereditary disdain for merely material rewards led him
to set up as an independent lecturer and essayist, a churchless
preacher. He bought a house in Concord, the village of his ancestors, remarried, and settled down to what seemed likely to be the
life of a crank. His literary taste, however, was fastidious, and when
he came to harangue his countrymen in secular sermons, his pro-
ductions showed no trace of the quaintness of the Puritan or the
naiveté of the home-schooled prophet.

At the same time his work betrayed a depth of ambition that he
was always reluctant to acknowledge. The writing with which he
made his name was the work of a deliberate sensationalist. "Books
are for the scholar's idle times," he informed the bookish Phi Beta

Kappas of Harvard in his 1837 lecture "The American Scholar." The next summer he told the Harvard Divinity School that "the priest's Sabbath has lost the splendor of nature; it is unlovely; we are glad when it is done." People's houses, he said, must be "very unentertaining, that they should prefer this thoughtless clamor."

The fireworks in "Self-Reliance," published in 1841, were less brilliant but in some ways more destructive. "Self-Reliance" is the most beloved of Emerson's essays, yet a number of the golden words are certainly outrageous. With all the malice of suppressed ambition, Emerson advised his readers to ignore salutary customs and usages. The egotism implicit in the words "Whoso would be a man must be a nonconformist," though it might suit a gentleman with an inherited income ($1,200 a year, in Emerson's case, paid out of his dead wife's estate), could only contribute to the ruin of those differently situated—the great majority of men who must learn humbly and patiently to earn their bread. Yet the careful reader will find a discrepancy between the laxity of Emerson's dogmas and the diligence of his style. His manner is superior to his wisecracks, and so, one comes to see, is his philosophy.

⌒

At the heart of the idea of Emersonian self-reliance is the belief, scarcely a novel one, that self-knowledge is the key to self-improvement. Emerson argued that the object of education is to help a person find the qualities in himself that are strong enough to *be* relied on; and to this end he drew on a number of old Western methods of introspective discipline, all of them intended to help a person discover what is strong and valuable in his character, and distinguish what is weak and pernicious in it. The challenge, for Emerson, was to make the old methods credible to Americans who were unversed in the ancient lore, and who, being caught up in practical American realities, might be tempted to scorn it.*

Like Goethe, who said "all that is outside is also inside," Emerson seized on the old Western idea that the natural world, rightly studied, supplies a key to the soul, and that the soul, once opened, yields truths about the moral structure of the universe. "The ancient Greeks," Emerson said, "called the world κοσμος, beauty." In his dialogue *Gorgias*, Plato has Socrates argue that the soul, like the world, possesses its own *cosmos*, its own pattern of beauty and order. Yet very often, Emerson said, we become conscious of this interior order only when we confront something in our external life that startles us into self-perception. "If the stars should appear one night in a thousand years," Emerson wrote, "how would men believe and adore; and preserve for many generations the remembrance of the city of God which had been shown!" But however familiar nature is, men still feel its power. In the first chapter of his first book, *Nature*, which he published at thirty-three, Emerson said that "crossing a bare common, in snow puddles, at twilight, under a clouded sky, without having in my thoughts any occurrence of special good fortune, I have enjoyed a perfect exhilaration. I am glad to the brink of fear."

What is outside, Emerson believed, teaches us to understand what is inside. He had experienced, in the Jardin des Plantes in Paris, an epiphany: gazing on the "bewildering series of animated forms" displayed there, he was struck by the fact that no species

---

*Emerson's philosophy is deeply rooted in the Western tradition; yet he drew, too, on the philosophy of the East. His idea of self-reliance was influenced by the teaching of the *Bhagavadgītā*, a poem which left its press on his thought: "Better is one's own law, though imperfectly carried out, than the law of another carried out perfectly. Better is death in (the fulfillment of) one's own law: for to follow another's law is perilous." *Bhagavadgītā*, ed. S. Radhakrishnan (New Delhi: HarperCollins, 1993), 146–147 (III, 35).

of plant or animal life was "so grotesque, so savage, or so beautiful but was an expression of some property inherent in man the observer,—an occult relation between the very scorpion and the man." "I feel," he said, "the centipede in me,—cayman, carp, eagle, and fox." If a man thought hard enough about the natural architecture that awed and inspired him, he would find, Emerson said, that it impressed him precisely because it disclosed to him an answering architecture in himself. Emerson spoke of the outer world as "this shadow of the soul, or other me. . . . Its attractions are the keys which unlock my thoughts and make me acquainted with myself."

Such experiences are so common, Emerson observed, that we too often dismiss them. "A man should learn," he wrote in "Self-Reliance," "to detect and watch that gleam of light which flashes across the mind from within, more than the lustre of the firmament of bards and sages." If, he said, you have the courage to "believe your own thought," you will come to credit the truth of your intuitions, and in doing so you will catch a glimpse of something more. You might not have the intensely developed vision of Dante, who in his ultimate apprehension saw, "like a wheel revolving uniformly," the force that "moves the sun and the other stars." But you will find that there is an idea of order at work both in the universe and your own soul.

The practical Yankee in every American will be tempted to scoff at Emerson's Platonic idea that all "the circles of the visible heavens represent as many circles in the rational soul." But follow to the root the "strange sympathies" you felt in a summer twilight or a January dawn and you will come closer, Emerson says, to understanding that beneath your own mind's "inharmonious particulars" lies a "musical perfection, the Ideal journeying always with us, the heaven without rent or seam." This was in many ways a restatement of what his friend Carlyle, in *Sartor Resartus*, called "natural supernaturalism," the belief that by penetrating the

anomalous surfaces of things one can apprehend a divine significance in nature and waken to the perception of a lyrical cosmos.
Having pierced the veil of sensuous appearance, the transcenden-
tal mystagogue discovers the inward poetry of his own soul. This
notion, with its roots perhaps in the primeval depths of the civilization, is almost a commonplace of Western self-culture; one finds
variations of it in Shakespeare and Dante, in Plato and the Bible,
in the patristic philosophy of the church fathers and the nature
poetry of the Romantic authors. Emerson, in rephrasing the idea
in the American vernacular, sought to make it one of the spiritual
pillars of a new democratic civilization.*

---

*Newman found in the patristic philosophy of Clement and Origen the belief that "the
exterior world, physical and historical, was but the manifestation to our senses of realities greater than itself. Nature was a parable." Nature, Carlyle says in *Sartor Resartus*, "is
a Volume written in celestial hieroglyphs." It is "the Time-vesture of God, and reveals
Him to the wise, and hides Him from the Foolish." "God invented and gave us sight,"
Plato says in the *Timaeus*, "to the end that we might behold the courses of intelligence
in the heavens, and apply them to the courses of our own intelligence which are akin
to them." For Dante the intelligence Plato describes is a form of transcendent love: it
binds the scattered leaves of the universe in one volume. A similar notion of "natural
supernaturalism" is found in the idea of sphere melody, the "language" or "music" of
the spheres. The heavens "uttereth speech," says the psalmist: "There is no speech nor
language, where their voice is not heard." Addison drew on the psalm when he composed the hymn, "The spacious firmament on high . . ." The "music" of the cosmos is
answered by a correlative music in the human soul, albeit one that men are not always
able to hear. Thus Lorenzo, in *The Merchant of Venice*, exclaims to Jessica:

> How sweet the moonlight sleeps upon this bank!
> Here will we sit, and let sounds of music
> Creep in our ears; soft stillness and the night
> Become touches of sweet harmony.
> Sit, Jessica: look, how the floor of heaven
> Is thick inlaid with patines of bright gold:
> There's not the smallest orb which thou behold'st
> But in this motion like an angel sings
> Still quiring to the young-eyed cherubins;
> Such harmony is in immortal souls;
> But, whilst this muddy vesture of decay
> Doth grossly close it in, we cannot hear it.

Poetry was for Emerson another element of self-culture. In this he followed both the Greeks, who looked upon poets as the supreme educators of a people, and the Romantics, for whom poetry was essential to *Bildung* or self-development. The true poet, Emerson said, is able to communicate his intimations of the soul's inward order with living words—words that "would bleed," Emerson says, if you cut them. Poetry, he argued, "unlocks our chains." The "poets are thus liberating gods." A master poet like Shakespeare is a supreme "translator of things in your [own] consciousness." Notwithstanding "our utter incapacity to produce any thing like Hamlet and Othello, see the perfect reception this wit, and immense knowledge of life, and liquid eloquence find in us all." Shakespeare, Emerson said, "saw the splendor of meaning that plays over the visible world; knew that a tree had another use than for apples, and corn another than for meal, and the ball of the earth, than for tillage and roads: that these things bore a second and finer harvest to the mind, being emblems of its thoughts, and conveying in all their natural history a certain mute commentary on human life."

Yet words by themselves can do only so much to open up the mind: music, for Emerson, is as essential to poetry as language. Its rhythms mediate between the outer cosmos and the inner one. Emerson followed the Greeks in arguing that a poem, like the soul itself, resembles a living organism, a pattern of reason (*logos*) ordered by rhyme and rhythm. Like the Greeks, Emerson insisted that the music of poetry is itself a profound educational force, and he took to heart Plato's assertion that the rhythms and harmonies of poetry "sink furthest into the depths of the soul and take hold of it most firmly by bringing it nobility and grace."

It "is not metres, but metre-making argument"—word and music together—"that makes a poem," Emerson said: "a thought so passionate and alive, that, like the spirit of a plant or an animal, it has an architecture of its own, and adorns nature with a new thing." Thus the virtue, for Emerson, of the classic poets: their patterns of words and rhythms form a miniature cosmos, "an abstract or epitome of the world." Because its structure resembles that of both the universe and the soul, a classic poem "throws light upon the mystery of humanity."

Emerson's contemporary, William Holmes McGuffey, another child of Protestantism and the Greek Revival, embodied the Emersonian spirit in the primers he designed for the nation's schools. McGuffey, a clergyman who taught Greek and Latin at Miami University in Ohio, published the first of his *Readers* in 1836. By 1879 some sixty million copies of America's premier school textbooks were in print.

Like Emerson, McGuffey believed that poetry is essential to education. Rhythm mattered to him hardly less than it did to Emerson. The verses that fill his *Readers*—generous servings of Shakespeare, Milton, Pope—were meant to be recited: each *Reader* begins with elaborate guides to "articulation," "inflection," "accent and emphasis," as well as "instructions for reading verse," and each extract is marked with a complex system of accents to indicate emphasis and meter. The stress marks might seem quaint to us; but McGuffey followed the Greeks in supposing that rhythm and harmony have not only an aesthetic but also an ethical value.

An apostle of the American gospel of self-improvement that runs from Franklin through Emerson and Lincoln, McGuffey orchestrated the music of his *Readers* in such a way as to stimulate his students' desire to better themselves by knowing themselves better. "The education, moral and intellectual, of every individual," one of his lessons reads, "must be, chiefly, his own work. Rely upon it, that the ancients were right; both in morals and intellect, we give the final shape to our characters, and thus become, emphatically, the architects of our own fortune."

In Emersonian fashion McGuffey sought to guide the student's inchoate desire to better himself. His primers are, like the early Greek poetry itself, intended to be shapers of *ethos*, character. The *Readers* praise hard work and thrift; they warn against intemperance, gambling, and procrastination; they teach the importance of patience, self-discipline, perseverance, and courage. Yet the *Readers* are not quite the caricatures of Victorian morality one might expect. Man "is born unto trouble," one of McGuffey's lessons (taken from the Bible) says, and God "woundeth" souls. Life has its full cup of sorrow: it is a state of "trial and discipline," at times a "prisonhouse of pain." But even as McGuffey glances at the abyss, he invokes John Milton's faith in the possibility of a "dark ascent" through chaos to the light that "shine[s] inward" and illuminates every mind.

McGuffey does not patronize his students; Lionel Trilling praised the sophistication and "intense literariness" of the primers. As in Emerson's essays, the poet is the principal tutor. McGuffey gives his students Rousseau on Jesus and Socrates, Portia's judgment in Shylock's suit ("the quality of mercy is not strained"), Dr. Johnson's comparison of Pope and Dryden, Gray's *Elegy*, and David's lament for his son ("O my son Absalom my son, my son Absalom! would to God I had died for thee"). Reading McGuffey's *Readers*, one comes to see that it is we, not the Victorians, who are weakly sentimental when it comes to the education of the young.

⌇

McGuffey, who had made bad bargains with his publishers, profited little from his *Readers*. He received a barrel of ham at Christ-
mas and died in obscurity. Emerson became a celebrity and one of
the most successful lecturers of his time. For all the intensity of his
own self-involvement, he managed to touch the minds of others.
"When he was breaking [with age] and I was still young," Oliver
Wendell Holmes recalled in 1917, "I saw him on the other side
of the street and ran over and said to him, 'If I ever do anything, I
shall owe a great deal of it to you,' which was true. He was one of
those who set one on fire."

It was perhaps inevitable that so successful an intellectual
entrepreneur would be vulgarized. John Dewey claimed to be
Emerson's disciple, but he was not an altogether faithful one: his
concept of the "child-centered" school is in many ways a caricature
of the Emersonian idea of self-reliance. Dewey, who had been born
in Vermont in 1859, was a forerunner of the celebrity academic.
As a writer and philosopher he never rose above mediocrity, but as
an advocate of "democratic socialism" he transformed America's
schools. In books like *Democracy and Education* he argued that
children must be emancipated from the "autocratic" authority of
the teacher and from the "chain-gang procedures" of traditional
schooling. He called for replacing the older methods of introspective self-knowledge with techniques that would permit the child
to direct his education through spontaneous, lightly supervised
play. McGuffey was to give way to Rousseau. "As long as any topic
makes an immediate appeal" to the student, Dewey wrote, it might
properly be included in the curriculum. Education should be
rooted in "satisfactory activity," and the most satisfactory activity
is that which the child likes best.

Once the Deweyesque seed—Paul Goodman described its essence as student "participation and self-rule," "group therapy as a means of solidarity," and "permissiveness in all animal behavior and interpersonal expression"—was planted in the American classroom, education ceased to be a process of helping young minds discover the best that is within them through exposure to "the best that has been thought and said in the world." The older tradition of self-knowledge gave way to a therapeutic philosophy of self-esteem.

Although Emerson himself used the word "self-esteem" (as did Milton), he could not have found the laxity of the modern theory appealing. Still one cannot entirely absolve him of culpability for the current educational debacle, for in a number of places he laid himself open to the misreadings of Dewey and his followers. Part of the problem lies in the vagueness of Emerson's writing. For every living sentence in his essays there are perhaps a dozen dead ones, yet he was always unwilling to bind himself more closely to flesh and bone as Carlyle urged him to do. The deeper difficulty is that in his loosest sentences Emerson turned away from all that was hard and true in the vision of his forebears. He flirted with the freedom of an absolute relativism. "Good and bad are but names very readily transferable to that or this," he asserted in "Self-Reliance." He dreamt of antinomian liberation. The "only right is what is after my constitution, the only wrong what is against it." The "sacred germ of [a man's] instinct" was "not inferior but superior to his will." It was one thing for this scion of the Puritans, a man who inherited all their temperate habits, to divert himself with such fantasies; enshrine them as dogmas in a school, and you have the makings of a catastrophe.

Dewey loved the Dionysian in Emerson, but he overlooked the ways in which his idol qualified the bacchanalia. Emerson, after his literary benders, was apt to sober up and to observe that there are limits to liberation. Our sensual existence, he believed, is probably an illusion, a veil which, like that of *mǎyǎ*, obscures a deeper truth; but while we live in thrall to what Wallace Stevens called "the present knowing," we can neither deny the reality of evil nor the inescapability of sin and suffering.* "Don't trust children with edge tools," Emerson wrote. "Don't trust man, great God, with more power than he has, until he has learned to use that little better. What a hell we should make of the world if we could do what we would!" And more darkly:

> The violations of the laws of nature by our predecessors and contemporaries are punished in us also. The disease and deformity around us certify the infraction of natural, intellectual, and moral laws, and often violation on violation to breed such compound misery. A lock-jaw that bends a man's head back to his heels, hydrophobia, that makes him bark at his wife and babes, insanity, that makes him eat grass; war, plague, cholera, famine, indicate a certain ferocity in nature which, as it had its inlet by human crime, must have its outlet by human suffering. Unhappily, no man exists who has not in his own person become, to

---

*It has been argued that St. Augustine, in the *Enchiridion*, maintains that evil does not actually, or rather metaphysically, exist. "The answer to the problem of evil that Augustine is to give," Romano Guardini wrote in *The Conversion of St. Augustine*, "is that metaphysically it is non-existent," for "God creates neither evil nor any evil thing." It may be true that evil does not exist, but in the physical world we inhabit it seems to us to exist, and we must act accordingly. If this reading of Augustine is correct, we are caught in a paradox. We must act as though evil exists, for our limited, our merely sensuous and physical, perception tells us that it does: in our quotidian natural or physical life we cannot say, as Hamlet does, "I know not 'seems.'" Yet our metaphysical or spiritual faith (if such we have) tells us that evil cannot exist, for God could never have suffered it to: it must therefore be an illusion of the "present knowing," the enigmatic glass, St. Paul says, through which we now darkly see. Emerson's conception of evil was in many ways a restatement of this paradox.

some amount, a stockholder in the sin, and so made himself liable
to a share in the expiation.

In order to understand why men suffered, in order to understand
why *he* suffered—and he suffered greatly after the death of his five-
year-old son Waldo in 1842—Emerson returned to his Puritan
forebears. Men are sinners, and so must be sufferers.

⌇

Emerson is often thought to be the most cheerful of philosophers;
but surely Nietzsche, who venerated him, could never have done
so had his optimism been easily attained. On the contrary, it was an
overcoming of despair. He wrote in his journal in 1842:

> *I am Defeated all the time; yet to Victory I am born.*

In certain moods Emerson looked upon self-reliance as a discipline
of loneliness. Man's solitude was at once his joy and his punishment. "The soul," he said, "is not twin-born, but the only begot-
ten. We believe in ourselves, as we do not believe in others." The
"great and crescive self, rooted in absolute nature, supplants all
relative existence, and ruins the kingdom of mortal friendship and
love. Marriage (in what is called the spiritual world) is impossible,
because of the inequality between every subject and every object."
Again: "There will be the same gulf between every me and thee, as
between the original and the picture." We know little about Emerson's second marriage, but he did aver that "Love is temporary,
and ends with marriage." One must, he said, "embrace solitude
as a bride," for "souls never touch their objects." "I think then
the writer ought not to be married; ought not to have a family," he

wrote. "I think the Roman Church, with its celibate clergy and its monastic cells, was right."

If wives were a distraction, so too were friends. Although "I prize my friends," Emerson said, "I cannot afford to talk with them and study their visions, lest I lose my own." Henry David Thoreau lived in Emerson's house for a time. He had his own room at the top of the stairs, and Emerson gave him permission to build, on his property, the cabin that *Walden* made famous. But Thoreau and Emerson were never precisely close. "I spoke of friendship," Emerson wrote in his journal, "but my friends and I are fishes in our habit. As for taking Thoreau's arm, I should as soon take the arm of an elm tree." He disparaged his tenant's pretensions to equality of intellect. "I am very familiar with his thoughts," Emerson said of Thoreau: "they are my own quite originally drest." And no less damningly: "If I only knew Thoreau, I should think cooperation of good men impossible."

"I know," he said,

> that the world I converse with in the city and in the farm, is not the world I *think*. We dress our garden, eat our dinners, discuss the household with our wives, and these things make no impression, are forgotten next week; but in the solitude to which every man is returning, he has a sanity and revelations, which in his passage to new worlds he will carry with him.

In its most extreme form, self-reliance becomes a kind of solipsistic hell, each man helplessly imprisoned in his own impenetrable cell.

We have to hope that he was wrong. It is not good that man should be alone: education rests on the premise that the teacher *can* touch a student's soul. Emerson might have needed little enough help from others in order to fulfill his destiny, but no man, however great, accomplishes anything by himself. The good offices of scores of others—parents, teachers, friends, relatives—go into making a person even modestly self-reliant. It is, however, a testament to the virtue of Emerson's darkness that it is even now a source of light.

Hannah Arendt in the Public Square:
The Tyranny of the Social Imagination

*I*n 1958 Hannah Arendt published *The Human Condition.* The book, part panegyric, part lamentation, is a meditation on what she called public "space" or the public "realm." What she meant by public space was not simply the buildings and gathering places that in a good town square or market piazza encourage people to come together. It was not even civic art viewed more broadly, the paintings and poetic ornament she attributed to *homo faber*, the fabricating soul who translates "intangible" civic ideals into "tangible" civic art, a Corinthian column or a Doric entablature, a tragic drama or a well-wrought urn. Public space, for Arendt, was also a metaphysical arena in which people realized their individual potential. They escaped necessity's pinch—the arduous biological round of life-sustaining labor—through a "sharing of words and deeds." This was the tradition of the Greek city-state, from which Arendt drew much of her inspiration—a place designed "to multiply the chances for everybody to distinguish himself, to show in deed and word who he was in his unique distinctness."

But a new Leviathan was, Arendt believed, devouring the old public spaces. With the advent of the modern nation-state, a social dispensation began to emerge, one whose adepts—sociologists, psychologists, planners—were skilled in techniques derived from the social sciences but whose motives were far from pure. The new social technician, part schoolmarm, part bully, sought not merely to study behavior but also, Arendt argued, to control it. The school of Pericles was giving way to the school of Pavlov.

The social managers, Arendt maintained, sought to impose behavioral norms on people through "innumerable and various rules"—bureaucratic harnesses intended to "normalize" men and women, to compel them to "behave," and to punish their "spontaneous action or outstanding achievement." Refractory spirits who failed to conform were to be stigmatized as "asocial or abnormal." In her more perfervid visions, Arendt foresaw a social apocalypse, a "leveling out of fluctuation" that would result in the "most sterile passivity history has ever known."*

Arendt's jeremiad had a good deal in common with the warnings of other mid-twentieth-century prophets, among them Lionel Trilling and Friedrich Hayek, who in their different ways foresaw the emergence of a servile population springing reflexively to the sullen Pavlovian bells of the social state. But Arendt had her own idiosyncratic understanding of the way public space could help block the road to serfdom. The old forums, in liberating so much potential, foiled those who desired "conformism, behaviorism, and automatism in human affairs."

---

*But is life in a world where the social imagination is as pervasive as it now is crueler, are its authorities more arrogant, than was the case when the older moral traditions were more prevalent in the West? The answer must be no. It ought, however, to be borne in mind that the institutions which today do the most to protect us from the cruelty and arrogance of those "that have power to hurt" were devised by men who, like the American Founders, lived before the social imagination came to dominate the culture, and who derived much light from the older moral traditions. I, for one, should not like to live under a constitutional regime devised by, let us say, the social mandarins of the United Nations or of the European Union.

The question that haunts the reader of Arendt's work is whether we can get the old spaces back.

Arendt was born in 1906 into a German-Jewish family living in Linden, in what is now the city of Hanover. She passed much of her childhood in Königsberg, in what was then East Prussia; at the outbreak of the war in 1914 she moved with her family to Berlin. She was still in her teens when she first heard the name Martin Heidegger. It was "hardly more than a name," she said, but it "traveled all over Germany like the rumor of the hidden king." In 1924 she enrolled in the University of Marburg to study under the master. He was thirty-five, married, and working on *Being and Time*; Arendt embraced him as teacher, mentor, and lover.

The traditional hostility of the philosopher toward the polis was, Arendt believed, "only too apparent" in Heidegger. The "most essential characteristic" of his pose, she said, was "its absolute egoism." Heidegger was a mountain prophet. He shunned the "gabble" of the valley. He retired whenever practicable to his cottage in Todtnauberg in the Black Forest, where he could live, he said, in the "solitude of the mountains," in the "elemental nearness of sun, storms, and heavens." "It's marvelous up here," he wrote in 1925. "Sometimes I no longer understand that down there one can play such strange roles."

Arendt soon left Marburg to study under Karl Jaspers in Heidelberg. She continued, however, to see Heidegger, briefly and furtively, on railway platforms and in provincial hotels. Even so, the breach between them widened. In January 1933 Hitler came to power, and in May Heidegger joined the Nazi party. "The Führer himself and he alone," he declared, "is German reality and law, today and for the future." In the same year the German police, suspicious of Arendt's researches in the Prussian State Library, where she was collecting material on anti-Semitism for the German Zionist Organization, arrested and interrogated her. Upon her release, she fled Germany and found refuge in Paris. After the German invasion of France in 1940, the French authorities imprisoned her in the notorious internment camp at Gurs. She escaped and made her way to the United States, which became her home for the rest of her life.

Experience and reflection led Arendt to question Heidegger's contempt for public space. His "existential solipsism" had prevented him from making responsible political judgments. Yet one should not exaggerate the break between the two: it was accomplished by degrees and was indeed never complete. Arendt would always regard Heidegger as the incarnation of the philosopher-king, and their bond persisted until her death in 1975. She called him "the last Romantic," not without admiration. German Romanticism left its print on her own spirit. She was contemptuous of mere biological existence, the life of those "enslaved" by the necessity of getting their bread, imprisoned "in the ever-recurring cycle of the life process." She wanted, as the German Romantics did, to soar into a higher, freer realm. She too was *Tochter aus Elysium*, a daughter of Elysium.

In the spring of 1961, twenty years after she came to the United States, Arendt traveled to Israel to attend the trial of former SS lieutenant colonel Adolf Eichmann. Her impressions were printed first in *The New Yorker* and later in her book *Eichmann in Jerusalem: A Report on the Banality of Evil*. By applying the theses of

The Human Condition to the Nazis' mass murder of the Jews, she caused a sensation, even a scandal.

Studying Eichmann in the dock, Arendt concluded that he was not an evil genius but a fool: "Despite all the efforts of the prosecution, everybody could see that this man was not a 'monster,' but it was difficult indeed not to suspect that he was a clown." He was "genuinely incapable of uttering a single sentence that was not a cliché," Arendt wrote; in his aphasic helplessness he could but repeat, in "officialese" ("my only language," he said), the formulas he had learned to parrot. "The longer one listened to him, the more obvious it became that his inability to speak was closely connected to his inability to *think*."

Such people exist in every era, but not until the flowering of the social bureaucracies did they come into their own. Eichmann shone in the sleek bureaucracy of the SS not despite his banality but because of it. Under the social dispensation, Arendt wrote, a "substitution" of "collective man-kind for individual men" takes place, achieved mainly by means of the "social sciences which, as 'behavioral sciences,' aim to reduce man as a whole, in all his activities, to the level of a conditioned and behaving animal." National Socialism was for Arendt an extreme form of the social impulse to condition human beings. Hitler, the historian John Lukacs has observed, believed that "modern populist nationalism can—and indeed must—be socialistic." The concentration camps, Arendt wrote in her 1951 book *The Origins of Totalitarianism*, were themselves vast conditioning experiments, "laboratories" in which "each and every person can be reduced to a never-changing identity of reactions, so that each of these bundles of reactions can be exchanged at random for any other."

Eichmann figures in *Eichmann in Jerusalem* as the incarnation of the new social man and thus the ideal Nazi administrator.

A less dull creature would have either broken under the strain or turned sadist, and thus upset the smooth efficiency of the operation; Eichmann plodded on, processing mass murder as though he were stamping passports. Arendt thought he deserved to hang, but her portrait nevertheless stirred outrage because the mulish mental dormancy she attributed to him seemed to mitigate his guilt. Carrying her theory to what many thought an extravagant length, Arendt argued that Eichmann, caught up in the atmosphere of National Socialism, was "perfectly incapable of telling right from wrong."

If Eichmann figures in Arendt's roman à thèse as the embodiment of the banal social man, his Jewish victims make a prop for her theory of the decline of public space. Probably nothing in *Eichmann in Jerusalem* caused so much distress as the pages in which Arendt described the assistance that the Jewish councils, the *Judenräte*, gave the Nazis in implementing genocide. "Wherever Jews lived," Arendt wrote, "there were recognized Jewish leaders, and this leadership, almost without exception, cooperated in one way or another, for one reason or another, with the Nazis."

Arendt showed little feeling for the predicament of the Jewish leaders, though she conceded that their "submissive meekness" was understandable. No "non-Jewish group or people had behaved differently," she noted. To rebel was to court a fate worse than death. She described how Dutch Jews were "tortured to death" after attacking a German police detachment in 1941. For "months on end they died a thousand deaths, and every single one of them would have envied his brethren in Auschwitz and even in Riga and Minsk."

Still, if by 1941 it was too late to rebel, why had Jews and Gentiles alike failed to stand up to the National Socialists earlier? Arendt attributed the failure of civic nerve to the decay of public space and, in particular, to the decline of the political traditions that flourished in such space. In *The Human Condition* she had defined the essence of political activity as "jurisdiction, defense, and administration of public affairs." The crucial word is "defense." Arendt admired the man of action who had the "courage" to enter public space and defend himself against aggressors. Courage, she said, was "the political virtue par excellence."

Arendt believed that some peoples had more of this civic bone and muscle than others. The Danes, for example, had an "authentically political sense, an inbred comprehension of the requirements of citizenship and independence." The Diaspora Jews, by contrast, "had no political tradition or experience." They figure in Arendt's writings as civic *castrati* whose lack of political experience left them vulnerable to the pogrom. Had the Jews possessed a more adequate public space, Arendt believed, they could have developed the civic machismo that she admired.

This part of her argument, though, is at odds with her recognition that polis arts, however beautifully developed, could not in fact have saved the Jews. Even if they had turned the ghetto into a facsimile of Periclean Athens, they could not have effectually resisted a gigantic nation-state determined to wipe them off the face of the earth. They were helpless, Arendt wrote, because they "possessed no territory, no government, and no army"—in other words, no nation-state.

Arendt's analysis of the plight of European Jewry lays bare the deeper tension in her thought. Public space, small and polislike, is for her the school of civic courage and distinctive individuality. Yet no polis can withstand the might of a nation-state. Build a nation-state to save yourself, however, and you sacrifice the humanity and civic vigor of the agora, the forum, and the town square. The nation-state, because of its size, requires a people to

undertake the very kinds of social administration that degrade the
civic artistry that makes them strong and self-reliant. "Large numbers of people, crowded together, develop an almost irresistible
inclination towards despotism, be this the despotism of a person
or of majority rule," Arendt wrote, "and although statistics, that is,
the mathematical treatment of reality, was unknown prior to the
modern age, the social phenomena which make such treatment
possible—great numbers, accounting for conformism, behaviorism, and automatism in human affairs—were precisely those traits
which, in the Greek self-understanding, distinguished the Persian
civilization from their own." It is the despairing crux of Arendt's
philosophy. The social methods of the nation-state will always
overwhelm the civic intimacy of agora culture, yet without national
forms to protect them, agora people are perpetually at the mercy of
their nation-state enemies.

Part of the difficulty is the fetish Arendt makes of politics. She
thought politics essential to public space, yet in a world dominated
by national governments she saw no way to preserve the political
tradition of the town square, the agora, and the piazza, which had
been stripped of their sovereignty by the social managers of the
capital. Of the two things which, she believed, go into making a
satisfactory public space—art and politics—politics was for her the
most important. Yet it is precisely political authority—the politics
of the town square, the polislike agora or piazza community—that
the nation-state, to a greater or lesser degree, always usurps. Some
federal systems, like the American one, are politer about this than
others, but when push comes to shove, the national authority gets

the better of it. When it fails to, it is suspected of weakness, and the federation falls apart.

It is here that Arendt went wrong. Her account of polis politics, the keystone of her civic arch, is easily the weakest part of her argument. Politics, she claims, teaches men "how to bring forth what is great and radiant." The public man realizes the ideal of Phoenix, who teaches Achilles in *The Iliad* to be "a speaker of words and a doer of deeds." Political deeds are "the greatest achievements of which human beings are capable." They transcend biological necessity and savor of true freedom; they are the highest form of action, the "one miracle-working faculty of man."

Norman Podhoretz has said that Arendt, in her "flights of metaphysical fancy," is not always able to find her way back to "commonsense reality." In her account of the miracle-working political actor, Arendt flirted with a millennial politics that, in Jacques Cazotte's prophecy of the French Revolution, always draws upon itself its own doom. At the same time she ignored the pork-packing arts Bismarck thought the essence of the political craft. She overlooked all the characteristic shabbiness of the political animal. Even in Athens the typical politician was a scoundrel. The deeds of Draco, Peisistratus, Cleon, *et alia* were not, as a rule, radiant: the run-of-the-mill Attic pol, when he was not actually on the take, was sure to be dreaming of tyranny. Pericles himself was not much more than a common huckster on the hustings, if we are to believe Plato. In the *Gorgias* he has Socrates make merry over Pericles' conviction for theft and conclude, "We do not know of *any* man who has proved a good statesman in this city."

Arendt could, it is true, have cited statesmen whose deeds have a claim to radiance—Washington, for instance, or Lincoln or Churchill. But these are the rarest thoroughbreds of the species. In dressing up in messianic costume the mountebanks and mediocrities who constituted the mean average of the breed, Arendt was the dupe of her dogmas. Her belief that in politics, as in art and philosophy, people at times transcend their biological natures is merely a truism that she pushes so far that it becomes an absurdity. When Shakespeare's Antony says that all things can be reduced to natural or biological necessity—that our greatest achievements are but "clay," for the "dungy earth alike / Feeds beast as man"— Cleopatra rightly rebukes the "excellent falsehood." Arendt falls prey to the opposite falsehood when she insists on a rigid division between the dungy biological imperium and the glorious sphere of supranatural political freedom. If in none of his activities is man utterly a brute, in none of them does he wholly slough his beastly skin. Politics is no exception: the greatest Athenian statesmen had constantly to muck about in the untranscendental politics of fish taxes, plagues, and sewage disposal.

The Athenian politician had also to make provision for trade, an activity which, though Arendt disdained it as low and utilitarian, gave the agora its vitality. To "go agora-ing," in Greek, meant not only to seek distinction and honor in the public square but also to buy and sell things. *The Human Condition* itself testifies to the interpenetration of commerce and the civic arts: Arendt wrote it with the support of the Walgreen, Rockefeller, and Guggenheim foundations, with cash originally earned by businessmen.

When Arendt left the philosophy seminar for the civics class, she brought with her a quantity of Romantic baggage that burdened her new public vision. She left Heidegger, the apolitical hermit, to his cave; but she merely substituted, for her hero worship of the philosopher, a new, no less dubious worship of the politician. She once, Elżbieta Ettinger wrote in her study *Hannah Arendt / Martin Heidegger*, "idealized Heidegger beyond measure." In forsaking the mountain sage for the public man, Arendt dispensed with the idol but not with the idolatry. The craving for an ideal masculinity remained: instead of Heracleitus she now adored Pericles.

She was looking in the wrong place. It was almost certainly the art, not the politics, of the old public spaces that made them prime begetters of civic culture and individual distinction. The artist, to be sure, had a place in Arendt's town square: his craftsmanship preserved the remembrance of civic deeds by turning them into created things, "into sayings of poetry, the written page . . . into paintings or sculpture, into all sorts of records, documents, and monuments." Yet Arendt's picture of the artist as handmaiden to the politician reduces the aesthetic miracle of public space to a résumé of political events, the *res gestae* of so many departed demagogues. It is simply not true to the reality of classic public spaces as we find them. Even a cursory glance at the history of the Athenian agora—or at the Piazza Navona in Rome, the Piazza San Marco in Venice, or the Place de la Comédie in Montpellier—proves that there is a good deal more to them than this.

Quite as much as *The Greek Anthology* or *The Golden Treasury*, the true marketplace is an accretion of poetic form: its buildings as well as its liturgical, dramatic, and festal arts have been molded by a shaping, poetic impulse. A Greek building, Jacob Burckhardt said, is a "rhythm of masses." Its friezes, cornices, and pediments are a sort of frozen music, akin in their intricacy to the lines of a poem. "Everything in a Greek or Christian building originally signified something," Nietzsche said, "and indeed something of a higher order of things: this feeling of inexhaustible significance lay about the building like a magical veil."

In *The City in History*, Lewis Mumford called the life of the old public spaces "many sided." He described the Piazza Navona as "a place for lovers to stroll, a market place, a playground for the children of the neighborhood, with sidewalk restaurants on both sides of the place, where whole families can dine and gossip and drink, all three generations together." Typically the public space will have an anchor institution that contributes to this complication of endeavor. The institution might be, as on the Piazza Navona, a church, or it might be, like the *hôtel-dieu* in a French town, a charitable foundation. It might be a library, like the Library of St. Mark on Venice's Piazzetta San Marco, or it might be a town hall, like the Palazzo Pubblico on Siena's Piazza del Campo. The activity of the market square is various, but its artistry makes for coherent and theatrically dramatic public space: it entices people, and so helps to gather in the civic flock. Visitors experience well-wrought civic design, Goethe says, as a work of art: Venice itself was for him the "latest and best painting of the Venetian school."

The poetry of the public space played a part in the maintenance of the civic life of the community and in the transmission of its civic culture. Philosophers have made stabs at understanding the principle of civic utility at work in the artistry of the traditional town square. Aristotle thought its rhythms and harmonies have a "power of forming character" and so licked the citizen into shape. The poetry of the agora had too, he supposed, a cathartic effect. It eased the psychic burdens of communal life: "all are in a manner purged and their souls lightened and delighted."* Nietzsche agreed; he credited the old civic poetry "with the power of dis-

---

*The tragedies of the Attic dramatists, which before the construction of the Theater of Dionysus were staged in the agora at Athens, contain both spoken passages and sung passages. As a rule the meter of the sung passages is lyric, and the rhythm of the spoken passages in iambic trimeter or trochaic tetrameter.

charging the emotions, of purifying the soul, of easing the *ferocia animi* (ferocity of the mind) precisely by means of rhythm." When "the proper tension and harmony of the soul" was lost, Nietzsche said, the Greek sought sanity in music and poetry. He "had to *dance*, following the singer's beat."

We shall have to wait a little longer to get to the bottom of the biochemical mystery. But science has at last begun to comprehend the genius, and perhaps the genetic basis, of the agora culture of the public square. (Scientific inquiry cannot, of course, shed light on the question of its moral value.) Scientists speculate that music, rhythm, and gossip—the lifeblood of the marketplace and the chief constituents of its poetry—satisfy some need or natural requirement of human nature. The neuroscientist Daniel J. Levitin thinks that the instinct for rhythm and harmony may have been selected by nature because it promotes "bonding and cohesion," "group togetherness and synchrony." The anthropologist Robin Dunbar supposes that music, language, and gossip evolved as "vocal grooming" tools in early hominid groups that had grown too large to rely on tactile grooming techniques to promote cohesion. If Levitin and Dunbar are right, the agora succeeds in part because it is a big biological grooming factory.

⌒

Arendt attributed the decay of public space to the degeneration of politics, but her case would have been stronger had she fingered instead the decline of public poetry. The standard of politics in the West's public spaces has always been rather low, while that of their poetic molds and meters was once astonishingly high. Over the last few hundred years, however, there has been a falling-off in every department of public poetry—choral, dramatic, liturgical—as well as popular and proverbial.* Traditional town-square transmitters of poetic culture, such as schools and houses of worship, have ceased to perform the poetic office. Rock concerts and iPods we have in abundance, but our public spaces are unmusical.

In *The Human Condition* Arendt tried but failed to refute Dante, who knew from his own experience that it was not politics that made Florence a "fair sheepfold" but its civic-pastoral culture. Mars, he said, was always lurking in the dark places of the city's politics, ready to use his art to make the city sad (*sempre con l'arte sua la farà trista*). Dante sought to kick politics upstairs.†
He envisioned a world in which agora-piazza city-states would be subject to the temporal jurisdiction of the Holy Roman Empire and the spiritual jurisdiction of the papacy but would retain their own distinctive cultural and poetic traditions. Rejecting the idea that "each city can and should function as an autonomous, self-legitimating, and self-constituted sovereign whole," Dante put his faith, the scholar John Najemy has written, in the authority of a universal emperor capable of overcoming what we now call political Balkanization. This was an attempt to reinstitute the structural principles of the Roman Empire, yet in advocating it Dante looked forward to the federal nation-state. Where the nation-state

---

*Aristotle remarked on the value of proverbial poetry as an educative device and as a stimulus to ethical reflection, but these primitive forms of poetry—the ballad, for example, and even the nursery rhyme—are rapidly becoming extinct. The singing of ballads was until quite recently a staple of pub life in England, as Hardy, in *The Mayor of Casterbridge*, shows in his account of the Three Mariners, with its twelve-bushel-strength ale and evening singing, and as George Orwell makes clear in his essays on English pub life in the 1930s and '40s. Orwell lamented the fact that, "with its elaborate social ritual, its animated conversations and—at any rate in the North of England—its songs and weekend comedians," the pub was gradually being replaced "by the passive, drug-like pleasures of the cinema and the radio."

†Dante was himself a victim of the capricious politics of the agora-piazza city-state. He was in Siena when he learned that a rival faction at Florence, the Black Guelphs, had brought trumped-up charges against him. When he did not appear to answer the accusations he was sentenced to death. He never saw Florence again, he said, "save in dreams."

has been established on a benign constitutional foundation, its politics have been more stable, and more humane, than the agora-piazza politics of the ancient Greek and medieval Italian cities, the ill-starred statesmanship that condemned Socrates to death and Dante to exile.

The American Federalists who put the Constitution in place over the objections of the Anti-Federalists agreed. The Federalists sought to make the United States a federal nation-state; the Anti-Federalists sought to preserve the polis politics of the agora-piazza city-states, which they looked upon as crucibles of civic virtue. There is little doubt that the Federalists were right about this. The Anti-Federalists would have been wiser to point not to the political arrangements of the old public spaces (which Hamilton and Madison showed were quite defective) but to their cultural excellence. *

Jefferson, though he was not without sympathy for the Anti-Federalists, showed that it was possible to preserve the cultural virtues of the agora without insisting on the political emasculation of the nation-state. To protect civic artistry in a changing America, Jefferson sought to recreate the cultural intimacy of the communities he had known in his youth. As a college student in colonial Williamsburg he had been drawn into little cenacles of sympathetic scholarship which he was always to characterize in Athenian terms: "They were truly Attic societies." It was in communities of this kind, he believed, that men's civic-artistic impulses could

---

*See *The Federalist*: "Had the Greeks, says the abbé Milot, been as wise as they were courageous, they would have been admonished by experience of the necessity of a closer union, and would have availed themselves of the peace which followed their success against the Persian arms, to establish such a reformation. Instead of this obvious policy, Athens and Sparta, inflated with the victories and the glory they had acquired, became first rivals, and then enemies; and did each other infinitely more mischief than they had suffered from Xerxes. Their mutual jealousies, fears, hatreds, and injuries, ended in the fatal Peloponnesian war; which itself ended in the ruin and slavery of the Athenians, who had begun it."

flourish as they could not in a larger space. "A great deal of love given to a few," he wrote, "is better than a little to many." Jefferson's University of Virginia reflected this ideal; he intended it to be an "academical village," and in designing its "Lawn" he made an ingenious use of the classical arts to frame one of America's most beguiling public spaces.

Arendt offers little prescriptive guidance for those seeking to reclaim public space in a world dominated by the nation-state and its vast social machineries; certainly she did not follow Jefferson in seeking an apolitical agora, a purely cultural haven in which people might meet face-to-face and participate in the transmission of particular civic, artistic, and moral traditions. Yet her work remains a useful statement of the part public space might play in resisting the social revolution, if only a way could be found to salvage it. A new generation of civic artists is now attempting to revive the old public spaces: "New Urbanist" architects, among them Léon Krier, Andrés Duany, and Elizabeth Plater-Zyberk, are working to restore the town square to its old pride of public place. The effort is undoubtedly an important one, but Arendt shows us just how difficult the task is likely to be.

In Defense of Rhyme-Time

*N*ot so very long ago children in schools across the United States committed classic verse to memory. They declaimed passages from Shakespeare and Milton, Wordsworth and Keats; even in the earliest grades they learned by heart verses from such poems as Longfellow's "The Midnight Ride of Paul Revere" and Browning's "Abou Ben Adhem." By 1970, however, the tradition was largely dead.

The disappearance of rhyme-time might seem a relatively insignificant matter. Yet before we consign it to the ash-pit of superseded educational theories, we would do well to remember that for more than twenty-five centuries it formed an important part of elementary education in the West. Its origins can be traced to classical antiquity, when the Greeks discovered that words and sounds, and the rhythmic patterns by which they are bound together in poetry, awaken the mind and nourish its powers of perception.

Rhyme-time rests on the theory that (in the words of Plato) "rhythm and harmony find their way to the innermost soul and take strongest hold upon it, bringing with them and imparting nobility and grace." This theory has never been and perhaps cannot be proved, but there is little doubt that people instinctively believe it to be true, for education has from time immemorial begun with the primitive poetry of the nursery rhyme. Before a two-year-old can understand the meaning of Little Jack Horner's plum or Little Miss Muffet's tuffet, he delights in the rhythm and rhyme of the verse; and by hearing the music of particular verses often enough he comes gradually to understand first the sounds and eventually the words of which the verses are composed. Without knowing it, a child who has learned a scrap of verse has been drawn into the civilizing interplay of music and language, rhythm and sound, melody and harmony.

The Greeks made this instinctive faith in the educative powers of music and poetry a foundation of their system of education. They did not distinguish between music and poetry as we do; poetry was for them a form of music, as was indeed any art undertaken under the inspiration of the Muses. "In Greek culture," the Greek scholar Werner Jaeger wrote in *Paideia*, "poetry and music, 'blest pair of sirens,' were inseparable. The same Greek word, *music*, designates them both." Music and poetry were for the Greeks the profoundest of educational forces: poets were for them the chief educators of a people.

It was necessary to begin early, because the mind, when young, is specially receptive. So Plato says in the account of Greek education in the dialogue *Protagoras*. Boys in Athenian primary schools studied not only reading, writing, and arithmetic but also poetry. They were required by their teachers (*grammatists*) to commit passages of poetry to memory and recite them aloud. The teachers "set the works of good poets before them on their desks to read and make them learn by heart." After studying Homer's epic poetry, students turned to lyric poetry, which familiarized them with a new set of rhythms and harmonies. By this means, Plato said in his précis of the Greek theory of rhyme-time, the children become more civilized, more balanced, and better adjusted in themselves and so more capable in whatever they say or do, for *eurhythmia* [a word which, in addition to good rhythm, signifies order, balance, proportion, and gracefulness] and harmonious adjustment are essential to the whole of human life.

In every epoch of Western history until our own we find educators insisting that their pupils serve an apprenticeship in the work of master poets. The Romans who took over Greece took over also its *paideia*, its culture, which they called by the Latin word *humanitas*. The Christians who overthrew the paganism of the Roman Empire did not repudiate this culture. Just as the agora and the forum of Greco-Roman civilization evolved into the piazza, the plaza, and the town square of European Christendom, so the practices of the Greek grammarians begot the grammar, the Latin, and the cathedral schools of old Europe.

As a schoolboy in Roman North Africa in the fourth century St. Augustine studied only a very few Latin classics, principally Vergil's *Aeneid*, great chunks of which he learned by heart. But within its "narrow limits," the historian Peter Brown wrote, the education the young Augustine received was "perfectionist." "Every word, every turn of phrase of these few classics," Brown observed, "was significant and the student saw this." The "aim was to measure up to the timeless perfection of the ancient classic."

Dante, too, went to school to Vergil. In the *Inferno* he saluted Vergil as "*lo mio maestro e 'l mio autore*" (my master and my author), the teacher whose poetry awakened in him the "*grande amore*" (great love) which inspired his "*lungo studio*" (long study) of the *Aeneid*. In a grammar school in Stratford-upon-Avon, Shakespeare received a similar education. Michael Wood observed that the poet "was the product of a memorizing culture in which huge chunks of literature were learned by heart." Such "learning by rote," Wood wrote, "offers many rewards, not least a sense of poetry, rhythm and refinement—a heightened feel for language," as well as a familiarity with tales and myths, imaginative resources that are among the "most exciting gifts" a young person can receive.

Nearer to our own time Edmund Gosse showed how enchanting the rhythms of verse may be found by a child to be. In *Father and Son* he described how one day his father took down from the shelf an old Delphin Vergil and

> began to murmur and to chant the adorable verses by memory.
> *Tityre, tu patulae recubans sub tegmine fagi,*
> he warbled; and I stopped my play, and listened as if to a nightingale, till he reached,
> *tu, Tityre, lentus in umbra*
> *Formosam resonare doces Amaryllida silvas.*
> "O Papa, what is that?" I could not prevent myself asking.

"A miracle had been revealed to me," Gosse wrote,

> the incalculable, the amazing beauty which could exist in the *sound* of verses. My prosodical instinct was awakened, quite suddenly that dim evening, as my Father and I sat alone in the breakfast-room after tea, serenely accepting the hour, for once, with no idea of exhortation or profit. Verse, "a breeze mid blossoms playing," as Coleridge says, descended from the roses as a moth might have done, and the magic of it took hold of my heart forever.

The practice of requiring children as young as seven or eight to recite and memorize the work of master poets was transplanted to America, where it was incorporated in the readers and primers used throughout the country in the nineteenth and early twentieth centuries. Well into the 1920s rhyme-time occupied an important place in the New York City public schools. Citing Edgar Allan Poe's dictum that poetry is "the rhythmical creation of beauty," the Board of Education, in its 1927 *Course of Study in Literature for Elementary Schools*, insisted on the importance of memorizing both poetry and prose orations. "The teacher," the Board said, "should emphasize the rhythm, the beauty of diction, and the beauty of imagery [in a poem]. . . . Teachers should read a group of five poems somewhat similar in style and related in subject matter, so that the pupils may choose their favorite for memorization." A "class may memorize only a part of a longer poem, or one or more selected stanzas, for the whole poem may not be suitable for memorization. Whenever possible, the lullabies and poems of the lower and middle years should be sung or presented by phonograph records. Much of our stirring patriotic verse has been set to music. Records of such songs are available."*

The culture of recitation and memorization that prospered for centuries did not survive the progressive revolution in the

---

*The standard of literacy in the 1927 *Course of Study in Literature for Elementary Schools* is astonishingly high. Poems "for reading and memorization" by first-graders include those of Robert Louis Stevenson ("Rain" and "The Land of Nod"), A. A. Milne ("Hoppity"), Christina Rossetti ("Four Pets"), and Charles Kingsley ("The Lost Doll"). Second-graders recited poems by Tennyson ("The Bee and the Flower"), Sara Coleridge ("The Garden Year"), and Lewis Carroll ("The Melancholy Pig"). In third grade came Blake's "The Shepherd" and Longfellow's "Hiawatha," while fourth grade brought Elizabeth Barrett Browning, Emily Dickinson, and Kipling. In the grades that followed, students read and recited poems by Arnold, Browning, Burns, Cowper, Emerson, Keats, Macaulay, Poe, Scott, Shakespeare, Southey, Whitman, and Wordsworth.

schools. Rhyme-time, progressive educators argued, was a sterile and unfruitful discipline, one that promoted a culture of servility harmful to the free creative play of the mind. "The true center of correlation on the school subjects," G. Stanley Hall said in 1901, "is not science, nor literature, nor history, nor geography, but the child's own social activities."

Paul Goodman argued that progressive education is in many ways an extension, into the classroom, of the techniques of the social imagination: progressive teaching, he observed, is founded on the belief that children are "human social animals" who must be "socialized" and "adjusted to the social group." "Permissiveness in all animal behavior" is therefore encouraged: such permissiveness, by bringing out the "social animal" in a child, makes it easier for the child to merge his identity in that of the social pack.* Rhyme-time is anathema to progressive educators because it inhibits this development: it develops not the child's animal faculties but his

---

*Goodman demonstrates how intimate is the connection between the social imagination and the animal or natural imagination: both stand in an equivocal relation to the moral imagination and the customs and traditions that sustain it. Such a social progressive as Dewey worships nature quite as much as Edmund in *King Lear*: no more than Edmund will Dewey stand "in the plague of custom." The same intimacy may be observed in Rousseau. Rousseau worshiped nature, and he thought that the natural man, who was uncorrupted by custom and civilization, was superior to the civilized man of his day; yet his neo-Spartan politics anticipated Dewey and prepared the way for the social discipline of the nanny state. The nature worship Rousseau inspired must be sharply distinguished from the efforts of those who, like Wordsworth and Emerson, tried to read in nature's mystic book. Wordsworth and Emerson sought to find a transcendent purpose in the universe. Nature was to provide the spiritual key that would unbar the locks: the resulting revelation of overarching purpose would illuminate the inward laws of man's moral and spiritual nature. The mystic naturalists saw *through* the world of *physis* to something that lay beyond it. Thus Wordsworth sings of "the faith that looks *through* death," the visionary power that overcomes the "laws of vulgar sense" and beholds that which "is divine and true." Thus Emerson speaks of a man's spiritual "passage to new worlds." The nature worship of the social progressive, by contrast, is founded in a materialism that either denies that such a transcendent purpose exists or is indifferent to its significance.

civilized ones. We read in Plato of the music-less man who is also an uncivilized one, a hater of *logos*, a despiser of words, language, and reason, a

> stranger to the Muses: he no longer makes any use of persuasion by speech but achieves all his ends like a beast by violence and savagery, and in his brute ignorance and ineptitude lives a life of disharmony and gracelessness.*

T. S. Eliot said that when a people has become insensitive to poetry, their ability "not merely to express, but even to feel any but the crudest emotions, will degenerate." The progressive educator despises rhyme-time just for this reason: it is an initiation in civilization, and civilization, for the progressive educator, is more or less corrupt. (Human nature, on the other hand, is for the progressive educator originally and intrinsically good; the conservative educator, by contrast, believes that human nature is originally and intrinsically corrupt, and he finds in tradition, which embodies the cumulative wisdom of the civilization, a moral discipline that enables man to flourish in spite of his flaws.) Rousseau, who has some claim to being the first progressive educator, believed that man was good and that civilization was bad: he sought to banish literature from primary education because it was too intimately involved in the corruptions, the hypocrisies, and the falsenesses of civilization. In *Émile* he said that children should be kept away from the refining influence of books and poems. Émile himself

---

*Shakespeare echoed the sentiment in *The Merchant of Venice* :

> The man that hath no music in himself,
> Nor is not moved with the concord of sweet sounds,
> Is fit for treasons, stratagems, and spoils;
> The motions of his spirit are dull as night,
> And his affections dark as Erebus:
> Let no such man be trusted.

(Rousseau's fictitious educational guinea pig) "at twelve years old
will hardly know what a book is."* When progressive educators
argue that rhyme-time is a "chain-gang" technique, they are echoing Rousseau.

Are the progressives right? Edmund Wilson was at first
inclined to think so. But his old Greek teacher at the Hill School,
Alfred Grosvenor Rolfe, who was staunchly committed to teaching traditions that had been handed down from the old grammar
and Latin schools, led him to reconsider the matter. When Rolfe
began to write against progressive education, Wilson, who was at
the time an editor of *The New Republic*, "had a sort of idea at first
that I ought to be on the other side, since my magazine supported
John Dewey." But the more he read of Rolfe's satire on progressive
education,

> the more I felt there was something to be said for his position.
> Wasn't it true that, in order to train children to do anything really
> well, you had to break them to an exacting discipline as [Rolfe]
> had done with us in Greek? Without that you couldn't do any-
> thing with Greek—you couldn't do anything with anything. How
> great were the chances that a schoolboy could be counted on to
> choose what he needed . . . or to acquire [the requisite] disci-
> pline through natural bent?

Wilson conceded that Rolfe might "have misunderstood and mis-
represented what was proposed for progressive education; but
when I came later on to see something of the teaching both in progressive institutions and in the ordinary kind, I was appalled by
the slackness of the training." Certainly Wilson never shared the
progressives' antipathy to rhyme-time; in his diaries he tells how

---

*Rousseau made an exception for Defoe's *Robinson Crusoe*, which he believed would
teach Émile self-reliance.

he gave his young daughter, Helen Miranda Wilson, verses from Emerson's *Concord Hymn* to learn by heart.

Rhyme-time is an initiation rite, one by which the young are initiated in the mysteries of language and civilization. It is not really news that the civilization into which they are inducted is imperfect, nor is it strange that those of us who have already entered it should sometimes wish to escape it, to go off with Huck and Jim on the raft, or to be "Nature's Priest," as the youth in Wordsworth's poem is in the days before "the prison-house" closes upon him. "But I reckon I got to light out for the Territory ahead of the rest," Huck says, "because Aunt Sally she's going to adopt me and sivilize me, and I can't stand it." No one, however, can be boy eternal. One must grow up, and the attempt to protract beyond their natural limit the untamed pleasures of childhood can only involve us in difficulties greater than those we would escape.

~

Plato, it is true, sometimes speaks of "molding" the young soul with poetry.* The words suggest that rhyme-time involves the imposition, on the mind, of standards external and perhaps alien to it. But Plato knew very well that "nothing that is learned under compulsion stays with the mind," and he more often described

---

*It is sometimes said that Plato sought to banish poetry from his ideal city. The reality is somewhat more complicated; Plato taught that the *harmonia* and *rhythmos* of poetry must be subordinated to *logos*, to language, to reason, and ultimately to truth. Thus he has Socrates condemn, in the *Republic*, verses that are "neither moral nor true." Such verses ought to be excised, for "there is no lying poet in God." "Observe," G. A. Hight wrote in his analysis of the question, "that there is not a word about forbidding all poetry, but only of expurgating certain passages which tend to degrade the minds of the hearers." G. A. Hight, "Plato and the Poets," *Mind*, New Series, vol. 31, no. 122 (April 1922), 195. This bowdlerization of poetry, repugnant though it is to freedom, may have some justification when the poetry in question is being used to educate children.

poetic education as a means of uncovering, in the soul, a mold that is already there. The soul, having been thus inspired (or awakened), "supplies its own deep melodies." A man finds "the true rhythm and harmony of his being." Rhythm and harmony "have an *ethos*, a moral character," Werner Jaeger wrote in his précis of Plato's theory, one that enables the mind to discover its own interior poetry, "the hidden law of its own structure."

Peter Brown, in his study of the education of Augustine, conceded that the methods of poetic tuition are likely to strike a modern mind as "servile." But the paradoxical result of this early servitude was, he said, mental liberation. Augustine came "to love what he was learning." He "developed, through this education, a phenomenal memory, a tenacious attention to detail, an art of opening the heart, that still moves us as we read his *Confessions*." One suspects, indeed, that progressive educators resist rhyme-time just because it *is* a liberating exercise, and so frustrates the "socialization" of the child in a way that banal courses in "social studies," which never touch the deepest places in the imagination, do not. The social techniques of the progressives tend to homogenize us: the poetic techniques of traditional education tend to bring out our latent individuality. So far from oppressing the spirit of the young person, rhyme-time helps him fulfill the injunction of Pindar: "Become what you are."

~

"*One thing is needful,*" Nietzsche said. "'Giving style' to one's character—a great and rare art!" It "is the weak characters without power over themselves who *hate* the constraint of style." They "are always out to interpret themselves and their environment as *free* nature—wild, arbitrary, fantastic, disorderly, astonishing . . ."

But this "thrilling disorder," Nietzsche said, is a cultural dead end. Poetry is necessary because it brings out the latent order and artistry of the soul: poets, he said, are "tamers of the will, transformers of animals, creators of men, and in general sculptors and remodellers of life."

If poetic education was useful in the past in counteracting the spirit of "thrilling disorder" Nietzsche dreaded, it is perhaps even more necessary now, when children are from their earliest years exposed to entertainments that do little to cultivate, in the mind, a sense of order, proportion, measure, and harmony.* On the contrary, the cartoons for children that one finds both on television and in contemporary children's books are, with their misshapen figures and contorted faces, dim parodies of the *bizarre cubiques* of Picasso or Braque: all is fragmented, abrupt, cacophonous. From the hallucinogenic carnival of *The Wiggles* or *The Doodle-bops,* which recreate, in a stupider form, the anarchic spectacles of Kandinsky, to the contorted figures of *Charlie and Lola,* which burlesque the canvases of Chagall and de Kooning, the children's TV shows retail a genially degraded modernism.

Wordsworth in his preface to *Lyrical Ballads* said that "a multitude of causes, unknown to former times, are now acting with a combined force to blunt the discriminating powers of the mind" and "to reduce it to a state of almost savage torpor." Wordsworth had in mind "frantic novels, sickly and stupid German Tragedies, and deluges of idle and extravagant stories in verse." Today's entertainments for children would of course be out of his star of

---

*"A change to a new type of music or lyric poetry is something to be wary of, as a hazard to all our fortunes. Modes of music are never disturbed without unsettling the most fundamental customs, usages, and laws of the community." Plato, *Republic*, 424c. Shelley's saying, "Poets are the unacknowledged legislators of the world," should perhaps be read in this light, as should the saying of Fletcher of Saltoun, that if "a man were permitted to make all the ballads, he need not care who should make the laws of a nation."

comprehension: their music is of a kind which (to borrow Plato's words) "seems to maim the minds of those listeners who do not possess as an antidote a knowledge of its real nature." The poetry of rhyme-time could be such an antidote, but children no longer possess it.

⟿

Progressive educators today are no less opposed to rhyme-time than were their predecessors. It is not uncommon for children in American public schools to reach their tenth year without having encountered, in the classroom, a single line of classic English poetry or prose. The most recent challenge to recitation and memorization exercises comes from a theory called "constructivism." Based on the work of Swiss developmental psychologist Jean Piaget, constructivism rests on the belief that objective knowledge does not exist; students must therefore "construct knowledge for themselves." Education professor Linda Darling-Hammond of Stanford calls constructivism the "new paradigm" and argues that because "learners actively construct" their own knowledge, teachers "must construct experiences for" their students that enable them to learn. The teacher who gives a student Wordsworth's "Daffodils" or Coleridge's "Kubla Kahn" to memorize fails to "construct" an atmosphere in which "dynamic" or "authentic" learning can occur. "Constructivist teachers," one educator declares, "must create an open, nonjudgmental environment that permits students to construct, disclose, and expose their constructions to scrutiny." Darling-Hammond echoes this sentiment when she advises teachers to "make sure the emphasis is on powerful learning, not rote memorization."

But the progressives' educational philosophy is only superficially a philosophy of liberty. The exercises in "guided fantasy" and "sensitivity training" that under the progressive regime have replaced rhyme-time do little to open a child's mind. Exposure to classic poetry, by contrast, gives a child a language, at once subtle and copious, in which to articulate his own inchoate feelings. Augustine said that "all the various emotions of the heart" have rhythms which find their analogs in the rhythms of "verse and song." The rhythms of poetry, he believed, have the power to bring the dormant emotions of the heart to life. (Thus we speak of knowing a poem "by heart," a formulaic tribute to its power over us.) The literary culture that rhyme-time perpetuates is a record of how men and women have, in various times and places, struggled to understand themselves and to make sense of the complexities of the human heart. Such culture does not repress or enslave: it enlarges and strengthens and frees.

Conservative Compassion
versus Social Pity

A remarkable feature of George W. Bush's pronouncements, in the days before he became unequivocally a war president, was his unashamed use of the "L" word. As a candidate for the White House, Bush called his political philosophy "compassionate conservatism." But he was not afraid to utter the stronger word that gives that philosophy its meaning. The word is love.

Bush used the word when, during the presidential campaign, he was confronted by a man who spoke of illegitimate children and the welfare system. When the man used the word "bastards," Bush became angry. "First of all, sir," he said, "we must remember that it is our duty to love all the children." Many conservatives, however, are understandably skeptical of the notion of mixing love and politics. T. S. Eliot said that *amor* was above all others "the key word for Dante": it was for him "a principle of order in the human soul, in society and in the universe." This may be true; but memories of the love fests of the 1960s might cause even the most generous heart to reassess the virtues of hatred.

The taint goes deeper. Long before the emergence of the sixties' counterculture, progressive thinkers sought to make love a first principle of politics. Socialists invoked the idea of love in their struggle against market liberalism: they believed that the modern system of loveless labor could be replaced by a model of community grounded not in competition but in mutual care. In painting a picture of the "communal" or "social" man who would emerge after the downfall of capitalism, the socialists disclosed the deeper image of their hearts, the idea of the loving man, the man who is not alienated either from himself or the things and people around him.

In the twentieth century many liberals adopted this vision of love's place in society. They embraced the modest, Fabian socialism of the welfare state partly because they hoped to stave off more draconian forms of socialist organization, but also because they genuinely sympathized with the plight of the less fortunate, whose condition they hoped to improve through social legislation. In nationalizing almsgiving, the liberals were motivated, too, by the belief, so characteristic of the last century, that compassion exercised under the supervision of government experts is more likely to be effective than the charitable impulses of private individuals. Charity, under the new social dispensation, would be no longer a gift but a right. The liberals hoped, through this change of terms, to make the taking of alms less humiliating to the taker. They failed to see that the taking of charity is always humiliating, except, perhaps, when the gifts are accompanied by an affection so palpable as to diminish the shaming quality of the transaction.

~

The error the socialists and the welfare-state liberals made was to suppose that love's efficacy could be gradually extended beyond the bounds of the family and the tribe, where it spontaneously creates desirable patterns of order, into larger communities, where it does not. Wherever love has been obliged to perform a large and public role, it has always degenerated into mere pity. Hannah Arendt illuminated the distinction between love and pity when she drew attention, in her book *On Revolution*, to a theme in Dostoevsky's *The Brothers Karamazov*. Arendt described how the novelist, in the story of the Grand Inquisitor, contrasted the loving compassion of Jesus with the eloquent but disastrous pity of the Inquisitor:

> For *compassion*, to be stricken with the suffering of someone else as though it were contagious, and *pity*, to be sorry without being touched in the flesh, are not only not the same, they may not even be related. Compassion, by its very nature, cannot be touched off by the sufferings of a whole class or a people, or, least of all, mankind as a whole. It cannot reach out farther than what is suffered by one person and still remain what it is supposed to be, co-suffering. Its strength hinges on the strength of passion itself, which, in contrast to reason, can comprehend only the particular, but has no notion of the general and no capacity for generalization. The sin of the Grand Inquisitor was that he, like Robespierre, was "attracted toward *les hommes faibles*," not only because such attraction was indistinguishable from lust for power, but also because he had depersonalized the sufferers, lumped them together into an aggregate—the people *toujours malheureux*, the suffering masses, et cetera. To Dostoevski, the sign of Jesus's divinity clearly was his ability to have compassion with all men in their singularity, that is, without lumping them together into some such entity as one suffering mankind. The greatness of the story, apart from its theological implications, lies in that we are made to feel how false the idealistic, high-flown

phrases of the most exquisite pity sound the moment they are confronted with compassion.

Pity, Arendt argued, is a concern for the misery of another unprompted by intimacy with, or love for, the sufferer. Compassion, by contrast, is a love directed "towards specific suffering" and concentrates on "particular persons." It can be exercised only by individuals or small groups, not by agencies or bureaus. Pity, Arendt wrote, "may be the perversion of compassion." Because the pitier "is not stricken in the flesh," because he keeps his "sentimental distance," he has often shown "a greater capacity for cruelty" than the confessedly cruel.

The type of compassion modern liberals claim as their own peculiar virtue is really a form of pity, milder perhaps than that which lies at the heart of the socialist orthodoxies, but dangerous in its own right. David Hume said that pity was a "counterfeited" love. It is the false compassion that results when men exercise their kindness by committee: it is the look in the eyes of the welfare clerk or the public housing official. To be pitied by another man is to stand humiliated before him; however well intentioned programs grounded in pity may be, they always end by laying low their intended beneficiaries. Pity does not lead to a flourishing in the pitied, though it may provoke their resentment, even their rage; the act of pitying is always a kind of strength condescending to weakness. Love awakens; pity oppresses.

∽

As a candidate for the White House, Bush pledged to overcome the culture of pity, "the soft bigotry of low expectations," and to mobilize America's little platoons of compassion on behalf of the

wayward, the needy, the outcast. The platform on which he cam-
paigned—as I understood it—was not a conservative apology for
the welfare state, or a plea for the extension of its social services;
it was an attempt to revive forms of pastoral care that flourished in
the market squares—in the villages and shtetls—of the West before
the great expansion of commerce and industry that began in the
eighteenth century, and before the emergence, in the late nineteenth and early twentieth centuries, of the social state.

Ever since the days of Voltaire and d'Alembert, it has been the
fashion to disparage pastoral institutions that had their origins in
the benighted times, in the Dark and Middle Ages. Yet the keepers
of those old market squares and village greens developed an array
of first-rate charitable institutions, most of them quite independent
of the state. These institutions were at once humane in scale and
rooted in the local knowledge of particular people and conditions.
They effected, the historian William E. H. Lecky said, "a complete
revolution" in the care of the downtrodden and were crucial to the
maintenance of the fabric of civic life. Such voluntary associations
as the confraternity and the sodality, the guild and the *charité*, were
hospitable in the widest sense. In old French towns the *hotels-dieu*—
"hostels of God"—offered refuge to the weak and the sick, and to
those who were "cast down amidst the sorrows and difficulties of
the world." In Venice the Scuole Grandi—the "Great Schools"—
brightened the city's piazzas not only by sponsoring civic festivals
and processions but also by distributing alms, succoring paupers,
and administering hospitals. The Low Countries had their frater
houses, the English shires their almonries and chantries.

This pastoral ethos was by no means the exclusive property of
the Christian populations of old Europe. In his novel *The Bridal
Canopy*, S. Y. Agnon described, in a beautiful and affecting way,

the pious charity of the Hassidic Jews of Galicia. No one who has read Agnon's account of Reb Yudel and the "renowned men . . . who study Torah in dire poverty and distress and solitude and loving-kindness" is likely to forget their benefactions—how Joshua Eleazar "forgot" to eat the potatoes, that he might share them with a guest, or how Moshe Leib of Sasov "shared the sufferings of all men as though they were his own," and "used to support orphans from his own pocket and cover their heads and cure them of boils."

The same pastoral ideal inspired the mendicant orders whose adepts devoted themselves to the service of the community, the various friars (Black, White, Grey, Brown, Austin, Capuchin) who went forth into the marketplace to feed the hungry, clothe the naked, and heal the sick. Supported by the generosity of the prosperous members of local communities, the friars, Dom David Knowles has written, "for at least two centuries surpassed all other members of the clergy in spiritual energy, doctrinal knowledge and pastoral ability."

In *Les Misérables*, Victor Hugo described the power of these kinds of faith-based charity not simply to feed and clothe but to heal and transform. Hugo made his character Monseigneur Myriel, bishop of Digne, a model of religious charity, and showed how his compassion forever changed the life of the convict Jean Valjean.

"You need have told me nothing," [the bishop assured Valjean.] "Why should I ask your name? In any case I knew it before you told me."

The man [Valjean] looked up with startled eyes. "You know my name?"

"Of course," said the bishop. "Your name is brother."

"Monsieur le curé," the man cried, "I was famished when I came here. Now I scarcely know what I feel. Everything has changed."

Les Misérables is a novel, and it may be that Hugo's account of the compassion of the bishop of Digne is overly sentimental. Consider, however, the work that is even now being performed by Father Peter Raphael and Sister Simone Ponnet in Abraham House in New York City. This organization, in the Mott Haven section of the Bronx, is home at any given time to a dozen or so previously incarcerated convicts who, in exchange for early release, have agreed to live by the rules of the house—its regimen of work, education, and drug testing—before regaining their full liberty. When I mentioned Hugo's bishop of Digne to Father Raphael, who was for many years a prison chaplain on Rikers Island, I found that he knew the story by heart. Hugo's picture of compassion, he insisted in French-accented English (Father Raphael was born in the Languedoc), "is not fiction." He has seen the transformations take place. In New York State some 70 percent of released offenders return to crime. Of more than one hundred Abraham House graduates, only one has so far gone back to prison for a fresh offense.

George W. Bush promised to revive, in contemporary America, the pastoral ideal that has allowed Abraham House to rescue so many strayed souls; but as president he was unable to overcome the institutionalized pity of the social state. Faith-based proposals intended to permit religious institutions to play a part in the distribution of public assistance languished in legislative limbo. Religious institutions are in many ways better equipped than purely secular ones to help people solve certain kinds of problems; but Bush never persuaded the nation to embrace his pastoral project. Proselytes of the secular religion of the social state continue to dominate the heights, and everyone else is supposed to acquiesce in the fiction that the social bureaucracies they have established are as effective in helping people as the older institutions they superseded.

Very often, when I read an account of some particularly wretched man, one who has committed a terrible crime or has fallen into a miserable way of life, I try to connect the figure of ruin with the child he must once have been, full of promise and possibility. This certainly takes an effort of imagination; but how much greater must be the force of will that associates the fallen man with the idea of a loving God who purposefully gave him life and who yet desires his regeneration. Not many people, I suppose, have such a power of imaginative will, but it is incontestable that some people do. Father Raphael is one of these. "God," he tells me, "came to call sinners."

More perhaps than any other quality, it is this quality of religious faith that turns pity into charity. It does this, I think, because it enables the dispenser of charity to see, in the recipient who takes it, something more than degraded human flesh. Whatever one's idea of the truth of particular religious creeds, society benefits when a person engaged in charitable work is able to see promise in the person he is charged with helping: is able to see in him "a living soul," created in the image of his maker. Faith in God, Father Raphael says, is essential to the pastoral work of the nondenominational Abraham House. He calls the place a "little parish, a parish of offenders."

His faith, Father Raphael says, not only helps him see the "grace God can work" in fallen men; it helps him also overcome the fear a man naturally feels when he works under the ever-present threat of violence. Here, too, Hugo understood the problem. After the bishop of Digne has offered Valjean a bed for the night, Hugo relates how the convict "swung round upon his elderly host, folded his arms, glared at him," and exclaimed,

> "This is wonderful! You're putting me to sleep in a bed next to your own." He broke off to laugh, and there was a monstrous quality to his laughter. "Have you thought what you're doing? How do you know I have never murdered anyone?" The bishop replied quietly: "That is God's affair."

Father Raphael tells me that when you visit a prisoner on Rikers Island, "You don't go by yourself over there." He believes that God goes with him.

The effect of a compassionate gaze is to make the beneficiary conscious of something in himself he did not know he possessed. Hugo's bishop of Digne sees past Valjean's grime and perceives what Hugo called his "soul." Through the bishop's charity, Valjean is himself brought to "see his own soul, hideous in its ugliness." Yet as "he wept a new day dawned in his spirit." Melodrama? If so, we need more of it: according to one study, one in every thirty-two adults in the United States is under some form of supervision by the criminal justice system; more than two million people are behind bars.

Compassionate assistance cannot, of course, be a substitute for the punishment of criminal acts. And whenever we speak of the healing virtues of *caritas*, we must always remember the ineradicable element of evil in our sensuous nature. No doubt most of us do too little to resist the evil in ourselves; but for the few who actually embrace the malignant power they discover in their hearts, even acts "of kindness and of love" may fail to redeem. Still, in many cases a compassionate charity *can* heal, and it is therefore unfortunate that institutions which have the power to do more than pity those who suffer continue to be shut out of public almsgiving. Abraham House receives no government money. In order to qualify for the funds that NGOs committed to some variant of the social imagination are eligible to receive, Abraham House would have to compromise the pastoral culture that makes it effective. "We tried many, many times," Father Raphael says. "We went to Albany. We saw the people from the state and from the city, telling us, 'Oh, you have to compromise with us, to change a little bit your philosophy, because we can help you.' But our philosophy is that we cannot erase the spiritual way we deal with human beings."

Compassion is as important in education as it is in almsgiving. It is the teacher's sympathetic insight into the mind of his student that enables him to perceive the student's potential. We do not, when we are young, know who we are; it is in the course of growing up and being educated that we come to understand what we must be. The teacher whose vision is sharpened by compassion helps to awaken, in the student, the processes of self-culture that will enable him to develop his own peculiar gifts and aptitudes.

This work of doing justice to others, impossible in a crowd, is not easy even in a classroom. A teacher must have sufficient discernment to penetrate the masks that young people so often wear. Such discernment is a by-product of compassion. Only love, the German philosopher Johann Georg Hamann said, can reveal the true nature of anything. "My experience tells me," Coleridge said, "that little is taught or communicated by contest or dispute, but everything by sympathy and love." Educators whose teaching is an extension of their powers of sympathy very often develop the most remarkable faculties of perception. Shakespeare has one of his characters reflect on the folly of taking love out of learning, for love "adds a precious seeing to the eye." In the same spirit Dickens dramatized the compassion of the true teacher in the character of Marton, the schoolmaster in *The Old Curiosity Shop*. Like Hugo's bishop of Digne, Marton is the soul of charity, and he has awakened in little Harry, his "favourite scholar," a love of learning and of "poring over books." Yet Harry's reciprocated affection for his teacher perplexes Marton. "How did he ever become so fond of me?" the schoolmaster asks. "That I should love him is no wonder, but *that he should love me . . .*" The reader understands what Marton himself does not: it is what Dickens calls Marton's "compassion" that has made Harry love him and desire to please and emulate him. Harry ends by calling his teacher his "dear kind friend." "I hope I always was," Marton replies. "I meant to be, God knows."

The teacher who today shrinks from challenging his students because he is afraid to injure their self-esteem might seem to resemble a character like Marton. But the resemblance is superficial; the teacher who does not urge his pupil to go up higher is not really a compassionate figure; there is, in his failure to hold his students to his own private standards, a frigid pity, and a secret contempt. Yet it is not easy to see how teachers who have been trained under a social regime can do much better. Teachers in the public schools practice their craft in a highly centralized system that inhibits the development of sympathetic insight. Anyone who has tried to fit his personality into the mold of such a system knows how difficult it is to keep intact even his consciousness of his own humanity. Only by an effort of will can he bring himself to see that the human raw material he is charged with processing has also its unique human potential.

The reign of public pity has given the United States its share of shabby housing projects and grim schoolhouses, yet those who continue to exalt the social imagination have gained a reputation for compassion while their conservative critics are generally supposed to be callously indifferent to human suffering. Part of the problem is that for many years conservatives, unnerved by the success of the progressives in imposing their social ideals on society, reasoned that, since they could not beat their opponents, they must join them. Only by doing so could they hope to "dish" their enemies. "If there is to be a revolution," Bismarck said, "we would rather make it than suffer it."

Welfare-state liberals built up their regimes of bureaucratic pity both to prevent the enactment of more extensive forms of socialism and to assuage their own guilty consciences. The pessimistic conservatives, by contrast, embraced the social imagination in order to outmaneuver their opponents. Bismarck was not, strictly speaking, a conservative: he was an idiosyncratic reactionary who, in the words of his English biographer, A. J. P. Taylor, followed by turns Marx and Metternich. In the 1880s, a decade after he unified the German nation, Bismarck implemented a program of social insurance. The reforms were admirable in theory, and had they been implemented in a different spirit they might have proved beneficial in practice. But the Iron Chancellor enacted his reforms in a manner calculated to diminish personal liberty and increase the authority of the state. Bismarck, Taylor said, did not "promote social reform out of love for the German workers." His object was to make workers "more subservient" to the state. "Whoever has a pension for his old age," Bismarck remarked in 1881, "is far more content and *far easier to handle* than one who has no such prospect."

Bismarck succeeded in outmaneuvering his enemies and in laying the foundation of the *Sozialstaat* envisioned by the nineteenth-century German economist Johann Karl Rodbertus, one of the earliest theoreticians to reconcile nationalism and socialism in a romantic vision of administrative *étatisme*. The Iron Chancellor "provocatively rejoiced," Taylor wrote, "in echoing Frederick the Great's wish to be *le roi des gueux*, king of the poor." But the merriment was deceptive, for the old Junker was a romantic pessimist. With his nervous anxieties, his gastric ulcers, his cigars, and his "Black Velvet" (a combination of stout and champagne he concocted himself), Bismarck was not at home in the modern world he felt powerless to stave off completely, nor was he in the least sympathetic to its aspiration to lift up the masses through social legislation. "I have spent the *whole night hating*," he announced one day when he was the most powerful man in Germany and perhaps in Europe, and might be supposed to have been on good terms with his planet.

A century after Bismarck's reforms, Richard Nixon made a similar series of calculations. His domestic proposals were faithful to the social ideal: a larger welfare state, a high tariff, new regulatory agencies, more federal spending, wage and price controls. When spending pushed prices up, Nixon's answer was, "Kick the chain stores." As part of his Family Assistance Plan he contemplated the ultimate form of public pity, a government-supplied minimum income unconnected either to exertion or achievement. Although Congress never enacted the proposed guaranteed-income legislation, Nixon succeeded in opening the government's sluice gates. Spending on social programs, 28 percent of the budget at the end of Lyndon Johnson's term, consumed some 40 percent of it by the time Nixon left office. Under his administration the dreams of the Great Society became a reality.

Nixon had been influenced not by Rodbertus but by Nietzsche. Borrowing a copy of Nietzsche's *Beyond Good and Evil* from his assistant, Monica Crowley, in 1992, Nixon said, "I must have lent [my copy] out to someone. I can't believe I'm missing my Nietzsche! I always try to look at his stuff during a presidential campaign to remind me of why I went through the damn fire." Nietzsche's theory of decadence found fertile soil in Nixon's mind. In remarks in Kansas City in July 1971, Nixon recalled how, on visits to Athens and Rome, he had mused on the decline of American civilization. The "great civilizations of the past," he said, "as they have become wealthy, as they have lost their will to live, to improve," have "become subject to the decadence which eventually destroys a civilization." The United States, he said, was "now reaching that period." The policies he proposed for a "decadent" America were contrived in an atmosphere of impending doom and have about them, as so many things in his life do, a quality of ruin.

Attempts to portray Nixon as a reactionary populist are unconvincing in part because they overlook the Nietzschean quality of his politics. In his book *Nixonland* the historian Rick Perlstein argues that Nixon forged "a public language that promised mastery of the strange new angers, anxieties, and resentments wracking the nation in the 1960s." He saw that the "wave of the political future was an ambivalent reactionary rage," and he created a framework for future Republican victories "by focusing people's resentments." In dwelling on the kicked puppy in Nixon—the "tormented" loser who was rejected by the Franklins (the socially prestigious fraternity at Whittier College)—Perlstein accepts at face value Nixon's contention that he was "one of us." This was the slogan of his ur-campaign against Jerry Voorhis in 1946. Conrad, in *Lord Jim*, glossed the talismanic phrase. Jim, Marlow says, "was one of us. He stood there for all the parentage of his kind, for men and women by no means clever or amusing, but whose very existence is based upon honest faith, and upon the instinct of courage."

Nixon might have pretended that he was "one of us." But the man who found his vade mecum in *Beyond Good and Evil* was convinced that he was a superior man—a tiger, albeit one in jackal's clothing. He was not, in self-conceit, a man of the people; he was an aristocrat, one who as the result of some existential error had not been assigned his rightful place in the master class. Not for nothing did he watch the film *Patton* over and over again. Here was the kind of *Übermensch* he believed himself to be. *Patton*, like *Beyond Good and Evil*, liberated his inner superman. Flying back to Washington with the movie fresh in his mind, he vowed to strike the enemy harder in Cambodia. "Cut the crap on my schedule," he said. "I'm taking over here. Troop withdrawal was a boy's job. Cambodia is a man's job." His sadness alone might make him question his Caesarian vocation. "He who is really possessed by raging ambition," Nietzsche said, beholds "its image with *joy*." This perhaps explains the curious spectacle of Nixon composing, in the White House, a memo to himself concerning the "need for joy."

A true herd politician respects the cattle. Nixon disdained them. He embraced the paternalist policies of the social state precisely because his own private attitude was as patronizing as that of Bismarck and the Roosevelts. The cattle could not be expected to make it on their own; someone had to kick them. He himself belonged not among the degraded *Volk* but in the Nietzschean club of heroic world-shapers. He flattered Mao as though the old man were chairman of the membership committee. "The chairman's writings moved a nation and have changed the world," Nixon said unctuously when he was admitted to the book-filled sanctum in the Forbidden City. Mao teased the overeager applicant: "I've only been able to change a few places in the vicinity of Peking." When Mao hinted that they had got rid of the troublesome Lin Biao by arranging for his plane to crash, Nixon knew that he had made the grade. "The chairman can be sure," he said, "that whatever we discuss . . . nothing goes beyond the room." He was one of them.

To miss this element in the Nixonian fantasy is to miss the core. To raise the blood pressure of electoral cattle with culture-war politics was child's play. The morons on the White House staff could do that. Even Agnew could do that. The great object was to be a statesman after the fashion of Bismarck and Metternich, and to design a new balance of power for the world, a work of geopolitical art. Plenty of presidents have used their diplomatic skills as an instrument in the service of their country. Nixon might have been the only one to use the country as an instrument in the service of his diplomatic skills.

⸎

In the years since Nixon's fall, conservatives have put forward a telling critique of the inadequacies of the social state, but they have failed to address the problem of compassion in a conservative way. They continue to find themselves in bidding wars with the champions of the social imagination, and under George W. Bush the social state and its entitlement machineries grew rapidly. Conservatives today perceive the radical wrongness of bureaucratic pity, but they have yet to find a way to revive the habits of pastoral care. One of the objects of conservative thinkers in the coming years must be to find a way of adapting, to modern conditions, the older, better culture that Dante knew when he called Florence a "fair sheepfold," and which St. Francis extolled when he composed his Prayer.

Obama, Shaman

*T*he really striking thing about the charismatic leader is the extent to which his followers regard him as a healer of wounds, an alleviator of pain. In this sense, surely, President Obama is a charismatic figure. The carefully knotted ties and conservatively tailored suits only accentuate the exoticness of his shamanism; he has entered the American psyche not as a hero but as a healer.

The country, or much of it at any rate, has longed for such a figure, a man from the once-oppressed race whose rise to power will atone for the sins of slavery and racial stigmatization. But Obama's rhetoric encompasses more than a promise of racial healing. He is not the first politician to argue that politics can redeem us. But in posing as the Adonis who will turn winter into spring, he revives one of the more questionable political conceits: the belief that a charismatic leader can ordain a civic happy hour and give a people a sense of community that will make them feel less bad.

~

In his unfinished treatise *Economy and Society*, Max Weber defined charisma as "a certain quality in an individual personality by virtue of which he is set apart from ordinary men and treated as endowed with supernatural, superhuman, or at least specifically exceptional powers or qualities." Weber was able to do little more, before he died in 1920, than give a pseudoscientific élan to an idea that had been kicking around for centuries. Most of what he said about charismatic authority was stated more cogently in Book III of Aristotle's *Politics*, which described the great-souled man who "may truly be deemed a God among men" and who, by virtue of his greatness, is exempt from ordinary laws.

What both Aristotle and Weber made too little of is the mentality of the charismatic leader's followers, the disciples who discover in him, or delusively endow him with, superhuman qualities. "Charisma" was originally a religious term signifying a gift of God: it often denotes (according to the seventeenth-century scholar-physician John Bulwer) a "miraculous gift of healing." James G. Frazer, in *The Golden Bough*, demonstrated that the connection between charismatic leadership and the melioration of suffering was historically a close one: many primitive peoples believed that the magical virtues of a priest-king could guarantee the soil's fertility, and that such a leader could therefore alleviate one of the more elementary forms of suffering, hunger. The identification of leadership with the mitigation of pain persists in folklore and myth. In the Arthurian legends, Percival possesses an extraordinary magic that enables him to heal the Fisher King and redeem the wasteland; in England the touch of the monarch's hand was believed to cure scrofula.

It is a sign of growing maturity in a people when, laying aside these beliefs, it acknowledges that suffering is an element of life that sympathetic magic cannot eradicate, and recognizes a residue of pain in existence that even the application of technical knowledge cannot assuage. Advances in knowledge may end particular kinds of suffering, but these give way to new forms of hurt—milder, perhaps (one would rather be depressed than famished), yet not without their sting. We do not draw closer to a painless world.*

One of the objects of a mature political philosophy is to reconcile people to the painful limitations of their condition. The American Founders recognized this, as did the English statesmen who presided at the Revolution of 1688: they rejected utopianism. And yet, precisely because they knew that human beings are by nature far from perfect, they allowed a degree of scope in their constitutional settlements for the mysterious, quasi-magical qualities that Weber associated with charisma—rather as an architect, as a concession to human frailty, might omit the number thirteen when labeling the floors of a building. The "magic" of the post-1688 English constitution, Walter Bagehot observed, lay in the pageantry of the monarchy, a relic of the mysterious grace of the healer-redeemer chiefs of old. The American Founders, after experimenting with weaker forms of executive power, created the presidency, an office spacious enough for a charismatic leader to work his wizardry, but narrow enough to prevent delusory overreaching.

＿＿

Unlike the English Whigs and the American Founders, the modern champions of the social imagination regard suffering not as an unavoidable element of life but as an aberration to be corrected by up-to-date political, economic, and hygienic arrangements. Rather than acknowledge the limitations of our condition, the

*The "pain which is essential to life cannot be thrown off," Schopenhauer says. "The ceaseless efforts to banish suffering accomplish no more than to make it change its form." If we succeed in removing pain in one of its forms, "it immediately assumes a thousand others."

social visionary is continually contriving panaceas that will enable us to transcend it.

Barack Obama, in taking up the part of regenerative healer, is the latest panacea. Our schools, he says, are "crumbling." There are "lines in the emergency rooms" of the hospitals, and our corporate culture is "rife with inside dealing, questionable accounting practices, and short-term greed." He points to the millions of Americans who, in struggling with life's difficulties ("high gas bills, insufficient health insurance, and a pension that some bankruptcy court somewhere has rendered unenforceable"), have become bitter and unhappy. Obama attributes these problems to a failure of government and more especially of politics—a politics that breeds "division, and conflict, and cynicism" and has become a "dead zone" in which "narrow interests vie for advantage and ideological minorities seek to impose their own versions of absolute truth."

The solution, he says, lies in a political reformation. Unless we "begin the process of changing politics and our civic life," we will bequeath to our children "a weaker and more fractured America" than the one we inherited. Hence his mantra, "Change we can believe in." Like the Nicene Creed, Obama's doctrine begins in belief. *Credo.* Once we believe in the possibility of a transformative politics, "the perfection begins." The selfish politics of the present yields to the selfless politics of the future. We discover that "this nation is more than the sum of its parts—that out of many, we are truly one." So believing, we can replace a politics that breeds division, conflict, and cynicism with one that fosters unity and peace. In Obama's "project of national renewal," government can become an expression of "our communal values, our sense of mutual responsibility and social solidarity."

In June 2008 Obama elaborated on the premises of his political thought when he said that his victory in the race for the

Democratic nomination would in the future be regarded as the moment "when we began to provide care for the sick and good jobs to the jobless," a golden age "when the rise of the oceans began to slow and our planet began to heal." Yet even as he suggests that a new communitarianism can heal not only America's pain but even the world's, he is careful to anticipate the charge of utopian delusion. Just when he seems to embrace in the most fantastic way the notion that he is a figure sprung from the *Fourth Eclogue* of Vergil, he draws back and relegates the social prophet in him to his cave. He will not, he says, deceive us: in his sober, lawyerly way he tells people that government cannot "solve all their problems." But the candor of the confession seems only to heighten his followers' faith in his powers.

The danger of Obama's healer-redeemer fable lies in the hubris it encourages, the belief that gifted politicians can engender new forms of communitarian solidarity that will make our lot less painful. Such a renovation of our national life would require not only a change in constitutional structure—the current system having been geared to conflict by the Founders, who believed that the clash of private interests helps to preserve liberty—but also a change in human nature. Obama's conviction that it is possible to create a beautiful politics, one in which Americans will selflessly pursue a shared vision of the common good, recalls the belief that Dostoevsky attributed to the nineteenth-century Russian revolutionists, who supposed that, at the coming of the revolution, "all men will become righteous in one instant." The perfection would begin.

In rejecting the Anglo-American politics of limits, Obama revives a political tradition that derives ultimately from Niccolò Machiavelli. In the *Discourses on Livy* and *The Art of War*, Machiavelli argued that it is possible to create a communitarian republic like the one whose outlines he glimpsed in Livy's (highly romanticized) version of Roman history—a polity in which citizens, forsaking their own swinish pursuits, would become happy in the pursuit of a common good. Wise laws, he maintained, would "make citizens love one another." The virtuous *res publica* of the Romans could be conjured anew.

To liberate a people from the bondage of pain and establish a new communal order, a statesman must possess, Machiavelli argued, a kind of charisma he called *virtù*. He described the most charismatic statesman with whom he was (personally) acquainted, Cesare Borgia, in Weberian terms, as one who "exhibits a fortune unheard of, a *virtù* and confidence [so much] more than human that he can attain all he desires."

Jacob Burckhardt credited the luminaries of the Italian Renaissance with envisioning the state as a work of art. More tragically, they envisioned it as a machinery of redemption. Machiavelli's prince was the first intimation of a modern charismatic type, the demiurge who uses a demonic *virtù* to overcome divisive self-seeking in the name of social solidarity. Self-interest led to market capitalism and alienation; civic selflessness led to public-spirited communitarianism and happiness. The "Machiavellian vocabulary," the historian J. G. A. Pocock argued in *The Machiavellian Moment*, became the "vehicle of a basically hostile perception of early modern capitalism." Machiavelli rejected as unrepublican the pursuit of private interest which the leading Anglo-American statesmen accepted.

In doing so he anticipated modernity's childish dream of an anodyne world. His communitarian state is the distant prototype of the workers' paradises of Marx and Lenin and the Nordic Valhallas of Hitler and Houston Stewart Chamberlain. His influence is evident in both the enlightened despot celebrated by the continental philosophes and the socialist wizard admired by such intellectuals as Edmund Wilson, who hailed Marx as a combination of "Prometheus and Lucifer," a heroically diabolic figure who could redeem the wasteland of modern capitalism. The Machiavellian ideal of a communitarian paradise haunts, too, the welfare-state philosophy that Bismarck (for his own cynical reasons) promoted when he established the world's first *Wohlfahrtsstaat*, a model for socialists in Germany and welfare-state liberals in England and the United States. The idea of community is even now a touchstone of activists and academic writers on politics; they have refreshed the older vision by phrasing it in the language of civic virtue rather than social solidarity. But it is no less spurious a vision. True community, the most intimate and local of civic forms, can scarcely be promoted by something as clumsy and bureaucratic as the administrative machinery of a great nation-state.*

In breathing fresh life into the communitarian daydream, Obama revives a style of charismatic leadership that fell out of favor in the

---

*The social expert is typically loathe to see communities develop independently of the state; he looks to the government to foster local civic culture by means of programs administered by the expert castle class to which he himself belongs. Thus the British Tories, in their efforts under David Cameron to promote community in Britain, have placed at the center of their program a policy calling for the establishment of "a powerful Office for Civil Society to fight for the interests of charities and community groups," to be staffed by the usual social-scientific gurus.

United States after the death of FDR. Of the three presidents since 1945 most often regarded as possessing charismatic qualities, the first, Kennedy, was a tax cutter who questioned liberal utopianism when he said that "life is not fair," and the second, Reagan, sought to curb the hubris of New Deal *étatisme*. The third, Clinton, said that he could feel our pain but retreated from his pledge to heal it when he scrapped a plan to nationalize medicine. Obama, by contrast, is faithful to the old-style charismatics, whose slogans ("social solidarity," for example) he has taken out of cold storage.

Of course, he would not have gotten as far as he has had he simply defrosted the ideas of Henry Wallace and George McGovern. Obama's charisma is tuned to the mood of the moment. The charisma of American political leaders has typically rested on images of unflinching strength and masculine authority: Teddy Roosevelt in the North Dakota Badlands; Kennedy, the naval hero whose sexual prowess was acknowledged even in his Secret Service code name ("Lancer"); Reagan, the man on horseback whom the Secret Service called "Rawhide." Obama's charisma, by contrast, is closer to what the critic Camille Paglia has identified with today's television talk-show culture, in which admissions of weakness are offered as proof of empathetic qualities. Talk-show culture is occupied with the question of why we feel so bad when it is our right under the social dispensation to feel eternally good. The man who would succeed in such a culture must appear to sympathize with these obscure hurts; he must take pains, Paglia writes in *Sexual Personae*, to appear an "androgyne, the nurturant male or male mother."

Obama has evidently found a new way to bottle the old wine. He knows that experience has taught Americans to suspect the masculine healer-redeemer who bears collectivist gifts; no one wants to revive the caudillos of the thirties. Studiously avoiding the tough-hombre style of earlier charismatic figures, he phrases his vision in the tranquilizing accents of Oprah-land. His charisma is grounded in empathy rather than authority, confessional candor rather than muscular strength, metrosexual mildness rather than masculine testosterone. His power of sympathetic insight is said to be uncanny: "Everybody who's dealt with him," columnist David Brooks says, "has a story about a time when they felt Obama profoundly listened to them and understood them." His two books are written in the empathetic-confessional mode that his most prominent benefactress, Oprah, favors; he is her political healer in roughly the same way that Dr. Phil was once her pop-psychology one. The collectivist dream, Obama instinctively understands, is less scary, more sympathetic, when served up by mama (or by mama in drag).

With the triumph of Obama's postmasculine charisma, the patriarchal collectivism of the New Deal has finally given way to a new vision of liberal community, the empathetic mommy state that Balzac prophesied in *La Comédie humaine*. The leader of the future, Balzac foresaw, would be a man who, like his diabolically charismatic Jacques Collin, possesses a capacity for maternal love. When his protégé Lucien dies, Collin exclaims: "This blow has been more than death to me, but you can't understand what I'm saying. . . . If you're fathers, you're only that and no more. . . . I'm a mother, too!" Collin ends his career as a functionary of the state—and a policeman. The Grand Inquisitor of the future, Balzac intimates, will undertake his inquisitions in the name of matriarchal pity.

Yet if Obama has made redemptive communitarianism attractive in an age of sagging sperm counts, he has done nothing to correct the underlying flaw of the collectivist ideal: its incompatibility with the older morality of limits. The politics of consensus that Obama favors is incompatible with the Founders' adversarial system, which permits those whom he disparages as "ideological minorities" to take stands on principle that, at times, frustrate the national consensus. Obama believes there is no place in politics for moral and ethical "absolutists" who would defy the community. The "ideological core of today's GOP," he writes, is "absolutism, not conservatism," an absolutism driven by those who prize "absolute truth" over "communal values."* This commitment to absolute truth, he argues, stands in the way of a politics that can solve our problems and change our lives.

Obama goes so far as to argue that the Constitution itself is "a rejection of absolute truth." His moral relativism is intimately bound up with his conviction that we can transcend those limitations in human nature that the Founders acknowledged when they drafted the Constitution. The charismatic redeemer, Machiavelli observed, is all but bound to reject older moral standards. It is not simply that adherence to traditional morality will prevent such a leader from being properly ruthless in the pursuit of his ideal; it is that the old morality, with its emphasis on the limits of man's fallen condition, makes his communitarian paradise seem quixotic—an instance of utopian overreaching.

Machiavelli was ready with a solution. He prepared the way for the politics of redemptive healing by working to overturn the older morality. In particular he undermined the West's most potent myth of diabolic amorality and delusory hubris. Two years after he completed *The Prince*, Machiavelli composed a fable, *Belfagor, or the Devil Who Took a Wife*, in which he ridiculed the idea that

---

*A number of President Obama's defenders have argued that his Republican adversaries are "nihilists" because they have refused to cooperate in the enactment of his legislative agenda. Whatever else the politician who embraces a vision of "absolute truth" may be, he cannot with justice be characterized as a "nihilist."

the devil can take possession of a man's mind and corrupt those around him. In assuming (correctly) that the diabolic qualities of his redemptive prince would be easier to swallow once the devil himself became a joke, Machiavelli blazed a path that Voltaire, Diderot, Goethe, and Shaw afterward trod. No one fears the devil that Voltaire refused to renounce on his deathbed. ("This is no time to be making enemies.") Goethe's Mephistopheles is charming, as is Shaw's (in *Man and Superman*). Even those characters whom modern European artists have intended to be diabolic (such as Balzac's Collin) arouse sympathy in a way that older devil characters (Shakespeare's Iago, for example) do not.

Dostoevsky was among the few who grasped the momentousness of the change that Machiavelli initiated in the West's conception of diablerie.* Near the end of *The Brothers Karamazov*, he describes an encounter between the devil and Ivan Karamazov. The devil appears not with claws and horns but in the guise of an elegant man of the world: he phrases his taunts in French and laughs at modern intellectuals who believe that he doesn't exist, or who worry that to admit his existence would harm their "progressive image." Dostoevsky implied that it was precisely when the devil became a wit that the intellectual classes of the West succumbed to the most familiar form of diabolic temptation: the belief that men can transcend the limits of their condition and "be as gods."

Obama has revived a cruel mirage, but the country has defenses against his brand of redemptive politics. Some of these defenses

---

*Maritain was another: "The unconcealed and palpable influence of the devil on an important part of contemporary history is one of the significant phenomena of the history of our time."

are constitutional, others cultural. The very strength of America's religious ideal of redemption has restrained, though it has not entirely forestalled, the development of alternative secular ideals of redemption. A religiously inspired belief in original sin has made Americans wary of succumbing to the Pelagian notion that a mere mortal, however charismatic, can build the New Jerusalem out of purely secular materials. The country's constitutional system, itself founded on the theory of original sin, has created a perpetual conflict of factions and interests that has so far prevented any single party from imposing a monolithic unity from above, such as Europe's collectivists were able to do.

And then there is the devil himself, the West's traditional symbol of evil. He is taken a good deal more seriously on these shores than he is in Europe. A 1991 survey by the International Social Survey Programme found that 45.4 percent of Americans believed in the devil (61 percent, according to a 2005 Harris poll), compared with 20.4 percent of Italians, 12.5 percent of Russians, 9.5 percent of West Germans, and 3.6 percent of East Germans. We often read of differences between America and Europe with respect to belief in God, but differences with respect to belief in diabolic evil may be even more revealing. It is significant that belief in the devil is lowest in those countries (Russia and Germany) that suffered, during the twentieth century, most acutely from forms of evil that might without exaggeration be called diabolic. Europeans, it may be, have proved more susceptible to the element of diabolic temptation in charismatic leadership precisely because they are less likely to believe in the reality of diabolic evil.

Yet Obama has undoubtedly found a weakness in America's defenses. His postmasculine charisma is likely to flourish in a political environment that has come to resemble not only a TV talk show but a TV reality show, one in which the candidate rarely escapes the camera's eye. The masculine leader of old had to conceal his weaknesses. "I rather tell thee what is to be feared," Shakespeare has Julius Caesar say, "than what I fear, for always I am Caesar." When scrutiny was less intense, the man on horseback could hope to get away with it. Shakespeare's Cassius laments that the public never knew how weak Caesar really was:

> He had a fever when he was in Spain,
> And when the fit was on him, I did mark
> How he did shake; 'tis true, this god did shake . . .

Today a camera would capture the image of the shaking god. Superman, Norman Mailer said in his famous essay on Kennedy, can thrive in the supermarket—but in cable TV and YouTube, the *Übermensch* may finally have met his match. The practitioner of the new postmasculine charisma has no such problem: the very images of frailty that undermine the conventional masculine leader's pose of strength help his postmasculine successor, whose object is to appear human, all too human. Softness has become an asset for candidates who have molded themselves on the exhibitionist model of the Oprah matriarchy.

Hence Obama's spectacular rise. But he is bound in the end to disappoint: what he calls the "audacity of hope" Schopenhauer more persuasively calls "the delusion of hope." Not only does Obama's cult of secular redemption teach us to despise our political system's recognition of human frailty, it encourages us to seek for perfection where we will not find it—in politics, in the hero worship of a charismatic shaman, in the speciousness of a temporal millennium. Lacking the moral parables that made our ancestors wary of those delusions in which overweening pride is apt to involve us, we pursue false gods and turn away from traditions that really can help us to make sense of our suffering lot.

~~

A final observation. One of the tests of a leader is whether he has a capacity to mobilize his people's myths. Thomas Jefferson, Abraham Lincoln, Martin Luther King Jr., and Ronald Reagan all reworked biblical parables of healing and redemption in their rhetoric. Obama's ability to work successfully in this vein is evidence of his uncommon political skills. But in revising the politics of redemption he has concentrated it more relentlessly than his predecessors on the radiance of a particular kind of shamanistic magic, one that inheres in the person and figure of the binder of wounds.

Obama's revision of the redemptive style helps explain why, more perhaps than any president since Kennedy, he is a favorite of those members of the elite classes who manage the social state or sympathize with its ideals. Their compulsive ardor is likely to puzzle those who do not find the catchwords of the president's redemption rhetoric—"journey," "real change," "that's what hope is, imagining"—especially persuasive. They fail to see how rich is the vein of archaic sentiment he has tapped. One could imagine an anthropologist, centuries hence, sifting through the ruins of our civilization and concluding something like this: "The rise of the cult of Obama, a young legislator from one of his people's Midwestern metropolises, suggests parallels with the earlier progress of the Egyptian cult of Osiris and the Greco-Phrygian worship of Adonis-Attis, in which civilizations which had forsaken their original spiritual inspirations sought

rejuvenation in the figure of a beautiful young man who promised to redeem a barren age. The Obama cult was especially
popular among those citizens who, in the scribal forms of the
day, marked the box designated 'some college or more' in their
communications with the central authority."

Today's well-to-do churchless elites, particularly those who
inhabit the bluish seacoasts, are as apt to be dissatisfied with their
unregenerate state as those who turn to religion in the effort at the
perfect. Unlike the religiously inclined, however, the blue elites
find little consolation in the civilization's older spiritual disciplines: they have as a rule learned to cherish secular substitutes for
religion. In a blue state like Connecticut, income and church atten-
dance are negatively correlated: in blueland it is the poorer folk
who are more likely to be conventionally pious. The elites in these
regions, precisely because they are conscious of a spiritual void—
an emptiness that even the choicer forms of Epicureanism cannot
fill—were among the first to anoint Obama a secular healer.

The same elites have used a reading of the establishment clause
of the First Amendment to relegate the traditional spiritual culture
of the West to an obscure corner of the American public square. It
is in many ways only to be expected that they should now look to
a swami to effect the miraculous regeneration of a spiritual wasteland their own policies have done so much to create.

Blood and Iron or the Mending of Nature? The Case of Lincoln, Bismarck, and Darwin

> Liberty of action, sir? There is no such thing as liberty of action. We are all slaves and puppets of a blind and unpathetic necessity.
> —Mr. Glowry, in Peacock's *Nightmare Abbey*

*I*n September 1862 Otto von Bismarck, the new prime minister of Prussia, went to the Prussian Chamber of Deputies to confront the Budget Committee. His face still sunburned from a trip to the south of France, he urged the lawmakers not to waste time in political debate while Germany remained ununited. "It is not to Prussia's liberalism that Germany looks," he said, "but to its power. . . . It is not by means of speeches and majority resolutions that the great issues of the day will be decided—that was the great mistake of 1848 and 1849—but by *Eisen und Blut*" (iron and blood).

Across the Atlantic, Abraham Lincoln reached a similar conclusion, or so Edmund Wilson argued in his 1962 book *Patriotic*

Gore. In Wilson's reading, Lincoln too used "iron and blood" to achieve his goals: both he and Bismarck "established a strong central government over hitherto loosely coordinated peoples. Lincoln kept the Union together by subordinating the South to the North; Bismarck imposed on the German states the cohesive hegemony of Prussia."

Was Wilson right to find a similarity of method and purpose in the two greatest statesmen of their age? Bismarck carried out his policy by going to war with neighboring states and using fighting words to stimulate German nationalist sentiment, the chauvinism that enabled him to unite the German Reich in January 1871. He himself pronounced the definitive judgment on the morality of the first of these wars, that with Denmark in 1864. A French diplomat called on him in the Wilhelmstrasse and struggled to express his disapproval of Prussia's conduct without violating the canons of diplomatic politeness. "Don't put yourself out," Bismarck told the Frenchman. "Nobody but my king thinks that I acted honorably."

No less devious were the Bismarckian machinations that led to the war with Austria in 1866 (a manufactured dispute over the administration of the conquered Danish duchies of Schleswig and Holstein) and the war with France in 1870 (which had its origin in the Hohenzollern candidature for the Spanish throne, which Bismarck himself secretly promoted). All of Bismarck's victims shared the frustration of Austria's Franz Josef. "How can one avoid war," the Habsburg emperor asked, "when the other side wants it?"

Underlying Bismarck's policy of blood and iron was the belief that a nation is a quasi-biological organism with a morally unconditional right (in his words) "to live and to breathe." In order to become a nation, Bismarck believed, a people may, on one pretext or another, prey upon other peoples. The right of conquest, he said, was "sacred," and never more so than when undertaken in order that the German nation might "live." Prussia's actions, he declared in 1866, followed from the "right of the German nation to exist, to breathe, to be united; it is the right and the duty of Prussia to give the German nation the foundation necessary for its existence."

The thesis that Lincoln, like Bismarck, was a blood-and-iron statesman rests on the notion that his statecraft was a variation on the Bismarckian theme. Lincoln, in this interpretation, believed that in order to survive, or simply in order to vindicate its founding ideals, a nation has a right to make war on those of its citizens who reject either the nation itself or its ideals.

This, however, was not what Lincoln believed: the thinking that led him to wage the Civil War was quite different from that which led Bismarck to wage his wars. The question of Lincoln's responsibility for the Civil War turns ultimately on his policy toward the seceding states. According to such historians as Lord Acton, if Lincoln had really been the freedom-loving statesman he claimed to be, he would have recognized the right of the secessionist populations to choose their own destinies for themselves. More recently, paleoconservative writers have revived Acton's argument and depicted Lincoln as an enemy and not a friend of freedom.

Are Acton and the paleocons right? In deciding where his duty lay, Lincoln on becoming president had first to determine the criteria by which he was to judge the morality of secession. Was the moral fitness of secession a matter of numbers? If so, how large did the numbers have to be? I, a lone citizen of the United States, may announce that I am seceding from the Union and attempt to make off with such federal property in my neighborhood as I fancy.

If I do this, I will almost certainly be seized, tried, and jailed. No president would judge my act of secession morally legitimate. But does secession become legitimate if, say, 51 percent of a particular population approves it? Sixty-seven percent? One hundred percent? May particular segments of this subpopulation—blacks, for example, or slaves, or blue-eyed people, or Buddhists—be excluded from the calculus of legitimacy? By what procedure is popular approval of secession to be manifested? Must its expression take the form of a plebiscite, or is it sufficient that conventions composed of notable citizens decide?

Lincoln could have pronounced a purely personal judgment on the moral legitimacy of secession, but that, he conceived, was not his job. He had his station and knew its duties: when he became president, he swore to preserve, protect, and defend the Constitution of the United States. The only criterion, he supposed, that he could reasonably use in judging the legitimacy of secession was that of the Constitution itself. James Buchanan, Lincoln's predecessor, concluded that the Constitution forbade secession; Lincoln reached the same conclusion. The Yale constitutional scholar Akhil Amar, in his book *America's Constitution: A Biography*, argues that Lincoln's interpretation was correct and that the Constitution prevents "subunits from unilaterally bolting whenever they [become] dissatisfied." When the war came, it came not because of Lincoln's predilection for blood and iron but because of his interpretation of the law of the land—a fundamental expression of its *mores*—and his application of it to a particular case.

One can, as in a law-school exercise, split hairs ad infinitum. Was the Constitution itself a legitimate law, given that *it* was a by-product of treason and rebellion? Can a charter that recognizes, as the Constitution does, a right of withdrawal from an older instrument (the Articles of Confederation), foreclose, with any show of justice, the same right of exit from the compact that it has established in its place? And even if Lincoln was right about the *letter* of the Constitution, was he not, in prosecuting the Civil War, violating the *spirit* of freedom that gave birth to it? Did a point not come, after quantities of blood had been spilled and the Confederacy had given so many proofs of devotion to its Cause, when Lincoln ought to have concluded, as Mr. Gladstone did, that the Southern people had "made a nation," and to heck with the Constitution?

It is possible that Lincoln would have reached such a conclusion if he had believed that nothing more than the fate of the Constitution was at issue. But there was something else to be weighed in the balance. "For my own part," he told John Hay, "I consider the first necessity that is upon us, is of proving that popular government is not an absurdity." Lincoln believed that if the United States were broken up by internal dissension, the result would be a setback for the cause of free government from which it might not soon recover. The question, he said, was

> whether a constitutional republic, or a democracy—a government of the people, by the same people—can, or cannot, maintain its territorial integrity, . . . whether discontented individuals, too few in numbers to control administration, according to organic law, . . . [can] break up their Government, and thus practically put an end to free government upon earth. . . . When ballots have fairly, and constitutionally, decided, there can be no successful appeal, back to bullets; . . . there can be no successful appeal, except to ballots themselves, at succeeding elections.

Lincoln's point was that if you can opt out of a democracy whenever you lose an election, democracy will never work. The moral case for the Union was even stronger, he believed, given that those who were trying to break out were doing so not because their own liberties had been violated—they had not been—but merely because they objected to Lincoln's belief that slavery ought not to be extended into the national territory.

It is true that Lincoln suspended the writ of habeas corpus. It is true that his secretary of state boasted that, by touching "a bell [at his] right hand," he could have persons deemed obnoxious to the regime incarcerated without due process. But if there were Bismarckian touches in Lincoln's statecraft, he was not, on the whole, a Bismarckian statesman. Bismarck himself sensed this and never liked Lincoln. The two men were on different sides of a great political and philosophic divide. An earlier generation had a better sense of this than ours does. "We have been at war with Metternich and Bismarck," the British historian George Macaulay Trevelyan wrote after World War I. "Cavour and Garibaldi gave us Italy for an ally, while Washington and Lincoln gave us America."

Trevelyan, like his great-uncle Macaulay, was what is called Whiggish in his approach to history: he analyzed the moral choices statesmen made and described how those choices enlarged or restricted the individual's liberty of action. By contrast, our contemporary approach to history is almost Darwinian. Edmund Wilson anticipated the trend in *Patriotic Gore*, in which he urged historians to

> interest themselves in biological and zoological phenomena. In a recent Walt Disney film showing life at the bottom of the sea, a primitive organism called a sea slug is seen gobbling up smaller organisms through a large orifice at one end of its body; confronted with another sea slug of an only slightly lesser size, it

ingurgitates that, too. Now, the wars fought by human beings are stimulated as a rule primarily by the same instincts as the voracity of the sea slug.

If Bismarck offered a sea-slug apology for his statesmanship, others have attributed a sea-slug vision to Lincoln himself, who (in their view) differed from Bismarck only in the way that he veiled the Darwinian *Machtkampf* with a spare but poetically appealing rhetoric of moral idealism. Paraphrasing the thesis of a recent study of Lincoln and Darwin, the critic Richard Eder pointed to the "larger tragedy at the root" of Darwin's and Lincoln's work: "Universal death as the necessary agent of natural selection; vast death as the agent of emancipation." Lincoln, in this reading, derived his ethics from nature, and nature, Leslie Stephen observed in his book *The Science of Ethics*, has "but one precept, 'Be Strong,'" and "but one punishment, decay culminating in death and extirpation." If the interpretation that Eder describes is right, Lincoln's philosophy resembles nothing so much as that of Edmund in *King Lear*:

> Thou, Nature, art my goddess; to thy law
> My services are bound.

Just as nature uses death to enforce its regime, so Lincoln used death to enforce his.

Nature, whatever else she may be, is a goddess who possesses a sense of humor. Rarely has she shown an acuter sense of fun than when she arranged for the assembly of the genetic material that became Abraham Lincoln at roughly the same time the fertilized egg that was Charles Darwin first leapt into the womb. Both men

were born on February 12, 1809. But attempts to find correspon-
dences between the very different, in some ways antithetical, types
of evolution in which each man specialized—biological evolution
in Darwin's case, ethical evolution in Lincoln's—prove not in the
end to be very persuasive.

Lord Annan has argued that theories that confuse biological
evolution with human ethics are as a rule "worthless." The problem lies in the effort to compare the actions of organisms that have
developed a conscience and a moral imagination to the actions of
organisms that lack such conscientious power. It is one thing if
your cat playfully torments a wounded animal, quite another thing
if you yourself do. Conscience enables its possessor to sit in judgment on the characteristics that have won him a spot in the race for
genetic victory: it enables its possessor, at times, to reject naturally
selected traits that have helped pay for the winning ticket (if such it
be) he holds in the lottery of life. History and ethics are the record
of the moral acts of morally conscientious organisms; biology is
the record of the biological acts of morally unconscious organisms.
The confusion of the two realms is a symptom of our time.

From the perspective of history and ethics, Bismarck's attempt
to formulate a crude form of Social Darwinism, a Prussia-as-sea-
slug style of statesmanship, was a step backward. The fittest, T. H.
Huxley observed, is not necessarily the best; nature—"*la nemica
Natura*"—is a power without a conscience. A trait selected by
her—finesse, for example, in preying on the weak—is not necessarily one worthy of moral approbation. It might, for example, be
some day proved that the capacity for crime is a selected trait, that
the deviousness, the bold badness, of the criminal intellect has
resulted in genetic mutations that have contributed to the evolutionary fitness of the human organism. Stupidity too might prove
to be such a trait. If intelligence has at times served an evolutionary
turn, so undoubtedly has the stupidity that is, after all, far more

common—the stupidity that shields the mind from life's horrors and so enables the unintelligent person to thrive and reproduce, in contrast to the too-sensitive perceptiveness, the acute nervous delicacy, of his more intelligent brother, who very often makes a hash of things. "Yes, nature is ironical," Hippolite says in Dostoevsky's *The Idiot.* "Why does she create her very best human beings only to make fools of them later?"

"Evolutionary ethics are fraudulent," Annan argues. "Ethics tell us what we ought to do, they deal with the problem of obligations; evolutionary ethics tell us nothing about obligation." To write history under the inspiration of Darwin is take the "ought" out of the story. One is left only with a pervasive "must."* Lincoln's rhetoric of liberty and democracy becomes either purely hypocritical or deeply delusory: whatever he might have said that he and his tribe were doing, they were in reality fighting for biological mastery, for victory in a struggle in which only the fittest survive.

⟶

A Darwinian can of course argue that our conscientious morality is itself an evolutionary artifact, and that our moral imagination is simply a higher expression of the natural imagination. Thus Shakespeare's Polixenes, in *The Winter's Tale*, tells Perdita:

Yet nature is made better by no mean
But nature makes that mean: so, over that art,
Which you say adds to nature, is an art
That nature makes. You see, sweet maid, we marry

---

*Schopenhauer says, "Necessity is the kingdom of nature; freedom is the kingdom of grace." By "grace" he means the state of having overcome nature.

A gentler scion to the wildest stock,
And make conceive a bark of baser kind
By bud of nobler race: this is an art
Which does mend nature, change it rather, but
The art itself is nature.

The moral art that "mends" our merely instinctual, biological, genetically striving nature may itself, paradoxically, be a product of that nature. But if so it proves only that the law of evolution can transcend the motives in which it began and develop, in its highest evolutionary creations, a sense of moral purpose that leads the created thing to turn its back on the primitive traits that midwifed it.

Lincoln was not, like Edmund in *King Lear*, an adorer of nature; he is perhaps better understood as a mender of nature. Such a moral reading of his statesmanship, it is true, is unlikely to find approval in some quarters. The trend in historical scholarship during the last century and a half has been to substitute determinist readings of history for moral ones: for the most accomplished modern historians, "renown and grace is dead." In his book *The American Political Tradition*, Richard Hofstadter argued that the Founders' rhetoric of liberty and constitutional government concealed a conscious or unconscious desire to preserve their own economic power. Their status as members of the rich, propertied classes determined their politics and explains what Hofstadter called their "rigid adherence to property rights." In similar fashion historians have argued that Lincoln's rhetoric of liberty was a mask for Northern economic interests. These interpretations are products of a variant of the social imagination—its most familiar expression is Marxism—which reduces men and women to social and economic automatons whose actions are determined by the interests of the classes to which they belong.

It is possible that, where history is concerned, Darwin will become the new Marx. Marxism has been largely discredited; but those who remain faithful to the social imagination continue to resist any return to the moral interpretation of history, which seems to them Whiggish and naive. A history inspired by biology—one in which Washington and Lincoln become slaves of nature—would enable those who continue to derive inspiration from the social imagination to discredit historians who in their work have carried on the moral tradition of Tacitus and Thucydides, of Macaulay and Gibbon. In the past such aficionados of the social imagination as Rousseau turned to nature worship in their struggle against the moral imagination and its "plague of custom." A debased Darwinism would enable today's social philosophers to carry on the fight with new, supposedly scientific weapons. It would also perpetuate the paradox of progressivism. The social progressive seeks to liberate man from his lower self—his biological or class-inspired rapacity—through a process of secular redemption. Yet in order to achieve this reformation he makes a fetish of humanity's animal nature, its merely biological and carnal—its merely material—characteristics. Thus he exalts particular biological, sexual, racial, and social types, as Marx and Lenin did when they exalted the proletarian, as Dewey did when he exalted the child as a social animal, as today's progressives do when they offer up encomia to the gay pride of the homosexual or the special knowledge of the wise Latina. Such is the barrenness of a merely material philosophy: its adepts may dream of secular redemption, a new heaven and a new earth to be achieved by social devices, yet practically they are always descending to the cruder worship of unredeemed nature, or to the idolatry of gross matter.* The social visionaries may prophesy a universal

---

*Marx, though he sought to repudiate the classical political economists, went much farther than they did in making man into a socio-economic machine and a creature of his

freedom, but they are always exalting not the common humanity of
the species but particular carnal and sexual distinctions, as though
the essence of our being were to be found in the complexion of our
skin or the constitution of our genitalia.

At all events, the new Historical Darwinism, should it gain
ground, is likely to prove as blind an alley as the old Social Darwinism. Certainly it can do little to illuminate the statesmanship
of Lincoln. "Let us have faith that right makes might," he said in
1860. You cannot Darwinize Lincoln, who insisted that biological might is not necessarily the same as moral right. Still less can
you Bismarckize him. And yet it may be that once an organism has
developed a moral imagination, what is Darwinian and Bismarckian in its mental organization can be Lincolnized.

---

social class: society for him is destiny. The disciples of Darwin, in applying Darwinism
to man's social life, have made man into a biological machine: biology for them is destiny.
Samuel Butler said of Darwin that he "banished mind from the universe." The same
thing could be said of Marx.

Hearts of Darkness:
Exporting the Welfare State

*P*aternalism was supposed to be finished. The belief that grown men and women are childlike creatures who can thrive in the world only if they submit to the guardianship of benevolent mandarins underlay more than a century's worth of welfare-state social policy, beginning with Otto von Bismarck's first *Wohlfahrtsstaat* experiments in nineteenth-century Germany. But paternalism's centrally directed systems of subsidies failed to raise up submerged classes, and by the end of the twentieth century even some liberals, surveying the cultural wreckage of the Great Society, had abandoned their faith in the welfare state.

Yet in one area—foreign aid—the paternalist spirit is far from dead. A new generation of economists and activists is calling for a "big push" in Africa to expand programs that in practice institutionalize poverty rather than end it. The Africrats' enthusiasm for the failed policies of the past threatens to turn a struggling continent into a permanent ghetto—and to block the progress of ideas that really can raise up Africa's miserable populations.

The intellectual justification for the new paternalism comes from economists such as Columbia's Jeffrey Sachs, who in his recent best-seller *The End of Poverty* argues that prosperous nations can dramatically reduce African poverty, if not eliminate it, by increasing their foreign-aid spending and expanding smaller assistance programs into much larger social welfare regimes. "The basic truth," Sachs says, "is that for less than a percent of the income of the rich world"—0.7 percent of its GNP for the next twenty years—"nobody has to die of poverty on the planet."

Sachs headed the United Nations' Millennium Project, created in 2002 by Secretary General Kofi Annan to figure out how to reverse poverty, hunger, and disease in poor countries. After three years of study, the project's ten task forces concluded that prosperous nations can indeed defeat African poverty by 2025—if only they spend more money. "The world already has the technology and know-how to solve most of the problems faced in the poor countries," a Millennium report asserted. "As of 2006, however, these solutions have still not been implemented at the needed scale." Translation: the developed nations have been too stingy.

We have heard this before. The "response of the West to Africa's tragedy has been constant throughout the years," observes the economist William Easterly. From Walt Rostow and John F. Kennedy in 1960 to Sachs and Tony Blair today, the message, Easterly says, has been the same: "Give more aid." Assistance to Africa, he notes, "did indeed rise steadily throughout this period (tripling as a percent of African GDP from the 1970s to the 1990s)," yet African growth "remained stuck at zero percent per capita."

All told the West has given some $568 billion in foreign aid to Africa over the last four decades, with little to show for it. Between 1990 and 2001 the number of people in sub-Saharan Africa below what the UN calls the "extreme poverty line"—that is, living on less than a dollar a day—increased from 227 million to 313 million while their inflation-adjusted average daily income actually fell, from 62 cents to 60. At the same time nearly half the continent's population—46 percent—languishes in what the UN defines as ordinary poverty.

Yet notwithstanding this record of failure, the prosperous nations' heads of state have sanctioned Sachs's plan to throw more money at Africa's woes. In July 2005, G-8 leaders meeting in Gleneagles, Scotland, endorsed Sachs's Millennium thesis and promised to double their annual foreign aid from $25 billion to $50 billion, with at least half the money earmarked for Africa. This increased spending, the Gleneagles principals proclaimed, will "lift tens of millions of people out of poverty every year." No doubt, too, Africans will soon be extracting sunbeams from cucumbers.

It is doubtful whether the G-8 leaders themselves believe all the gaseous rhetoric that emanates from their meetings. But a sort of fifth estate, composed of actors and aging rock stars, has emerged, determined to hold the prodigal statesmen to their word. The new Africrats include the pop empress Madonna, the actress Angelina Jolie, and U2 singer Paul Hewson, better known as Bono, who has emerged as Sachs's leading promoter and enforcer. After attending this year's G-8 summit at Heiligendamm, Germany, Bono pronounced himself "skeptical" of the pledges made at Gleneagles. The skepticism was reasonable, given that the document in question was not intended to be credible. But Bono, who wrote the foreword to Sachs's *The End of Poverty*, has made it his life's work to force the G-8 to take its oratory seriously. At Heiligendamm he got into what he called a "huge row" with the Germans, whom he accused of "playing a numbers game" with their aid contributions.

Bono has had better luck with U.S. leaders. In 2002 he and then–treasury secretary Paul O'Neill traveled together to Africa on a widely publicized twelve-day "fact-finding" mission to study the

AIDS epidemic. In 2007 President George W. Bush, who reportedly discussed increasing American aid to Africa with Bono at the G-8 summit in Heiligendamm, announced that he would expand the centerpiece of his Africa policy, the President's Emergency Plan for AIDS Relief. Bush launched the initiative in 2003 with a five-year, $15 billion commitment; in May 2007 he asked Congress to double the commitment to $30 billion over five years.

⌐⌐

Like earlier practitioners of paternalist charity, today's Africrats propose policies that treat the material effects of Africa's problems—disease, dirty water, hunger—not their underlying causes, which the West too once struggled with. For centuries high rates of death from infectious diseases were found throughout what is now the prosperous world. Hunger too once darkened the landscape, though so effectively has the problem been solved that countries like the United States face a looming obesity crisis.

No benign magician descended, à la Jeffrey Sachs, on the prosperous nations to shower them with money. They developed laws and freedoms that enabled people to take their futures into their own hands. In his book *The Mystery of Capital: Why Capitalism Triumphs in the West and Fails Everywhere Else*, the Peruvian economist Hernando de Soto argues that the world's poorest countries remain poor in part because they lack legal protections—property rights foremost among them—that enable Western peoples to tap the potential of "dead" capital and invest it in wealth-generating enterprises.

The Kenyan economist James Shikwati agrees that handouts thwart the emergence of a culture of self-reliance. When a drought afflicts Kenya, he says, Kenyan politicians "reflexively cry out for more help." Their calls reach the United Nations World Food Program, a "massive agency of apparatchiks who are in the absurd situation of, on the one hand, being dedicated to the fight against hunger while, on the other hand, being faced with unemployment were hunger actually eliminated." When the requested grain reaches Africa, a portion of it "often goes directly into the hands of unscrupulous politicians who then pass it on to their own tribe to boost their next election campaign." Much of the rest of the grain gets dumped at less than fair market value. "Local farmers may as well put down their hoes right away," Shikwati says. "No one can compete with the UN's World Food Program."

CARE, one of the world's largest charities, would agree. In August 2007 it rejected some $45 million in U.S. government financing to distribute subsidized food in Africa, saying that the subsidies hurt African farmers. "If someone wants to help you, they shouldn't do it by destroying the very thing that they're trying to promote," George Odo, a CARE official, told the *New York Times*. The American government, however, has no plans to abandon the practice.

Shikwati's observations have been borne out most recently in Ethiopia, where the government's collectivist agriculture policies have unsurprisingly resulted in famine. Foreign nations duly sent aid, which, according to a July 2007 report in the *New York Times*, government soldiers duly squandered: "Soldiers skim sacks of grain, tins of vegetable oil and bricks of high-energy biscuits from food warehouses to sell at local markets. The cash is distributed among security officers and regional officers. . . . Then the remaining food is hauled out to rural areas where the soldiers divert part of it to local gunmen and informers as a reward for helping them fight the rebels. . . . To cover their tracks, the soldiers and government administrators who work with them tell the aid agencies that the food has spoiled, or has been stolen or hijacked by rebels."

The cycle is vicious. The aid that ends up in corrupt rulers' bank accounts enables them to stifle both free markets and the political and legal reforms that free markets need to operate efficiently. A recent Heritage Foundation study found that, of the seventy least-free countries on earth, nearly half have received U.S. foreign aid for more than three decades. The result is more poverty, more aid money, and more corruption. In Zimbabwe, for example, foreign aid enabled strongman Robert Mugabe to destroy property rights, introduce a command economy, and create a kleptocracy where the inflation rate recently reached 11,000 percent. Once southern Africa's breadbasket, Zimbabwe now depends on subsidies to feed its people.

Sachs points to his "Millennium Village clusters"—twelve sites located in Ethiopia, Ghana, Kenya, Malawi, Mali, Nigeria, Rwanda, Senegal, Tanzania, and Uganda—as evidence that he will succeed where earlier centrally directed efforts failed. The Millennium Village initiative, its apologists claim, does what "has never been done before." It "addresses an *integrated* and *scaled-up* set of interventions covering food production, nutrition, education, health services, roads, energy, communications, water, sanitation, enterprise diversification and environmental management."

If this doesn't sound like a conceptual breakthrough, it's because it isn't. The Millennium Project, like earlier paternalist programs, is a collectivist enterprise run by bureaucrats and subject to—or, as the apparatchiks prefer to say, "scaled up" by—central governments abroad. These "colossally expensive, nonreplicable" villages, contends Bunker Roy, founding director of India's Barefoot College, have been imposed on locals by governments and academics seeking "installations that are friendly to globe-trotting celebrities."

Sachs boasts that the village of Sauri, in Kenya, recently "celebrated its first harvest as a 'Millennium Village'" with a bumper crop. With sufficient money and attention it is always possible to create a Potemkin village. But no centrally directed program has yet been able to create and sustain a sprawling network of prosperous villages, towns, and cities, such as we take for granted in the United States.

Why? One reason is that the amount of information required to administer so extensive a prosperity will baffle even the most careful plan and the most thoughtful administrator. "We know little of the particular facts to which the whole of social activity continuously adjusts itself in order to provide what we have learned to expect," Friedrich Hayek wrote in *The Constitution of Liberty*. Only by renouncing bureaucratic control, Hayek maintained, can a country make the most efficient use of the knowledge that its citizens collectively possess. It is for this reason that a free society can employ "so much more knowledge than the mind of the wisest ruler could comprehend."

Another reason that Millennium Villages won't succeed is that they fail to foster a climate of innovation. Four centuries ago Francis Bacon, analyzing the emergence of problem-solving cultures, observed that the solutions they lighted upon were often "altogether different in kind and as remote as possible from anything that was known before; so that no preconceived notion could possibly have led to the discovery of them." But the preconceived notions imposed by large, bureaucratic programs too often thwart the unforeseeable breakthroughs that result when people are free to pursue their own destinies. According to a candid report issued in July by a group of NGOs, aid initiatives in the Sahel, along the southern perimeter of the Sahara, "are almost always driven by externally imposed ideas for development" intended to make donors look good; the architects of the programs approach problems in "narrow and inflexible ways" which ignore the ideas of local populations.

Yet even if all this is conceded, shouldn't the prosperous nations at the very least underwrite African health care to stem the tide of death? Perhaps, but the real question is whether subsidized medicine is the best way to raise life expectancy—or whether political and legal reforms that promote the creation of wealth do more. Nor is it clear that, even if subsidized health programs do work in some circumstances, they are likely to be effective in Africa, given the corruption that so often prevents aid from reaching its intended recipients.

Not only do the Africrats' policies fail to address the real causes of Africa's troubles, but they also treat the people whom they are trying to help as children. *Vanity Fair*'s July 2007 "Africa Issue" described how Sachs, in a southwestern Ugandan village in January 2007, addressed the inhabitants as though they were slightly dim kindergartners: "And we have seen the bed nets in your houses. Do you have bed nets in your houses?"

"Yes!"

"We are happy to see that. And are they working? Do they help?"

"Yes!"

"We are happy to see that."

Yes, Kimosabe! Sachs is not the only *sahib* who invites us to view Africa through the prism of childhood. In 2004 Prince Harry of England visited Lesotho, a small, landlocked country in southern Africa, to befriend children with AIDS; standing before a battery of cameras, the prince gave a four-year-old boy a pair of Wellington boots and cradled a six-month-old girl in his arms. When Madonna traveled to Malawi in 2006, dripping dollars and sentiment, her publicist spoke candidly of her paternalist (or maternalist) aspirations: "She's kind of adopting an entire country of children."

Rotimi Sankore, a journalist who has written widely on Africa, points out that the Africrats' favorite poster child is "a skeletal looking two- or three-year-old brown-skinned girl in a dirty torn dress, too weak to chase off dozens of flies settling on her wasted and diseased body, her big round eyes pleading for help." Sankore calls such images "development pornography." The "subliminal message, unintended or not," he argues, "is that people in the developing world require indefinite and increasing amounts of help and that without aid charities and donor support, these poor incapable people in Africa or Asia will soon be extinct through disease and starvation."

The Kenyan writer Binyavanga Wainaina maintains that the relentless focus of the Africrats on the image of the pitiable, childish African distorts Africans' idea of themselves and their potential. "There must be a change in mentality," agrees Kenya's Shikwati. "We have to stop perceiving ourselves as beggars." At the same time Africrat rhetoric that depicts the continent as "one giant crisis" (Wainaina's phrase) obscures the progress that many Africans are making on their own. The African entrepreneurs who make up what Wainaina calls the "equity generation"—stock exchanges now thrive in Uganda, Kenya, Nigeria, and Ghana—are, by pursuing their own private interests, doing more to assure a prosperous African future than all the Africrats' programs put together. President Bush made subsidized medicine the centerpiece of his Africa policy; he might have done better to invest in Africa's rising entrepreneurs.

If paternalism doesn't work, why does the paternalist mentality persist? Joseph Conrad suggested an answer in his 1902 novella *Heart of Darkness*. Conrad's anti-hero, Kurtz, is a man of benevolent intention who goes to Africa with grandiose dreams of saving people but who ends by slaughtering those natives who resist his hunt for ivory. The story's narrator, Marlow, finds a report that Kurtz prepared for the International Society for the Suppression of Savage Customs. Kurtz, Marlow says, "began with the argument that we whites, from the point of development we had arrived at, 'must necessarily appear to them [savages] in the nature of supernatural beings—we approach them with the might of a deity,' and so on, and so on. 'By the simple exercise of our will we can exert a power for good practically unbounded.'" The thesis of Sachs's *The End of Poverty* is not essentially different. He too believes that Westerners "can exert a power for good practically unbounded" over people who have not reached our "point of development."

The patina of benevolence, Conrad suggests, often conceals a messianic narcissism, an incipient megalomania: Kurtz spent his days in Africa "getting himself adored." Egotism and the desire for adoration are useful stimulants when they cause people to produce things that other people want or need. But it is a tawdry ambition that deters, as the paternalist philosophy does, people from realizing their own potential.

Reading Conrad one is uneasily reminded of today's Africrats. Under the guise of helping Africans, they aggrandize themselves, burnish their fame—and, not least, get themselves adored. Their tours of Africa are exercises in hero worship, part Roman triumph, part Felliniesque spectacle. The landing of the jet on some remote shimmering tarmac; the heat of the African sun; the exotic savor of the desert or of the jungle air; the fawning masses: all contribute to the narcotic spell that these progresses cast over those who undertake them.

Then comes the encounter between the benign magician—the Prospero from the northern latitudes—and the Suffering African. Amid a glitter of flashbulbs, the august tourist, like a monarch touching for the King's Evil, lays hands on the dying AIDS patient or the undernourished child. Bobby Kennedy and Princess Diana perfected the art with which the superstar feels another's pain; Bono, Madonna, and Angelina Jolie have carried on the tradition. A messianic odor clings to Sachs's account of this celebrity satrapy, in which the superstars figure both as agents of grace and as high priests of a cult: "The Live 8 concerts, Bono's ONE campaign, Angelina Jolie's work for the United Nations, and many other acts of leadership and grace are drawing millions of eager individuals into a new commitment to work for the end of poverty, and thereby for a world of peace and shared well-being."

Paternalism persists as a psychology precisely because it satisfies the cravings of vanity in a way that real reform doesn't. (Where people have learned to save themselves, they do not need saviors.) So potent are paternalism's pleasures that they have beguiled even those who theoretically oppose them. Consider the regression of Sachs himself. Sachs was born, in Detroit, into a family of civic aspiration; as a young economist at Harvard, during the 1980s, he helped devise "shock therapy" for Bolivia, a country crippled by public-sector spending.

Today, however, he rejects his old faith in economic freedom, which he ridicules as "magical thinking." Repudiating his Bolivian policies, he now calls for curing African poverty LBJ-style, through massive transfers of wealth. Sachs has discovered that it is more glamorous to be a paternalist wizard, solving the little people's problems for them, than it is to help them, as in Bolivia, solve their problems for themselves. When he was advocating a Reagan-Thatcher program of spending cuts and smaller government in Latin America, the most he could hope for was an appreciative notice in the *Wall Street Journal*. Now he hangs with Bono and goes off into the bush with Angelina Jolie.

So prosperous have free nations become that not only their tycoons and superstars but even members of their middle classes are rich enough to taste the pleasures of paternalism—a fact that Madison Avenue has not failed to exploit. Companies like Gap, Converse, Motorola, and Armani—which were also sponsors of *Vanity Fair*'s Africa issue—have subscribed to Bono's "(red) manifesto," a promise that "if you buy a (red) product or sign up for a (red) service, at no cost to you, a (red) company will give some of its profits to buy antiretroviral medicine" for Africa. The curious (use) of (parentheses) in Bono's "manifesto" is apparently intended to give the ad campaign an edgy, agitprop flavor, enabling the consumer to flatter himself that, in purchasing his new cell phone or pair of sneakers, he is doing something more than engaging in a routine market transaction. An acquisitive bourgeois on the surface, he is at heart (or so he pretends) a spiritual guerrilla on Bono's long march to social solidarity.

The ambivalence about economic liberty that characterizes Bono's campaign points to a larger contradiction in Western charity in Africa. It is a paradox of the Africrats that they should long to retreat from the commercial civilization that has made them great to the primitive conditions of the jungle and the desert. They are plainly enchanted by the exoticism, the pastoral simplicity, of peoples who have not yet mastered the secret of market prosperity.

This longing for the supposed innocence and simplicity of more primitive cultures was an important element in the psychology of nineteenth-century romanticism, which emerged from the same cultural matrix that gave birth to nineteenth-century paternalism. Both paternalism and romanticism developed in reaction to the progress, in the West, of political and economic freedom and the unexampled prosperity that came in their wake. Slaveholders in the United States fashioned an apology for human bondage that was partly romantic and partly paternalistic: they were, they claimed, recreating the feudal splendors of *Ivanhoe* on the plantation while at the same time they were tending to the submerged class with a solicitude absent in the coldhearted world of free labor. Across the ocean, romantic aristocrats like Bismarck, confronted with the progress of liberty, sought to preserve the power of the patrician classes by means of a new method of paternal supervision, the social machinery of the *Wohlfahrtsstaat.*

Paternalism's most astute defenders have typically worked to disguise its coercive sting by framing their efforts as an attempt to save the little people—as yet unspoiled by capitalism—from the evils of freedom. In the proletarian novels of the 1930s, writers romanticized the alienated working class; other paternalists, like the "radical chic" philanthropists whom Tom Wolfe satirized in the 1960s, found their noble savages in the urban ghetto. Like their predecessors, the Africrats too romanticize their pets. In doing so they have worked out a new bucolic aesthetic to justify their disillusionment with a capitalism that has been the making of their own fortunes, even as they promote policies that promise to keep their wards in a poverty that bears little resemblance to Rousseau's fantasies of primitive innocence. It is a philosophy of mandarin pity, one that will do little to raise up the suffering Africans.

Lincoln as a Savior of Liberty

*I*n 1861 free institutions seemed poised to carry all before them. In Russia, Tsar Alexander II emancipated twenty-two million serfs. In Germany, lawmakers dedicated to free constitutional principles prepared to assert civilian control over Prussia's feudal military caste. In America, Abraham Lincoln entered the White House pledged to a policy of excluding slavery from the nation's territories.

The new machinery of freedom, though it was Anglo-American in design, was universal in scope. At its core was the idea, as yet imperfectly realized, that all human beings possess a fundamental dignity. This was a truth that, Abraham Lincoln believed, was "applicable to all men and all times."

In 1861 the faith that all men have a right to life, liberty, and the fruits of their industry was invoked as readily on the Rhine and the Neva as on the Potomac and the Thames. "The Germans were the last people that the liberal tide reached," Friedrich Hayek wrote in *The Constitution of Liberty*, "before it began to recede." This was true also of the Russians, or at any rate of certain sections of the Russian intelligentsia, which in the 1860s numbered such eminent classical liberals as Boris Chicherin and Nicholas Milyutin. Turgenev captured the flavor of the liberal Russia of the early sixties in his 1862 novel *Fathers and Sons*, in which he makes Bazarov, a nihilist, complain that the country was just then full of liberal talk of "parliamentarianism, the bar, and the devil knows what."

A reaction was nevertheless gathering momentum; privilege would not surrender its prerogatives without a fight. In Russia, in Germany, and in America, grandees with their backs against the wall met the challenge of liberty with a new philosophy of coercion. This philosophy was founded on two ideas. The first was paternalism. Landowners in Russia and in the American South argued that their domestic institutions embodied the paternal principle: the bondsman had, in his master, a compassionate father to look after him, and he was therefore better off than the worker in the cruel world of free labor. In Germany, Prussian aristocrats like Bismarck sought to implement a paternal code—it became known as the welfare state—intended to make the masses more subservient to the state ("easier to handle," in Bismarck's words).* The paternalists, Lord Macaulay said, sought to "regulate the school, overlook the playground, fix the hours of labour and recreation, prescribe what ballads shall be sung, what tunes shall be played, what books shall be read, what physic shall be swallowed."

The second idea was racial nationalism. At its core was the belief that certain (superior) peoples have a right to impose their

*In their book *Free to Choose*, Milton and Rose Friedman identified "the affinity between aristocracy and socialism." "It may seem paradoxical," they wrote, "that an essentially autocratic and aristocratic state such as pre–World War I Germany—in today's jargon, a right-wing dictatorship—should have led the way in introducing measures that are generally linked to socialism and the Left. But there is no paradox. . . . Believers in aristocracy and socialism share a faith in centralized rule, in rule by command rather than by voluntary cooperation. They differ in who should rule: whether an elite determined by birth or experts supposedly chosen on merit. Both proclaim, no doubt sincerely, that they wish to promote the well-being of the 'general public,' that they know what is in the 'public interest' and how to obtain it better than the ordinary person. Both, therefore, profess a paternalistic philosophy. And both end up, if they attain power, promoting the interests of their own class in the name of the 'general welfare.'"

wills on other (inferior) peoples. Planters in the American South dreamed of enslaving Central America and the Caribbean. Germany's nationalists aspired to incorporate Danish, French, and Polish provinces into a new German Reich. In Moscow and St. Petersburg, Pan-Slavic nationalists sought to rout the Ottoman Turks and impose Russia's will on Byzantium. The new nationalist chauvinism was propped by the racial philosophies of such thinkers as Enst Moritz Arndt and Joseph von Goerres in Germany, Nicholas Danilevsky in Russia, and Edmund Ruffin and James Henry Hammond in the United States. The romantic school of racial nationalism drew inspiration too from the philosophy of racial aristocracy propounded by the Comte de Gobineau, whose *Essai sur l'inégalité des races humaines* appeared in the 1850s, as well as from the theory of Germanic superiority espoused by the Comte de Boulainvilliers and the Comte de Rémusat.

Lincoln recognized that the West had reached a turning point. The decisive question of the epoch, he said, was whether free constitutions could survive and prosper in the world, or whether they possessed an "inherent, and fatal weakness" which doomed them to a premature degeneration. Could America—could any nation conceived in liberty and dedicated to the proposition that all men are created equal—"long endure"?

It was not improbable, Lincoln said, that if the new philosophy of coercion were permitted to advance, human bondage would become lawful in all the American "States, *old* as well as *new*—*North* as well as *South*." America would witness the "total overthrow" of free-state principles: it would become a country in which "all men are created equal, except negroes, and foreigners, and Catholics."

It was not only in America that free institutions were threatened. Lincoln repeatedly characterized the struggle between freedom and servitude as a global one. The outcome of the American contest between the two philosophies would, he predicted, have a great—possibly a decisive—influence on the future of liberty in other places as well. Were the American Republic to shatter on the anvil of slavery, men and women around the world would suffer. If, on the contrary, the United States were saved on principles of freedom, "millions of free happy people, the world over," Lincoln said, would "rise up, and call us blessed, to the latest generations."

Scholars have criticized Lincoln for exaggerating the threat to liberty, but it is important to understand how formidable, in his day, the odds against free institutions seemed. The new philosophy of coercion was dangerous precisely because it went to the heart of the free-state ideal: it attacked the principle that all men were created equal. The "definitions and axioms of free society" were, Lincoln said,

> denied, and evaded, with no small show of success. One dashingly calls them "glittering generalities"; another bluntly calls them "self evident lies"; and still others insidiously argue that they apply only to "superior races." These expressions, differing in form, are identical in object and effect—the supplanting of the principles of free government, and restoring those of classification, caste, and legitimacy. They would delight a convocation of crowned heads, plotting against the people. They are the vanguard—the miners, and sappers—of returning despotism. We must repulse them, or they will subjugate us.

If the free-state philosophy was founded on the belief that all men are created equal and that the laws of the state must apply equally to all, the new coercive philosophy, Lincoln said, grew out of a faith in the efficacy of "classification" and "caste." Under the coercive scheme, humanity was to be divided into various social or racial groups; it was the task of the state to make laws or impose regulations appropriate for each particular subunit. This theory of classification was in some ways merely a revision of the old feudal idea that divided humanity into those who fight, those who pray, and those who toil; but the new sociologies of race and political economy lent the feudal idea a fresh prestige. Critics of the free state used the new sociological vocabularies to dismiss free institutions as the invention of a particular socioeconomic class (the bourgeoisie), which had created them merely in order to conceal their own economic power.

When, in the fall of 1862, Lincoln told Congress, "We shall nobly save, or meanly lose, the last, best, hope of earth," the fate of liberty hung in the balance in three great nations: Russia, where Alexander II sought to promote liberal reform; Germany, where Otto von Bismarck applied his dark genius to the destruction of the *Rechtsstaat* (rule-of-law state); and America itself.

Those three powers—Russia, Germany, and the United States—would go on to dominate the twentieth century. Only one did not become a slave empire. Alexander II failed to liberalize his country and was assassinated. Liberal Russia gave way to reactionary Russia, reactionary Russia to Bolshevik Russia. Bismarck succeeded all too well in the tasks he had set himself. In his book *Gold and Iron*, the historian Fritz Stern showed how Bismarck prepared the way for National Socialism by stamping out the "dream of a liberal, humane Germany" and forging a "fatal and unprecedented" system of "constitutional absolutism," a "mighty, militaristic country that would idolize power." Lincoln, alone of the three statesmen, left his country freer than he found it.

Speculation is justified. Had Lincoln not forced his revolution in 1861 by refusing to compromise on the question of territorial slavery, human bondage, in some perhaps milder form, under some perhaps prettier name, might have survived in the United States into the twentieth century. Compulsory labor would have derived fresh strength from the new weapons in the coercive arsenal—"scientific" racism, Social Darwinism, and the ostensibly benevolent doctrines of paternalism. The coercive party in America, unbroken in spirit, might have realized its dream of a Caribbean slave empire. Cuba and the Philippines, after their conquest by the United States, might have become permanent slave colonies. Such a nation would have had little reason to resist Bismarck's Second Reich or Hitler's third one.

The historical probabilities would have been no less grim had Lincoln, after refusing to compromise on the question of territorial slavery, failed to preserve the United States as a unitary free state. The Southern Republic, having gained its independence, would almost certainly have formed alliances with regimes grounded in its own coercive philosophy; the successors of Jefferson Davis would have had every incentive to link arms with the successors of Otto von Bismarck.

None of this came to pass. The virtue of Lincoln preserved the liberties of America. In the decades that followed, the nation that he saved played a decisive part in vindicating the freedom of peoples around the world.

Ah, but *should* America have played that part? Was it wise of the United States to intervene in the wars to defeat Germany? Was the country right to wage a Cold War against Russia?

On July 4, 1821, John Quincy Adams, who was then secretary of state, addressed the House of Representatives. What, he asked, had the United States done for the benefit of mankind? America had, he said,

> in the lapse of nearly half a century, without a single exception, respected the independence of other nations while asserting and maintaining her own. She has abstained from interference in the concerns of others, even when conflict has been for principles to which she clings, as to the last vital drop that visits the heart. She has seen that probably for centuries to come, all the contests of that Aceldama the European world, will be contests of inveterate power, and emerging right. Wherever the standard of freedom and Independence has been or shall be unfurled, there will her heart, her benedictions and her prayers be. But she goes not abroad, in search of monsters to destroy. She is the well-wisher to the freedom and independence of all. She is the champion and vindicator only of her own.

The policy Adams advocated had merit at a time when the wars of Europe and Asia, though they might seriously inconvenience Americans and threaten their commerce, were not likely to bring them to their knees. The young Lincoln, in his 1838 address to the Young Men's Lyceum of Springfield, explained why:

> Shall we expect some transatlantic military giant, to step the Ocean, and crush us at a blow? Never!—All the armies of Europe, Asia and Africa combined, with all the treasure of the earth (our own excepted) in their military chest; with a Buonaparte for a commander, could not by force, take a drink from the Ohio, or make a track on the Blue Ridge, in a trial of a thousand years.

This was undoubtedly true at the time Lincoln spoke. But advances in technology would soon render the oceans a less formidable barrier than they once had been. The implication of these technological innovations was for a time effectually hidden from many American statesmen, for during the nineteenth century the British navy policed the seas. But in the twentieth century the threat to America's freedom and security could no longer be overlooked. Armies could be brought across the sea more rapidly and more efficiently than ever before; long-range bombers and intercontinental missiles could strike American cities; nuclear weapons could annihilate them.

As the world came closer, American statesmen were bound to consider the merits of the policy England had during many generations pursued. Unlike the United States, which in its youth relied on the oceans to protect her from whatever dangers the vast and populous Eurasian landmass presented, England could at no time in her history look with indifference on the upheavals of a continent from which she was separated by nothing more than a narrow stretch of water, one which Napoleon was pleased to call a ditch. England could not rely on natural barriers to protect her liberties; she was obliged to build up a good fleet. But even a good fleet would not be enough, her statesmen concluded, should a single state come to dominate the Continent. Such a power would have at its command such an array of resources, both human and material, as to render even the Royal Navy an insufficient protection, for the rival power could build up an even more formidable navy.

From the reign of Elizabeth until that of George VI, it was the policy of England to maintain the balance of power on the Continent by preventing the emergence of a great continental state with such a preponderance of might as to permit it to dominate the lesser states. Whenever it appeared that such an empire was beginning to emerge, English statesmen sought to form coalitions of states capable of resisting the pretensions of Leviathan. By such means William III sought to check the aggrandizements of Louis XIV, the younger Pitt those of Napoleon, Winston Churchill those of Hitler. Many Englishmen questioned the wisdom of this policy: they would have preferred to see England maintain a less costly aloofness from the affairs of the Continent. It was left to Macaulay to observe how dearly England would have paid had she adopted such a "strictly insular" policy and left the Continent to shift for itself. England's commitments abroad, he wrote, "in which shallow politicians imagined that we had no interest, were in truth the outworks of London."

America's commitments abroad during the last century were often justified in idealistic terms. Woodrow Wilson might have been St. George, so greatly did he come to relish the notion of slaying foreign monsters. But in reality America's policy was for the most part founded in a realistic appraisal of her position in an altered world. Her situation was now in many ways comparable to that of England: she was, in effect, an island off Eurasia. Henry Kissinger, a pupil of the geopolitical strategist Halford Mackinder, observed that America's position called for

> a global policy comparable to Great Britain's toward Continental Europe. For three centuries, British leaders had operated from the assumption that, if Europe's resources were marshaled by a single dominant power, that country would then have the resources to challenge Great Britain's command of the seas, and thus threaten its independence.

From a geopolitical perspective the United States, Kissinger argued, is as much "an island off the shores of Eurasia" as Britain.

He lamented only that America should so often have confused her perception of her interests with her moral aspirations. The country had an interest in resisting the "domination of Europe or Asia by one power and, even more, the control of *both* continents by the *same* power." In such circumstances, "it should have been the extent of Germany's geopolitical reach" and not her "moral transgressions" that prompted America to go to war with the Reich.

However that may be, it remains the fact that America's interventions abroad have very often promoted the freedom of other peoples. That these interventions were in reality (or so at least it can be argued) prompted less by the country's idealistic impulses than by her concern for her own security does not diminish the value of the achievement. Many things combined to make it possible for the United States to perform this historic service. Among those things, the statesmanship of Lincoln was surely not the least.

Dukedom Large Enough:
Jefferson in His Library

*I*t is the fashion in America to produce, every generation or so, a new Jefferson. Lincoln saw in the author of the Declaration of Independence a philosopher of liberty. Franklin Roosevelt, in his battles against "economic royalists," invoked the statesman who deplored the financial policies of Alexander Hamilton. More recently, Americans have snickered at the slave-driving sexual predator of the Sally Hemings scandals. It is time for a fresh edition. Why not look in the library?

"I labour grievously under the malady of Bibliomanie," Jefferson wrote in 1789. Like the *opiomane*, the *bibliomane* is hooked on his drug, and it is amusing to find Jefferson, an aging addict, pushing his habit on younger souls, ever eager to share with them the narcotic that eased his own path through life. Kevin J. Hayes, in *The Road to Monticello*, a study of Jefferson's devotion to books, argues that "literature is important in and of itself and that a literary life is a life worth living." Not that he thinks the literary hours of a man's life are severable from the rest of his existence. On the contrary, Hayes contends that Jefferson's interest in books improved his domestic life, his friendships, his political labors, his architecture, and his work as a farmer and gardener.

If Jefferson did not shut himself up in a book-lined tower as Montaigne did, he did spend a good deal of time alone in his study. The challenge for any bibliographic Jefferson scholar is to pierce the veil that obscures the activity of the book room, a place Jefferson's friend Margaret Bayard Smith thought "so sacred that I told him it was his sanctum sanctorum."

The veil is not easily rent. How "he employed his hours of study," Dr. Johnson said of Jonathan Swift, "has been enquired with hopeless curiosity. For who can give an account of another's studies? Swift was not likely to admit any to his privacies, or to impart a minute account of his business or his leisure." Jefferson was possibly even more secretive than Swift, and Hayes is too often reduced to supplying a sort of annotated catalog of the books he acquired. Tantalizing hints amount to little. Hayes argues, for example, that Jefferson, in composing the Declaration of Independence, was influenced not only by legal and political writing but also by poetry: "The influence of poets, devotional writers, and other belletrists on the *Declaration* cannot be ignored." Yet other than his observation that Jefferson alluded, in the Declaration, to the poet James Thomson's phrase "manly firmness," Hayes never explains how this influence manifested itself.

If Jefferson's literary vocation is difficult to penetrate, it is all too easy to exaggerate its scope. Hayes describes Jefferson's instructions to Meriwether Lewis on the eve of his Western expedition with William Clark as his "Passage to India." But while he calls the "imaginative vision" of the instructions as "stunning," he fails to persuade the reader that the work is an instance of creative power on the order of Whitman's poem or Forster's novel.

Hayes similarly exaggerates the literary merit of Jefferson's version of the Gospels, *The Life and Morals of Jesus of Nazareth*, which he thinks might be "the finest biography of Christ ever written." It is true that Jefferson, in depicting Jesus as a "sage of nature," anticipated Ernest Renan's *Vie de Jésus*, but one has only to compare the two books to see how far short Jefferson falls of Renan's literary standard.

Hayes gives Jefferson too much credit, too, for literary originality and artistic open-mindedness. He cites Jefferson's "stirring words" in a 1799 letter: "As long as we may think as we will and speak as we think, the condition of man will proceed in improvement." But the credit for stirring eloquence belongs to Tacitus, who in the introduction to his *Histories* said that he lived at a time when "you may think what you like and say what you think." Again: the "presence of Retzsche's Goethe in [Jefferson's] library," Hayes writes, "shows how open-minded he was to new forms of art and literature." The reader, however, is more likely to be conscious of the limitations of a sensibility on which some of the greatest writers of the age—Austen, Wordsworth, and Shelley, among others—seem to have made little impression.

~

Much of Jefferson's literary passion was of the antiquarian variety. This species of intellectual taste has gone out of fashion, but it is not quite the pedantic foolery George Eliot made it seem in her portrait of Mr. Casaubon in *Middlemarch*. Leopardi was one of the last exemplars of the tradition. "He came to know the world of two thousand years ago," his friend Giordani said, "before he knew that of his own time; and what is more surprising, from this lost ancient world he learned what his own was, and how to value it." It is almost heretical, in an age that worships originality and what is called authenticity, to suggest that apprenticeship in an ancient tradition of creativity may be fruitful, or to assert that the really creative spirits of the West will always find a stimulus in the "feeling that the whole of the literature of Europe from Homer" has a "simultaneous existence and composes a simultaneous order."* "I was not lacking in imagination," Leopardi said, "but I never thought of myself as a poet, until I had read the Greeks. . . . I did not lack enthusiasm, creative powers, and passion—but I did not believe myself eloquent, until I had read Cicero."

Jefferson was, like Leopardi, a close student of antiquity, and he was continually returning to the Greek and Latin classics. What did "all this classical erudition," as Hayes calls it, mean to him? One clue can be found in the way Jefferson will often render a Greek concept into English. He said of his friend Peyton Randolph that he was "cold and coy towards strangers, but of the sweetest affability when ripened into acquaintance. Of attic pleasantry in conversation, always good humored and conciliatory." By "attic pleasantry" Jefferson means *eutrapelia*—wit, liveliness, politeness in conversation; this "attic" standard was always his beau idéal of discourse. The Greek qualities of his literary imagination are evident too in his vision of an America where, "under our democratic stimulants," every citizen "is potentially an athlete in body and an Aristotle in mind." This is precisely the Greek ideal of *kalogathia*—beauty and excellence of mind and body—an idea which, though it was originally aristocratic, became in time the ideal of democratic Athens.

---

*Such was the formulation of T. S. Eliot in his essay "Tradition and the Individual Talent." In his essay "The Classics and the Man of Letters," Eliot argued that "the maintenance of classical education is essential to the maintenance of the continuity of English Literature."

Jefferson alluded to the Greeks and Romans not only in his writing but also in his architecture. It might be argued that his neoclassical tastes were a kind of derivative pedantry and reflected a servile attitude to the standards of the Old World. But such an interpretation does not do justice to Jefferson's belief that noble forms of art, wherever begot, nourish noble qualities of character. His invocation of the "light and choice" Attic taste was intimately connected to his vision of what America might become, and to his apprehension of the qualities of character that might flourish here. He knew, from his reading of Thucydides, that the Greek idea of *eutrapelia* stood for a conception of civilized life: the root word means "graceful turning" (hence our idea of the "well-rounded" man), and it implied a beautiful versatility in action. Matthew Arnold, in a lecture at Eton, defined *eutrapelia* as "a happy and gracious flexibility." A citizen who had been so educated as to be able to "turn," easily and gracefully, from one task to another perhaps very different one, will not, Thucydides has Pericles say in the Funeral Oration, be *idiotes*, an idiot, imprisoned in a fragmentary part-life. Such a citizen will, on the contrary, be a sort of universal man, sufficiently broad-souled to contribute to the life of the city.

It was this ambitious concept of citizenship, one that had something in common with the idea of moral, spiritual, and intellectual cultivation which thinkers like Coleridge, Mill, and Arnold were to advocate in England, that Jefferson sought to promote in America. Such citizenship was likely to be incompatible, he believed, with life in a mass manufacturing society, one that encouraged the specialization of labor, and he deplored Americans' "mimicry" of an "Amsterdam, a Hamburg, or a city of London." Just as Coleridge lamented the "Christian Mammonists" of England, so Jefferson wondered whether Americans would not "forget themselves, but in the sole faculty of making money." Yet, unlike many students of the civic arts, Jefferson did not seek to impose his ideal of citizenship from above: he did not look to the state to fashion a compulsory ethos of civic virtue. He devoted himself instead to the minor forms of community, ones in which men's civic, charitable, and creative impulses could flourish, freely and spontaneously, as they could not in larger groups.

Jefferson's conception of the University of Virginia reflected this communal ideal: he intended the university to be an "academical village." In another attempt to resurrect the Athenian vision, he proposed to divide America into communities called "wards" or "hundreds." Each hundred or ward, Jefferson said, would "be a small republic within itself, and every man in the State would thus become an acting member of the common government, transacting in person a great portion of its rights and duties."

~

Jefferson was not the only figure of the age to appeal to these minor forms of community. In 1811, two years after he left the White House, Jane Austen published *Sense and Sensibility*; in 1813 she published *Pride and Prejudice*. Largely ignoring the national politics of Pitt and Napoleon, she sought, much as Jefferson did, to carve out of the larger world of the nation-state what the philosopher Alasdair MacIntyre, in his reading of the novels, calls "enclaves for the life of the virtues." "What matters at this stage," MacIntyre wrote in his book *After Virtue*, "is the construction of local forms of community within which civility and the intellectual and moral life can be sustained through the new dark ages which are already upon us." Although Jefferson, as a good Whig, was devoted to the private rights of the individual and the larger politics of the nation-state, he too cherished the minor forms of moral and civic art.

"My library was dukedom large enough." As for Prospero, so for Jefferson: books were primers in the craftsmanship that each mastered in order to fashion his little well-ordered community (marred though each was by forced labor). Jefferson's literary work was closely connected to his desire to perfect the miniaturist arts (so different from the nation-making labors of the Declaration of Independence) that made possible the life of Monticello, a domestic community, and the University of Virginia, a community of learning, "a little academe / still and contemplative in living art." The bookish Jefferson is closely connected to the civic and communal Jefferson: the spaces he designed, public and private, may be the most original expression of his literary and artistic passion. We who today seek forums more intimate in scale, and more delicate in craftsmanship, than those we find around us have much to learn from him.

Lincoln, *Macbeth*, and the Moral Imagination

> All suffering, since it is a mortification and a
> call to resignation, has potentially a sanctify-
> ing power.
>
> —Schopenhauer

A few years before my grandmother died, she cleared out her house and gave me some of her souvenirs of Lincoln. There was nothing extraordinary in the collection: an unskillful oil painting of the president, a couple of framed copies of Brady portraits, a facsimile of the letter to Mrs. Bixby on the death of her sons in battle—the kind of things many Americans had in their houses a couple of generations ago. One item, however, struck me: the legend printed at the top of the Bixby letter. "The famous Bixby letter," the legend declared, "the model of perfect English." Reading it, I couldn't disagree. Some have contended that Lincoln's secretary, John Nicolay, drafted the letter; if he did, he succeeded in mastering his boss's style, in reproducing the severe grace of his sentences.

Lincoln was a model writer of English prose—but he was also something else: a model of how a decent man comes to terms with the doubtful aspects of his own character. In Lincoln's confession of his fascination with *Macbeth* he has left us a clue which, when taken together with certain passages from his speeches, and certain asides to his friends, amounts to a most elaborate confession. These clues allow us to reconstruct, however imperfectly, the inner drama of a man who was perplexed by his own ambitious yearnings—and permit us to glimpse the moral imagination of a civilized man in action.

It is, of course, no longer quite respectable to derive moral inspiration from the reading of poetry. Nietzsche, in *Daybreak*, said that whoever "thinks that Shakespeare's theatre has a moral effect, and that the sight of Macbeth irresistibly repels one from the evil of ambition, is in error. . . . He who is really possessed by raging ambition beholds this its image with *joy*; and if the hero perishes by his passion this precisely is the sharpest spice in the hot draught of this joy." In his book *Shakespeare: The Invention of the Human*, Harold Bloom cites this passage with approval: "moral contexts," he says, "are simply irrelevant to *Macbeth*."

Lincoln belonged to a generation that was not ashamed to find "moral contexts" in *Macbeth*; nor was it embarrassed to find in poetry a discipline in the refinement of moral sensibility. Matthew Arnold said that poetry is "the interpretress of the moral world." "How does one come by one's morality?" Virginia Woolf asked. "Surely by reading the poets . . ." Such an approach is not without its dangers; T. S. Eliot said that critics like Arnold are apt to confuse "poetry and morals in the attempt to find a substitute for religious faith." Lincoln did not, I think, seek in Shakespeare's plays a substitute religion; he did, however, find in them something that threw light upon his own motives.*

"For our time," Lionel Trilling wrote in *The Liberal Imagination,* "the most effective agent of the moral imagination has been the novel of the last two hundred years. It was never, either aesthetically or morally, a perfect form and its faults and failures can be quickly enumerated. But its greatness and its practical usefulness lay in its unremitting work of involving the reader himself in the moral life, inviting him to put his own motives under examination, suggesting that reality is not as his conventional education has led him to see it." Lincoln was not a great reader of novels; he turned rather to poetry, and particularly to the poetry of *Macbeth,* for the materials of moral initiation.

Macbeth was Lincoln's favorite play. Although he had a passing acquaintance with many of Shakespeare's plays, he was more familiar with some than with others, and he thought himself as intimate with a few of them as the scholars and actors who made it their profession to study them. "Some of Shakspeare's [*sic*] plays I have never read," Lincoln wrote James Hackett, an actor and author of a book called *Notes and Comments upon Certain Plays and Actors of Shakespeare,* "while others I have gone over perhaps as frequently as any unprofessional reader." Among the latter Lincoln included *King Lear, Richard III,* and *Hamlet.* But of all the

---

*Of course it might be that the trust which such thinkers as George Eliot, Matthew Arnold, Lionel Trilling, and perhaps Lincoln himself placed in the moral imagination was itself the product of a thwarted religious passion, a spiritual impulse frustrated by the inability of the moralist to believe in the truth of the old spiritual revelations of his civilization.

plays *Macbeth* was for him the most enchanting. "I think nothing equals *Macbeth*," he said.

Any comprehensive interpretation of Lincoln must acknowledge how central a place *Macbeth* occupied in his imagination. If the Lincoln whom Garry Wills conjured, in *Lincoln at Gettysburg*, Americanized the funeral oration of Pericles, if the Lincoln whom Edmund Wilson depicted, in *Patriotic Gore*, Americanized the King James version of the Gospels, we must set beside these Lincolns still another one—the Lincoln who Americanized *Macbeth*, and who acted out something of its drama in his life. Where a text has touched a man's passions in the way that *Macbeth* touched Lincoln's, we have only to look, closely and carefully, to see how many and strong are the text's connections to the circumstances of his life.

Lincoln, like Macbeth, was a man of "vaulting ambition." His law partner, William Herndon, thought him "inordinately ambitious," and likened the ambition that drove him to a "little engine" that "knew no rest." At low points in his career, when his ambitious desires went unsatisfied, Lincoln became sullen and dejected. In the dingy law office in Springfield he would sit, for hours at a time, "staring vacantly out the windows."

But Lincoln was not only an ambitious man; he was also a man who, during much of his life, was preoccupied by the question of what ambition is. As a young man he memorably sketched the character of the supremely ambitious man. In an 1838 address to the Young Men's Lyceum in Springfield, Lincoln observed that, unlike those whose ambition aspired "to nothing beyond a seat in Congress, a gubernatorial or a presidential chair," the supremely ambitious man found no "gratification" in "supporting and maintaining an edifice" that had been erected by others. The presidency itself, Lincoln said, would never "satisfy an Alexander, a Caesar, or a Napoleon." The "[t]owering genius" of such men disdains a beaten path. It seeks regions hitherto unexplored. It sees no distinction in adding story to story, upon the monuments of fame, erected to the memory of others. It denies that it is glory enough to serve under any chief. It scorns to tread in the footsteps of any predecessor, however illustrious. . . . Distinction will be . . . the paramount object [of the man who possesses such towering genius], and although he would as willingly, perhaps more so, acquire it by doing good as harm; yet, that opportunity being done, and nothing left to be done in the way of building up, he would set boldly to the task of pulling down.

Although the ambitious man will sometimes gratify his desire for greatness by "doing good," Lincoln says, he will "boldly" set about doing "harm" if he sees no other path to distinction. It is not an original insight; what is unusual about it is that it is the insight of a practicing politician.

If Lincoln was candid enough to admit that he was an ambitious man,* he was sufficiently sensitive of the imputation of ambition to conceal, at times, the passion that both drove and perplexed him. He took pains to demonstrate that ambition had not influenced the most critical of his public actions. Consider the lengths to which he went to convince the nation that he and his supporters had played in the coming of the Civil War was a passive one. In his second inaugural address he declared that on

the occasion corresponding to this four years ago, all thoughts were anxiously directed to an impending civil-war. All dreaded it—all sought to avert it. . . . Both parties deprecated war; but one of them would make war rather than let the nation survive;

*See Lincoln, "On Stephen Douglas," circa December 1856, in Lincoln, *Speeches and Writings 1832-1858* (New York: Library of America, 1989), 384 ("Even then, we were both ambitious . . .").

and the other would accept war rather than let it perish. And the war came.

The South, Lincoln maintained in his second inaugural address, made the war; the North merely accepted it. Or as Lincoln said to the South in 1861: "In your hands, my dissatisfied fellow country-men, and not in mine, is the momentous issue of civil war." Lincoln's attitude is that of Caesar: civil war was the other side's fault. "*Hoc voluerunt,*" Caesar grunted when, in the aftermath of Pompey's defeat, he surveyed the Roman dead at Pharsalus: "They would have it thus." As Caesar to his senatorial opponents, so Lincoln to his Southern ones. *Hoc voluerunt.*

But this was not true. The momentous issue of civil war had been in Lincoln's hands as well. There were things he might have done—things which might possibly have overted disunion and civil war—that he had not done. In the interval between his election to the presidency and his inauguration as president, a committee of thirteen senators attempted to negotiate a compromise between the sections. Senator Crittenden of Kentucky had superintended their efforts. Lincoln's future secretary of state, William Henry Seward, pursued a conciliatory line of his own. Lincoln quashed both demarches. "Let there be no compromise on the question of *extending* slavery," he wrote in December 1860. "The tug has to come, & better now, than any time hereafter."

Crittenden called for the restoration of the old Missouri Compromise line along latitude 36°30', and he proposed that the line be extended across the nation's Western territories to California. The effect of the proposal would be to make slavery unlawful in all the Western territory north of 36°30'. To conciliate the South, he proposed to guarantee slavery perpetually in all territory "now held, or hereafter acquired" by the United States south of the Compromise line, a concession that would permit slaveholding Fire Eaters to realize their dream of a tropical slave empire.

Seward too was quietly seeking a compromise. Shortly after Lincoln's election there appeared, in the *Albany Evening Journal,* a paper that enjoyed Seward's confidence, a proposal for reviving the Missouri line. A short time later the newspaper reiterated the proposal, and in private conversation Seward promised to support a bargain arranged on this principle. At about the same time he opened a negotiation with Lincoln, who had asked him to be his secretary of state. In December 1860 Seward dispatched his closest adviser, Thurlow Weed, to Springfield. Lincoln, who received Weed in his house on South Eighth Street, seemed genuinely to hope that Seward would become his secretary of state. But he would not compromise on the question of territorial slavery. At the end of December, Seward accepted the State Department and voted down Crittenden's proposal. Yet he seems later to have had a change of heart; in a speech in the Senate on January 12, 1861, he seemed to open the door to compromise on the territorial question. Only compromise, he suggested, could forestall a "disastrous revolution." To Baron de Stoeckle, the Russian envoy at Washington, he said that, in spite of the vote he cast against compromise in Senator Crittenden's committee, he remained sympathetic to a revival of the Missouri line. At a dinner party given by Stephen A. Douglas, he proposed a significant toast: "Away," he declared, "with all parties, all platforms, *all previous committals,* and *whatever else* will stand in the way of restoration of the American Union!"*

*The historian Glyndon Van Deusen, in his book *William Henry Seward,* has argued that Seward in November 1860 "felt compromise was not the answer" and that he changed his mind in December, when he proposed that the territories be divided into

It is certain that Lincoln himself was by this time alarmed. On February 1 he wrote to Seward to reiterate his policy. He was, he said, "baffled" by the confusion that had arisen concerning what he called the "vexed question" of territorial slavery. Congressman William Kellogg, he said, had come to him "in a good deal of anxiety, seeking to ascertain to what extent I would be consenting for our friends to go in the way of compromise" on the territorial question. "I say now, however, as I have all the while said," Lincoln wrote,

> that on the territorial question—that is, the question of extending slavery under the national auspices,—I am inflexible. I am for no compromise which *assists* or *permits* the extension of the institution on soil owned by the nation. And any trick by which the nation is to acquire territory, and then allow some local authority to spread slavery over it, is as obnoxious as any other. I take it that to effect some such result as this, and to put us again on the high-road to a slave empire, is the object of all these proposed compromises. I am against it.*

---

two parts, with "New Mexico coming in as a slave state, the rest of the territory north of the compromise parallel being free." Such an interpretation makes Seward's path still more tortuous. Unconvinced of the need for territorial compromise in November, he embraced it in December only after he learned that Lincoln was dead against it. It seems to me more likely that Seward was sympathetic to a revival of the Missouri line in November, when Weed first floated the idea in the *Albany Evening Journal*. In early December the rumor spread that Seward "wanted to make a great compromise like Clay and Webster!" See Seward's letter to Weed, December 3, 1860, in Thurlow Weed Barnes, *Memoir of Thurlow Weed* (Boston: Houghton Mifflin, 1884), 308. When Seward was summoned to a Republican caucus and asked whether he had authorized the proposals in the *Albany Evening Journal*, he pointedly refused to answer the question. "I kept my temper," he wrote to Weed. "I told them they would know what I think and what I propose when I do myself. . . . The Republican Party to-day is as uncompromising as the Secessionists in South Carolina. A month hence each may come to think that moderation is wiser."

*Lincoln was quietly prepared to compromise on several lesser questions, but on the critical question of territorial slavery he was uncompromising. New Mexico, the apparent exception to this uncompromising policy, in fact proves the rule. David Herbert

A few encouraging words from the president-elect about the compromise efforts might have diffused the crisis. But no words came. "They seek a sign," Lincoln said, "and no sign shall be given them."

⌇

Lincoln was, I think, morally justified in doing what he did, even though he risked civil war in doing so. A new philosophy of coercion was, he believed, advancing not only in the United States but throughout the West: it threatened to undermine the free-state principle that "all men are created equal." (See the essay "Lincoln as a Savior of Liberty" in this volume.) Yet even when a man acts in a morally justifiable way, he may still feel that a baser motive has influenced him. Lincoln was himself too morally sensitive not to be conscious of the problem. By allowing the "tug" to come when it did, he could hope to realize the historical greatness he craved.

Donald notes that Lincoln was "willing for New Mexico to be admitted without prohibition of slavery, 'if further extension were hedged against.' But on one point he was immovable: the extension of slavery into the national territories." David Herbert Donald, *Lincoln* (reprint; New York: Simon & Schuster, 1996), 270. New Mexico, Lincoln knew, was not the key to compromise: the key to compromise lay in the application of the Missouri line principal, not merely to territory now held by the United States but hereafter acquired by it, territory that could form the basis of a Caribbean slave empire. Lincoln could therefore offer the sop of New Mexico to the compromisers in his party without jeopardizing his position. His determination not to compromise any *significant* point was real. He believed that "the Missouri line extended [to territory now held or hereafter acquired], or Douglas's and Ely Thayer's popular sovereignty would lose us everything we gained by the election." Lincoln to Weed, December 17, 1860, in Barnes, *Memoir of Thurlow Weed*, 310–311. Lincoln said that, were he to consent to the extension of the Missouri line, the Fire Eaters would soon demand more: "a year will not pass," he said, "till we shall have to take Cuba as a condition upon which they will stay in the Union." Lincoln to James T. Hale, January 11, 1861, in David M. Potter, *Lincoln and His Party in the Secession Crisis* (reprint; New Haven: Yale University Press, 1962), 160, 233.

Lincoln's consciousness of the difficulty is evident in the dis-
ingenuousness of the rhetoric he employed after his election to
the presidency. He studiously maintained that his single overrid-
ing goal—his "paramount object" in the crisis before him—was
to preserve the Union. But Lincoln's paramount object, when he
assumed the presidency, was to prevent the extension of slavery
and thereby arrest the progress of coercion. His opposition to territorial slavery was the core of his mature political program. It had
reinvigorated his political career; it had enabled him to embarrass
Stephen A. Douglas in their great debates; it had won him the
Republican nomination for the presidency; it had been the first
principle of his presidential campaign.

If preservation of the Union really had been Lincoln's *paramount* object in the winter of 1860–1861, he would almost certainly have been willing to compromise on the supposedly subor-
dinate question of territorial slavery if by doing so he could have
preserved the republic from civil war. For as the Southern states
began, one by one, to secede from the Union—South Carolina was
the first to leave, on December 20, 1860—it was evident that his
position on the territorial question, together with the Southern
antipathy to it, were tearing the Union apart.

What is troubling, then, is not that Lincoln should have refused
to compromise on the territorial question, but that he should have
concealed the refusal beneath a rhetoric of Union.* Lincoln referred
to the territorial question only twice in his first inaugural address,
even as he conceded that that question was the "only substantial"

---

*Lincoln *explicitly* stated that his "paramount object" was to "save the Union" in his
August 22, 1862, letter to Horace Greeley: see Lincoln, *Speeches and Writings 1859–
1865*, 385. That the salvation of the Union was ostensibly his paramount object before
1863 is *implicit* in the first inaugural address: see Lincoln, *Speeches and Writings 1859–
1865*, 215–224.

one in "dispute" between the sections.* At first glance Lincoln's refusal to address in a more than cursory way what he called "the naked question," the "only substantial dispute" confronting the country, is striking; only gradually does it become apparent that Lincoln had reason to say as little about the dispute as possible. His opposition to territorial slavery had served its purpose: it had made him president, and as president he was in a position to thwart the progress of coercion.[†]

But of course his opposition to territorial slavery had also done something more. It had created the kind of crisis that an ambitious man could not help but love: a crisis that would enable Lincoln to realize all those visions of glory that had fascinated him since his youth, a crisis that would permit him to compete with Washington himself for a supreme place in the national pantheon.[‡]

⌒

The theme of *Macbeth*—the theme of the perversity of ambition—obsessed Lincoln. Even in other of Shakespeare's plays it is the theme of perverse ambition—the theme of *Macbeth*—that preoccupied him. "Unlike you gentlemen of the profession," Lincoln

---

*"One section of our country believes slavery is *right,* and ought to be extended, while the other believes it is *wrong,* and ought not to be extended. That is the only substantial dispute." Lincoln, First Inaugural Address, in Lincoln, *Speeches and Writings 1859–1865,* 221 (emphases in original).

†Lincoln might, it is true, have reasoned that the progress of coercion was a greater threat to the Union than civil war: he might have argued that his refusal to compromise on the territorial question—his resolution to accept civil war rather than change his territorial policy—grew out of his conviction that if civil war *might* destroy the Union, the progress of coercion would almost certainly do so by eating away the vital principles of the republic. This might indeed have been his reasoning, yet still he could not have been sure to what extent his ambitious will had influenced it. Reason may not, as Hume said, be the slave of the passions, but it is very often influenced by them.

‡Before he left Springfield to take up the presidency, Lincoln observed that the task before him was "greater than that which rested upon Washington."

wrote James Hackett in the summer of 1863, "I think the soliloquy in *Hamlet* commencing, 'O, my offense is rank, [and smells to heaven,]' surpasses that commencing, 'To be, or not to be.' But pardon this small attempt at criticism." In *Hamlet* it is the prayer of Claudius, the king who murdered a brother to gain a throne, that interests Lincoln, not the words of Hamlet himself, who in contrast to Claudius, Macbeth, and Lincoln himself found it difficult to translate ambition into action. Nor is it surprising that Lincoln should have cited *Richard III* as one of the plays that affected him most powerfully. Abraham Lincoln, as ambitious a man as any America has produced, was fully versed in the greatest literature of ambition.

After he had killed Duncan, Macbeth imagined that he would never sleep again:

> MACBETH: Methought I heard a voice cry "Sleep no more!
> Macbeth does murder sleep," the innocent sleep,
> Sleep that knits up the ravell'd sleave of care,
> The death of each day's life, sore labour's bath,
> Balm of hurt minds, great nature's second course,
> Chief nourisher in life's feast,—
> LADY MACBETH: What do you mean?
> MACBETH: Still it cried, "Sleep no more!" to all the house:
> "Glamis hath murder'd sleep, and therefore Cawdor
> Shall sleep no more, Macbeth shall sleep no more!"

Lincoln was drawn to *Macbeth*'s lines about sleep. In April 1865, after a visit to the headquarters of the army at City Point, Virginia, he returned to Washington aboard the steamer *River Queen* with Senators Sumner and Harlan and a young French nobleman, the Marquis de Chambrun. During the course of the voyage Lincoln read passages from *Macbeth* aloud to the party. Chambrun and

Sumner remembered that Lincoln dwelt particularly on Macbeth's meditation on the sleep of Duncan, which he read over twice:

Duncan is in his grave;
After life's fitful fever he sleeps well;
Treason has done his worst: nor steel, nor poison,
Malice domestic, foreign levy, nothing
Can touch him further.

Within the week Lincoln would himself be dead, and the words that so intrigued him in the last days of his life would come in retrospect to seem prophetic. But for Lincoln Macbeth's words were not prophecy: as much as Macbeth, he envied those who "slept well," for he himself did not. Like Macbeth he slept rather "in the affliction of . . . terrible dreams" that shook him nightly. He dreamt of an accident involving his son Tad's gun. "Think you better take 'Tad's' pistol away," he wired his wife from the White House. "I had an ugly dream about him." In March he dreamed that the White House was on fire. A few days before his death he had another nightmare, in which he saw a "crowd of people hurrying to the East Room of the White House." When he followed them there he "found his own body laid out and heard voices saying, 'Lincoln is dead.'"

The nightmares that disturbed Lincoln's sleep do not by themselves explain the fatigue he felt in 1865; nor do they explain the longing for the oblivion of sleep that led him to linger over Macbeth's words. When the journalist Noah Brooks suggested to the president that he needed rest, Lincoln replied, "I suppose it is good for the body. But the tired part of me is *inside* and out of reach." Nothing "touches the tired spot." On the *River Queen*, Lincoln marveled at how "true a description of the murderer" was Shakespeare's portrait: "the dark deed achieved," Lincoln said, "its tortured perpetrator came to envy the sleep of his victim." Our little life is rounded with a sleep; and it may be that Lincoln, too, was ready to die.

"Better be with the dead," Macbeth said, "Whom we, to gain our peace, have sent to peace." Duncan was at peace; but Macbeth, like Lincoln himself, lived to know "the torture" of a mind consumed in "restless ecstasy":*

O! full of Scorpions is my mind, dear wife!

"If there is a worse place than Hell," Lincoln said after Fredericksburg, "I am in it."

David Herbert Donald, in his life of Lincoln, paints a picture of a chief executive who was oddly contented in the late winter and early spring of 1865—a man who "showed no trace of any late-night anguish over his own responsibility for the conflict." But this contentedness was largely superficial. Edmund Wilson thought that Lincoln found the presidency "a harrowing experience." He was "shaken," Richard Hofstadter wrote, by the burden of the office, by "a burden of responsibility terrifying in its dimensions." He might even have been stricken, Charles W. Ramsdell suggested, "by an awareness of his own part in whipping up the crisis" that had led to the war. "Lincoln's rage for personal success," Hofstadter wrote, "his external and worldly ambition, was quieted when he entered the White House, and he was at last left alone to reckon with himself."†

---

*Shakespeare here uses the word "ecstasy" in its Greek sense of *ekistanai phrenon*, to drive a person out of his wits.

†This is one of the reasons Lincoln's life has the quality almost of a parable. He suffered and was changed. In most cases, Schopenhauer says, "the will must be broken by great personal suffering before its self-conquest appears. Then we see the man who has passed

He suffered. Visitors to the White House saw "anxiety and weariness" in his face, in the "drooping eyelids" that looked "almost swollen," in the "dark bags beneath the eyes." When his old friend Joshua Speed saw him ten days before the second inauguration, he was astonished by the president's altered appearance. "I am very unwell now," Lincoln told Speed, "my feet and hands of late seem always to be cold, and I ought perhaps to be in bed."

Lincoln did not, in his despair, become personally bloody in the way that Macbeth did:

I am in blood
Stepp'd so far, that, should I wade no more,
Returning were as tedious as go o'er.

He was, however, obliged to resign himself to rates of casualty from which even an ambitious man might have shrunk in the winter of 1860–1861, could he have foreseen them. Mary Chesnut, the diarist, said that she had been told, by an Englishman who had met Lincoln, that he had said "had he known such a war would follow his election, he would never have set foot in Washington nor have been inaugurated. He had never dreamed of this awful fratricidal bloodshed." The rates of casualty sustained during the Civil War were without precedent in American history; and they have never since been equaled. The anguished cry of Macbeth's Scotland was also the cry of Lincoln's America:

Bleed, bleed, poor country. . . .

---

through all the increasing degrees of affliction with the most vehement resistance, and is finally brought to the verge of despair, suddenly retire into himself, know himself and the world, and change his whole nature, rise above himself and all suffering, as if purified and sanctified by it, in inviolable peace, blessedness, and sublimity, willingly renounce everything he previously desired [for himself] with all his might, and joyfully embrace death." The note of peace and sublimity in Lincoln's life is found in the conclusion of the second inaugural address: "With malice towards none; with charity for all . . ."

The man who in 1865 composed the second inaugural address was haunted by the ocean of blood that had been spilt in four years' time:

> Yet, if God wills that it [the War] continue, until all the wealth piled by the bond-man's two hundred and fifty years of unrequited toil shall be sunk, and until every drop of blood drawn with the lash, shall be paid by another drawn with the sword, as was said three thousand years ago, so still it must be said "the judgments of the Lord, are true and righteous altogether."

This is a précis of Macbeth's own words: "blood will have blood." The sin to be expiated in the second inaugural address is the sin of slavery, not that of ambition: it is a sin for which the entire nation, and not simply the South, was to be punished. Lincoln observed that neither the prayer of the North nor the prayer of the South had been "answered fully." The Civil War, Lincoln said, could be ascribed to nothing other than "the providence of God": "He gives to both North and South this terrible War." But the belief that he was an "accidental instrument" doing the work of providence was not sufficiently consoling. Macbeth, in fulfilling the prophecies of the Weird Sisters, believes that the "air-drawn dagger" of fate has led him to Duncan: "Thou marshall'st me the way that I was going." But the consciousness of providential compulsion did not diminish the agony. The "obscure bird clamour'd," and "grace" was "dead." There was no longer anything "blessed" in mortality:

> I could not say "Amen." . . .
> But wherefore could I not pronounce "Amen"?
> I had most need of blessing, and "Amen"
> Stuck in my throat.

However providential his actions might have been, Lincoln had still the blood of a nation on his hands. There were times when even a conception of providential will did not sufficiently answer to the purpose of washing them clean:

> Will all great Neptune's ocean wash this blood
> Clean from my hand? No, this my hand will rather
> The multitudinous seas incarnadine,
> Making the green one red.

It is true that Lincoln believed he was implicated in the sin of slavery simply by virtue of the fact that he was an American, the citizen of a republic in which human bondage had been woven into the fabric of the Constitution. But it is difficult to believe that Lincoln's recognition of his own minor complicity in the institution of slavery was the primary cause of the anguish he felt when he contemplated the corpses. It was not for this reason that he was reading and rereading *Macbeth* in the spring of 1865, taking the poetry with him on boat trips on the Potomac, reciting the verses aloud to his friends, allowing its imagery to saturate his mind and penetrate his dreams. If Lincoln tells us, in the second inaugural address, that in God's eyes the Northerner is hardly less guilty than the Southerner where slavery is concerned, he also tells us that, in his own eyes, it is the Southerner who is far more viscerally guilty:

> Both read the same Bible, and pray to the same God; and each invokes His aid against the other. It may seem strange that any men should dare to ask a just God's assistance in wringing their bread from the sweat of other men's faces; but let us judge not that we not be judged. . . . The Almighty has His own purposes.

The Almighty might view a Northerner like Lincoln as no less guilty than a Southerner like Edmund Ruffin or Jefferson Davis. But Lincoln tells us that he himself has never been able to acquiesce in this belief. Lincoln says "judge not that ye not be judged" only after he himself has rendered very efficient judgment.

Lincoln's indirect complicity in slavery cannot explain the anguish he felt when he contemplated the tragedy of civil war. Knowledge that slavery "was, somehow, the cause of the War" rather assuaged than provoked his conscience. For insofar as slavery was the cause of the war, he was himself guiltless, or was no more guilty than any other American, and perhaps a good deal less guilty than the Southern ones; he had not the blood of six hundred thousand men personally on his hands. Lincoln anguished over the ocean of blood spilt in the course of the Civil War precisely because he could never satisfy himself that Southern recalcitrance was the sole cause of the war; he had always to wonder to what extent his own decision not to compromise on the question of territorial slavery had caused it.

◁══

In his moment of triumph, at the end of a war in which the forces under his command won a great victory, Abraham Lincoln reread *Macbeth* and reflected on how costly a thing is even a just ambition. This willingness to explore, at a time when a lesser man would have been conscious only of the glory of the moment, the "black and deep desires" latent within him is evidence of the sensitivity of Lincoln's conscience and the power of his moral imagination. He did not resolve the problem of ambition: no one ever will. But he acknowledged that the problem existed, and he used the resources of his civilization—resources that included the tragic poetry of *Macbeth*—to come to terms with it. His obsession with *Macbeth* explains as nothing else does why he was willing, in Hofstadter's words, to take upon himself "the moral burden of the War."

To be haunted by the concrete facts of one's own capacity for evil, to confront some ugliness in oneself, an ugliness previously suppressed, or successfully ignored, but now nakedly visible—is not the only way to attain self-knowledge. It is the tragic way. "To know my deed," Macbeth says, "'Twere best not know myself." The tragic protagonist goes mad, and eats grass; or he redeems himself through an act of expiation. Lincoln did not put his eyes out, as did Oedipus; nor did he "smote him[self] thus," as did Othello, or "by self and violent hands" take "off" his life, as Lady Macbeth is thought to have done. But how careless he was of his life, and how carelessly did he expose his figure to the fire of the rebel guns. If Lincoln did not, like Othello and Lady Macbeth, "take off his life," he yet dreamed of his death. Edmund Wilson thought he almost longed for it.* Lincoln, Wilson wrote,

---

*Sleep is in *Macbeth* more than once likened to death. It is "death's counterfeit" and "the death of each day's life." Death, in turn, is equated with peace. It is certainly possible that Lincoln, who longed for sleep, longed also for death. The ambitious man may end by discovering the vanity of ambition. Thus Gibbon writes of Severus: "He had been 'all things,' as he said himself, 'and all was of little value.'" (*Omnia fui, et nihil expedit.*) The wise man, T. S. Eliot says, comes, as Dante did, "to look to death for what life cannot give." "*Due cose belle ha il mondo: Amore e morte,*" says Leopardi: "The world has two beautiful things: death and love." When Schopenhauer speaks of the "joyful embrace of death," he means not suicide but the readiness to die. This, he says, "is the refined silver of the denial of the will to live that suddenly comes forth from the purifying flame of suffering. Sometimes we see even those who were very wicked purified to this degree by great grief; they have become new beings and are completely changed. Therefore their former deeds trouble their consciences no more, yet they willingly atone for them by death, and gladly see the end of the manifestation of that will which is now foreign to them and abhorred by them."

must have suffered far more than he ever expressed from the ago-
nies and griefs of the War, and it was morally and dramatically
inevitable that this prophet who had crushed opposition and
sent thousands of men to their deaths should finally attest his
good faith by laying down his own life with theirs.

When John Wilkes Booth, bred up in Shakespeare, assassinated
Lincoln, he thought in the obvious terms of *Julius Caesar*: *sic sem-
per tyrannis*. But Lincoln himself, who had also been bred up in
Shakespeare, and who had always about him a well-worn copy of
Shakespeare's works, could only have thought in terms of *Macbeth*:

> It will have blood, they say; blood will have blood.

We rightly view Lincoln not only as our greatest national hero but
also as our most totally and deeply tragic one. His was the tragedy
that leads through suffering to expiation and serenity.* There is a

---

*"Who leaves all," Emerson said, "receives more." There are, William James said, two
lives, "the natural and the spiritual, and we must lose the one before we can participate in
the other." The tragic exemplar of such a mortification is Hamlet. Having passed through
an interval of moral horror, he again sees the stars:

> There's a divinity that shapes our ends,
> Rough-hew them how we will . . .

Hamlet has by the end of the tragedy "surrendered" his life, for he is reconciled even to
the greatest terror it holds, its annihilation. He speaks of his own death with the equanimity of one who has embraced his sacrifice:

> Not a whit, we defy [reject] augury; there's a special providence in the fall of a spar-
> row. If it [death] be now, 'tis not to come; if it be not to come, it will be now; if it
> be not now, yet it will come: the readiness is all: since no man has aught of what he
> leaves, what is 't to leave betimes? Let be.

In the narrowest sense, Hamlet is rejecting Horatio's appeal to forestall the swordplay
with Laertes. "Let be" means "leave the arrangement as it stands." But if we examine
the injunction in the context of the entire utterance, as well as in the light of Hamlet's
earlier speculations about the value of being ("To be, or not to be"), we must, I think,
assign it a more comprehensive meaning. When Hamlet says "we defy augury," he rejects
Horatio's soothsaying desire to be "happily foreknowing," "privy" to the secrets of fate.

note of transfiguration in the words he spoke in March 1865, "With malice towards none; with charity for all . . ." They are arguably the most powerful words ever uttered by an American president. It would be absurd to claim for a practicing politician, a commander of armies, the beatitude of the mystic or the sweetness and serenity that, Matthew Arnold says, are found in a nature in which the "struggle and revolt" have ceased, and in which the whole man, "so far as it is possible to human infirmity," has been "swallowed up in love." But a revolution has nevertheless taken place. This is why, I think, the photographs taken of Lincoln during the last days of his life have a peculiar power and never fail to produce a tremor of emotion, even though one has seen them a hundred times. The feelings which the Gardner portraits of April 1865 provoke resemble those which Schopenhauer says we feel when we contemplate a "very noble character." Schopenhauer describes both the curious wasting of the flesh we find in such a character, and the otherworldliness of the character's gaze and expression. We imagine, Schopenhauer says, that we find in such a character a

> certain trace of quiet sadness, which is anything but a constant fretfulness at daily annoyances (this would be an ignoble trait, and lead us to fear a bad disposition), but is a consciousness derived from [the character's] knowledge of the vanity of all possessions, of the suffering of all life, not merely of his own . . . . When through some great and irrevocable denial of fate the will is to some extent broken, almost nothing else is desired, and the character shows itself mild, just, noble, and resigned.

Men, Hamlet counters, cannot outwit God's "special providence" concerning the disposition of their own being or that of others. They must accept such being: "Let be." The equanimity with which Hamlet confronts death is not morbid, for it coincides with a willingness "to be" that is remote from the antipathy to being he voices earlier in the play, when nonbeing ("*not to be*") seems to him "a consummation devoutly to be wish'd." "*Not to be*" has in him given way to the serenity of acceptance: "*Let be.*"

In the sorrow of such a noble figure there is

> a withdrawal, a gradual disappearance of the will, whose vis-
> ible manifestation, the body, [his grief] imperceptibly but surely
> undermines, so that [he] feels a certain loosening of the bonds, a
> mild foretaste of that death which promises to be the abolition at
> once of the body and of the will. [Nothing can] trouble him more,
> nothing can move him, for he has cut all the thousand cords of will
> which hold us bound to the world, and [in the form of] desire,
> fear, envy, anger drag us hither and thither in constant pain.

Such a character, Schopenhauer says, will "willingly atone" for
his deeds. The Macbeth in him dwindles to nothingness: he is
now Duncan. In his confession of his intimacy with *Macbeth*, Lincoln may be seen to have offered up a most subtle and profound
atonement.

> Yet who would have thought the old man to have had so much
> blood in him?

The Virtues and Vices of Messianism: What's Right and Wrong in America's Freedom Crusade

*G*eorge W. Bush's confidence in the global appeal of free institutions is now all but universally regarded as naive. The president's detractors ridicule as "Bush babble" the rhetoric of his second inaugural address, the high-water mark of his Freevangelical policy, and they point to his claim that "eventually the call of freedom comes to every mind and every soul" as evidence that he suffers acutely from a Messiah complex.

The criticism misses the mark. America was founded on a messianic idea. Whether John Winthrop was right or wrong when he crossed the ocean to build a city on a hill, it is too late to abandon the visionary business. Nor is it evident that we need, or ought to. The convictions the president expressed in his second inaugural address, utopian though they may be, have often, by a paradox that deserves but has never received careful study, inspired sound and pragmatic diplomacy. They are like the morbid secretion of the oyster, which proves to be a pearl. No, if Bush has gone wrong, his error lies not in his adherence to a Freevangelical faith that Lincoln, FDR, Truman, and Reagan all shared but rather in the

methods by which he has tried to implement that faith—methods
strikingly similar to those that brought two of his less happy predecessors, Woodrow Wilson and Lyndon B. Johnson, to grief.

—

The error of President Wilson was to exalt the technical machinery of democracy—the plebiscite and the ballot box—and to overlook the *demos* itself, its hopes and its hatreds, all those apparently
primitive impulses that do not fit neatly into a chart of *Homo sapiens*
progress but that are abundantly evident wherever actual human
beings are gathered together. Wilson, who had been bred a Calvinist, *ought* to have had a less pedantic idea of human nature. But he
was also a Ph.D. from Johns Hopkins, and he had been influenced
by the nineteenth-century faith in social science, a positivist vision
whose adepts regarded man's moral imponderables as vestiges that
would melt away in the sunshine of the dawning administrative
state. The technocrats, abjuring older moral vocabularies, looked
forward to the "scientific" solution of man's problems; social scientists would discover the laws that govern human nature, much
as biologists and physicists deduce such laws within their own
realms of study. Wilson's eminence grise, Edward Mandell House,
was a specimen of the technocratic type in one of its purer forms.
His 1912 novel, *Philip Dru: Administrator*, envisioned the emergence in the United States of a technocratic utopia. In the theory
of the technocrats, the promoter of free institutions had simply to
compile a mass of statistics concerning the "social development"
of a formerly oppressed people, sponsor an election or two, and a
free state would rise from the ashes of a fallen despotism.

Such was the intellectual equipment Wilson carried with
him when, in December 1918, he sailed to Europe on the *George*

Washington to preside over the greatest failure of American foreign policy in the twentieth century, the unsuccessful effort to create durable free states in central and eastern Europe. Jan Smuts, the South African statesman, warned Wilson that the central and eastern European peoples whom he hoped to save were "mostly untrained politically," and were "either incapable or deficient in the power of self-government." But Wilson failed to heed the warning. Winston Churchill spoke contemptuously of "the veneer of republican governments and democratic institutions" that Wilson, together with Lloyd George and Clemençeau, imposed upon the Germans after the war. Churchill and Smuts were proved right. The new Slav states of Czechoslovakia and Yugoslavia were never really satisfactory, and in Germany the Weimar regime, which put down no roots in the soil, was soon swept away. Two decades later Europe was again at war with itself, and free states were again in a death grapple with the forces of coercion.

The mistakes Wilson made in Europe were repeated, four decades later, in Vietnam, where the United States endeavored to prop a free state governed from Saigon. American policymakers, schooled, like Colonel House, in the assumptions of social science, sought to foist upon a largely uncomprehending people institutions that found no nourishment in the native soil. President Johnson, who had learned his trade from the technocratic artisans of the New Deal, promised in April 1965 to turn the Mekong River into a power plant to "provide food and water and power on a scale to dwarf even our own TVA." Descending into technobabble, Johnson asserted that a Vietnamese New Deal would "train people in the skills that are needed to manage the process of development." Neither LBJ, who never outgrew his youthful infatuation with the Rooseveltian administrative millennium, nor the Saigon politicians themselves, products of the French colonial system, were able to make the case for the free state in a way the indigenous population could understand. "Processes of development" meant very little to the peasant laboring in the rice paddy; Western institutions meant not very much more to the typical inhabitant of Saigon: he was no more interested in them than is Phuong in Graham Greene's *The Quiet American.* The result was another papier-mâché free state, one that was sustained largely by American will, and one that collapsed as soon as the last American troops were withdrawn.

George W. Bush entered office promising to change the sterile, social-scientific culture of the federal bureaucracy through programs (among them the quickly forgotten faith-based initiatives) intended to emphasize the constructive power of older moral and spiritual traditions, with their deeper roots in human nature. But he failed to make good his pledge to "change the tone" of the technocracy: certainly he never found a way to impose his vision on the mandarins charged with carrying out his policy. Bush has often been accused of messianism; but he never found a way to apply the virtues of the messianic temperament to the concrete problem of creating (in Iraq) a durable free state. In everything save sermon-making, he surrendered too easily to the technocratic impulses of his age.

The modern free state, Marx observed in *The Eighteenth Brumaire of Louis Bonaparte,* was midwifed by messianic figures driven by intense spiritual conviction. "The English people," Marx wrote, "borrowed speech, passions, and illusions from the Old Testament for their bourgeois [i.e., free-state] revolution. When the real aim had been achieved, when the bourgeois transformation of English society had been accomplished, Locke supplanted

Habakkuk." In deciding to invade Iraq in 2003, Bush overlooked the insight of Marx and made the same technocratic mistake Wilson and LBJ made before him. He attempted to give Locke to the people he intended to free without first having secured the services of Habakkuk, or the local equivalent thereof.

~

The failures of Wilson, LBJ, and (to date) Bush to create free states abroad are almost enough to persuade one to embrace the thesis of Harvard's Samuel P. Huntington, who in his 1996 book *The Clash of Civilizations* argued that certain civilizations, by virtue of their historic culture, are unsuited to the free institutions of the West. Disillusionment with the Freevangelical messianism of Wilson (or Johnson or Bush) leads naturally to Huntingtonism, perhaps to isolationism; Huntington himself has counseled American leaders to abandon the Truman Doctrine and "refrain from intervening in conflicts in other civilizations," even, or perhaps especially, when such interventions are intended to promote the growth of free institutions.

American history, however, supplies an alternative to the Freevagelical messianism that descends from Wilson. The principal source of the better tradition is the messianism that descends from another American president, Abraham Lincoln. Lincoln is quite unmistakably in the line of the Winthropian prophets. American institutions, he said, contained the "germ" of freedom, one that would "grow and expand into the universal liberty of mankind." Yet at the same time Lincoln had a delicate sense of the vagaries of human nature, and his feeling for the fragility of free institutions was almost tender. He was the product of an intellectual culture very different from that which molded Wilson. When he was a young man, the poetry of romanticism was just beginning to reach a wide audience, and his romantic training gave him a keen insight into the weakness of the constitutional machinery that the statesmen of the seventeenth and eighteenth centuries devised in their efforts to create a constitutional free state.

To remedy the deficiencies of this Enlightened craftsmanship, the young Lincoln proposed the development, in America, of public myths and rituals, a *"political religion* of the nation." He drew attention to the distinction Walter Bagehot was later to draw between the "useful" and "serviceable" parts of a constitution (in the contrivance of which such Enlightened statesmen as the American Founders have never been surpassed) and the "theatrical elements" that the Enlightened mind, for all its perspicacity, too often overlooked—those elements which, in Bagehot's words, are "mystic" in their claims and "occult" in their "mode of action." A constitution lacking such elements, Lincoln and Bagehot believed, will eventually perish if only from its own dullness.

As a mature statesman Lincoln refined his youthful intuition. He put aside the business of a political religion of the nation. In his effort to invest the American free state with those "mystic" and "occult" properties the Enlightened statesmen dismissed or slighted, he made his case for the American Union not in the Enlightened language of Madison or Montesquieu but in the accents of an older moral and spiritual vocabulary: he gave Americans Habakkuk rather than Locke. He invoked the King James Bible and suggested that the United States was a "chosen generation," a "holy nation," a "peculiar people." In the world-struggle between freedom and coercion, America, he said, had a providential part to play. If she played it well, "millions of free happy people, the world over," would "rise up, and call us blessed, to the latest generations." Paraphrasing the multiple-birth theory of John 3:3, he said that the United States, having expiated her sins in civil war, would experience a second nativity—a "new birth of freedom."

Lincoln's was a three-step messianism. Like all good seers, he first uttered a Prophecy. The Italian patriot Mazzini said that those who would defend the free state "must act like men who have the enemy at their gates, and at the same time like men who are working for eternity." Lincoln was as accomplished an eschatological stockjobber as Mazzini. In uttering his Prophecy—here we come to messianic step two—he did not omit, as free-state do-gooders too often do, to give his people scapegoats, viz., the evil slavedrivers. It is now the fashion to deplore the use of goats in politics; but as the advertisements of any election season demonstrate, one might as well deplore the weather. Besides, as Machiavelli observed, goats rightly used enable the statesman to channel popular energy constructively, and to prevent such energy from assuming more malignant forms. The third step of Lincoln's program was the most visionary. He promised that, after a purifying struggle with the goats, his people would reach the Destination—the palm grove, the milk-and-honey millennium, the New Jerusalem. After this "new birth of freedom," even the goats would be forgiven, and would be treated not with malice but with charity.

Lincoln's Prophecy, his goats, and his Destination have deep roots in the soil of the West. Odysseus, after a struggle with sundry goats, reaches Ithaca; Plato's adepts, after a similar process of expiatory strife, reach Virtue or God. Aeschylus and Vergil pressed the familiar pattern into the service of the state. In the *Oresteia* a cathartic struggle with goatish passions and a timely trip by Orestes to the seat of Apollonian prophecy culminate in the realization of a new civic ideal, that of Athens. In the *Aeneid* the pious hero clashes with an assortment of goatish villains and familiarizes himself, at Cumae, with Sibylline prophecy in order to found Rome. The

Hebrew version was in some ways grander. Where the Hellenes were limited by their cyclical conception of time, the Jews made the story linear. The Destination became ultimate and apocalyptic; the way was prepared for the "new heaven and new earth" that St. John the Divine glimpsed on Patmos. Protestantism revived these millennial desires. In seventeenth-century England the Protestant eschatology deposed the Stuarts and (as Marx observed) created the modern free state. In nineteenth-century America it drew fresh strength from the Second Great Awakening. Lincoln saw its force and laid his plans accordingly.

Of course he was working within the Western tradition; but the moral facts to which he appealed are universal. Every culture has its prophetic tradition, its goats, and its destinations. A Freevangelical diplomacy that succeeds begins with the recognition that what Lincoln did here can be done elsewhere.

Lincoln is the font from which the most accomplished of his successors have drawn in their attempts to promote free institutions abroad. At the Democratic convention in 1936, Franklin Roosevelt spoke of an American "rendezvous with destiny," a mission "to save a great and precious form of government for ourselves and for the world." The gathering world crisis put his rhetoric to the test. When a resurgent Germany began to subjugate Europe, Roosevelt was confronted with the question of whether to support the English. In retrospect his decision to embrace Churchill appears to have been foreordained. But of course it wasn't. When, in May 1940, Churchill became prime minister, influential figures in the English government—among them Sir Horace Wilson and R. A. "Rab" Butler—doubted the wisdom of resisting Hitler. Joseph P.

Kennedy, the outgoing American ambassador, succumbed to their defeatism. Democracy, Kennedy said, was "finished" in the United Kingdom. FDR disagreed. A leader, he saw, had emerged there, one who, like Lincoln, had painted the struggle between freedom and tyranny in a romantic language, the very archaisms of which, Isaiah Berlin observed, had created a "heroic mood" in Britain by "interpreting the present in terms of a vision of the past," as a "battle between simple good and simple evil."

America's decision to intervene in Europe was prompted of course by her sense of her own security interests. As "an island off the shores of Eurasia," Henry Kissinger has written, the United States has an interest in resisting the "domination of Europe or Asia by one power and, even more, the control of *both* continents by the *same* power," for such a power could marshal an array of resources that might bring America herself to her knees. Yet once he determined to intervene, Roosevelt was quick to characterize the intervention as a crusade for liberty. He did so not because he wished to disguise America's pursuit of her own interests but because he believed that those interests would be best served if the intervention promoted free institutions overseas. A freer Eurasia would, he seemed to believe, very likely be a more pacific Eurasia; and at all events a freer Eurasia would raise up allies who would almost certainly be helpful in any future struggles with aggrandizing despotisms.

Roosevelt found in Winston Churchill an ally who made his Freevangelical policy credible both to Americans and to Europeans. "I felt," Churchill said after King George VI asked him to form a government, "as if I were walking with Destiny, and that all my past life had been but a preparation for this hour and for this trial." Like Lincoln, Churchill was a vatic statesman. He uttered a Prophecy: after an interval of heroic suffering, the Nazi goats would be vanquished, and the Destination would be reached. "We cannot see how deliverance will come or when it will come," Churchill said in June 1941, "but nothing is more certain than that every trace of Hitler's footsteps, every stain of his infected, corroding fingers will be sponged and purged and, if need be, blasted from the surface of the earth."

The Freevangelical policy of Roosevelt succeeded. By backing the English prime minister he laid the groundwork for the redemption of Europe. Some will object that the bet he placed was not bold. Churchill, after all, was practicing his statecraft in the birthplace of the modern free state, where the culture of liberty had been long established and could be expected to be strong. True enough, but the Freevangelical policy of Roosevelt was intended not simply to preserve English liberty but to create free states on the Continent. In this FDR succeeded: free institutions, which had only a tenuous hold in Europe before 1945, now flourish there.

Germany, to be sure, was a difficult case, for under the Hohenzollerns it had been infected with the virus of Prussian militarism. Still, there was a free-state tradition in Germany. Liberal constitutional parties, by-products of the same Protestant traditions that inspired the freedom fighters of seventeenth-century England and eighteenth-century America, had thrived in Prussia before they were outmaneuvered by Bismarck in the 1860s. To give Germany's free-state impulses a chance to revive, it was necessary to extirpate the competitor tradition, the romantic paganism Bismarck had invoked in order to consolidate the German Reich. Bismarck himself was taken aback by the power of the genie he had conjured; he devoted himself, after 1870, to restraining it. But the romantic ideals of conquest and *Lebensraum* had by then found a home on Helmuth von Moltke's General Staff.

After Germany's defeat in 1918, Wilson, Clemençeau, and Lloyd George failed to dismantle the General Staff; the locus of the romantic cult of power remained largely intact. Truman and Churchill did not repeat the mistake. The Wehrmacht was broken up, and the National Socialists' goats (Slavs and Semites) and Destination (Valhalla and *Lebensraum*) were dropped from the national story. A mild Lutheranism was made to form the prophetic core of the new West German state. At the same time the victors resisted the temptation to which the peacemakers of 1919 had succumbed. They did not impose upon the defeated people a Carthaginian peace, and the subsidies of the Marshall Plan did much to reconcile ordinary West Germans to the new political order.

American leaders applied the same principles with no less success in Japan after its defeat by the Allied powers. In the face of considerable criticism, Douglas MacArthur and Harry Truman preserved the Chrysanthemum Throne and the Shinto tradition on which it rested—a moral and spiritual bedrock for the new Japanese free state. They had, indeed, no strong leader to back, such as Roosevelt found in Churchill, but the mystical prestige of his throne endowed the otherwise undistinguished Hirohito with all the prophetic authority with which nature had invested Churchill. The Americans bade the emperor revise his goats to bring them into line with free institutions; and in his 1946 New Year's Day rescript, Hirohito rejected as a "false conception" the belief "that the Japanese people are superior to other races and fated to rule the world." The monarch was no longer divine, or even sovereign; according to the new constitution, he was instead the "symbol" of the reformed Japanese state—what Bagehot would have called its theatrical component, charged with tempering daylight with magic. Japan's Destination itself, however, was unaltered; the continuity of the dynasty ensured that the country remained, in the eyes of the people, "blessed by the gods."

Four decades later Ronald Reagan came to power in America. The least technocratic of the modern presidents, Reagan likened himself to a mystic, and he was deeply committed to the Winthropian tradition of American messianism. America, he said, was a city on a hill. In his January 1974 address to the first Conservative Political Action Conference, he revived Winthrop's signature line. "You can call it mysticism if you want to," Reagan said, "but I have always believed that there was some divine plan that placed this great continent between two oceans to be sought out by those who were possessed of an abiding love of freedom and a special kind of courage."

Reagan belonged rather to the Lincoln-Roosevelt-Truman branch of the Freevangelical school than to the Wilsonian: he knew that free states need Habakkuks as well as Lockes. In the early 1980s some in his administration sought to challenge the Soviet empire in Cuba. Presidential aide Michael Deaver quoted Secretary of State Alexander Haig as telling the president, "Give me the word and I'll make that island a f—— parking lot." Reagan demurred. His instinct appears, in retrospect, to have been sound. However much ordinary Cubans might have yearned for a freer, better system, no leader had emerged, either in Cuba itself or in the diaspora, who had begun the work of reconciling the inchoate yearnings of the people with their traditional moral and spiritual vocabularies. None had translated Locke into the Cuban vernacular in a way that touched the Cuban soul.

Reagan made his principal thrust against communism not in Cuba but in Poland, where two leaders, Lech Walesa and Pope John Paul II, had emerged. They spoke of freedom in prophetical accents derived from the country's Catholic tradition, with its deep roots in the Polish character. In his book *The President, the Pope, and the Prime Minister: Three Who Changed the World,* John O'Sullivan offered a glimpse of the Lincolnian wisdom that underlay Reagan's statesmanship. "I have had a feeling," Reagan said, "particularly in the Pope's visit to Poland, that religion may turn out be the Soviets' Achilles' heel." Reagan did what he could to support the Polish free-state movement, and in doing so initiated the chain of events that led to the collapse of communism.

Romanticism is the catalyst of all the potent political myths of the modern period. In reviving the ideas and symbols—the goats and destinations—that the Enlightenment had relegated to the ashheap, Romantic poets supplied modern statesmen with the vocabulary they needed to touch the soul in an age of mass communication. Bismarck, Marx, and Bakunin used Romantic techniques to advance philosophies of coercion and terror that are not yet dead. Winthropian free-state messianism, revived by the Romantic counterconjuring of Lincoln during his struggle with the slaveholders, provides a salutary means of counteracting coercive Romanticism—or so the careers of FDR, Truman, and Reagan suggest.

President Bush attempted to apply the same policy in Iraq. The intervention was undertaken principally for reasons of national security. Intelligence suggested that Saddam Hussein possessed weapons of mass destruction: his record suggested that he would not hesitate to use them. If he did, the result would very likely be catastrophe in a region that supplies the West with a great deal of its oil. The question of the wisdom of the intervention need not detain us further; it is a question for the historians who, in the coming decades, will consider the nature of the intelligence on which the president relied in making his decision and the reason-ableness of the conclusions that he drew from it. What concerns us here is how the administration went about converting the war, once the president had resolved to undertake it, into a crusade for freedom.

Such a transmutation was always likely to be difficult, and the president and his advisers may be faulted for having failed to fore-see the extent of the difficulty. It was in many ways the same dif-ficulty Johnson encountered in Vietnam and Wilson encountered in Europe. You cannot give a people Locke if you have not first persuaded them that Locke is acceptable to Habakkuk, or to who-ever are his indigenous counterparts. A number of intellectuals in the Islamic world have attempted to reconcile the institutions of the free state with the historic traditions of Islam: they have tried to show that Islam's Habakkuks were crypto-Lockes, whose shades if summoned would bless free institutions. Their success has so far been limited. It is of course possible that Islam is simply incom-patible with liberty; but it would be rash, I think, to draw such a conclusion. The Islamic intellectuals who have worked up a syn-thesis of Mohammed and Montesquieu have typically been edu-cated in the French tradition; their language is remote from that of the Islamic masses; their vocabulary is too academic, too bookish, to stir the blood of masses of men and women. The Bush adminis-tration, having adopted a Freevangelical policy in Iraq, needed to translate the esoteric theories of the Islamic intellectuals into the vernacular idiom of Mesopotamia. They needed, too, to find lead-ers who could demonstrate that free institutions were compatible with the region's aboriginal goats and destinations.

Part of the difficulty lay in the neoconservative advice upon which the president leaned pretty hard in the days leading up to the commencement of Operation Iraqi Freedom. The neoconservative is a refugee from a romance that didn't work. Having broken with Marx and the god that failed, the neoconservative is like a jilted lover, wary of ever again succumbing to the seductions that kill. The neoconservative's skepticism toward the romantic modes is in many ways salutary, but it leads him to overprize the merely technical. He makes, very often, a kind of religion of Enlightenment. He may praise Lionel Trilling, but he is not as a rule sufficiently attentive to Trilling's warning that a politics that envisages the world in a "prosaic way" is unlikely to succeed.

The neoconservative seems to have hoped, when American troops marched into Baghdad, that reason and enlightened self-interest alone would persuade the citizenry to embrace the free-state ideals the troops brought with them. The neoconservative overlooked all that romantic effort and spiritual travail that Lincoln and Churchill, Mazzini and Gandhi, the seventeenth-century Protestants and the twentieth-century Zionists found indispensable in their efforts to vindicate the free-state ideal. In theory the president's Bible Brigades, schooled in the most Romantic poetry known to the West, ought to have enabled him to make good the psychological naiveté of the neoconservative, ought to have supplied that element of romance and spiritual acuity that was missing in the neoconservative's analysis. But it didn't happen that way.

⌒

This essay was written in 2007. In the interval since then I have become more sensible of the dangers in which a Freevangelical policy may involve the nation that pursues it too blithely and uncritically. The Freevangelical policy has its roots in prophecy and mysticism. Prophecy and mysticism have their place in a mature political philosophy; but care must be taken that they do not lead to the kind of utopian passion, the chiliastic fervor, that drives men to transgress salutary limits.

In a speech in the House of Representatives on July 4, 1821, John Quincy Adams warned that America, were she to play the part of apostle of freedom on the global stage, might well succumb to a pride that would have a demoralizing effect on her spirit and character. The United States, he said,

> well knows that by once enlisting under other banners than her own, were they even the banners of foreign independence, she would involve herself beyond the power of extrication, in all the wars of interest and intrigue, of individual avarice, envy, and ambition, which assume the colors and usurp the standard of freedom. The fundamental maxims of her policy would insensibly change from liberty to force. . . . She might become the dictatress of the world. She would be no longer the ruler of her own spirit.

In his book *Special Providence*, Walter Russell Mead identified Adams with the Jeffersonian school of American foreign policy. The Jeffersonians, Mead observed, "believe that the greatest danger facing the United States is the consequences of international overreaching. We can press our hegemony too far; we can insist too hard that our principles, whether Wilsonian ideals or Hamiltonian commercial values, be universalized into the practice of other countries." The warning is valuable. I do not believe that the United States ought to abandon its Freevangelical policy, which has done much good. But the keepers of our state traditions must take care to resist the temptation to complacency and even arrogance that a providential policy is apt to nourish in those who espouse it without a sufficient degree of humility and moral self-awareness.

Obama's Lincoln

*N*o one begrudges a statesman a degree of latitude in the manipulation of his precedents. FDR's Jefferson was largely a fantasy; Sir Edward Coke, in his struggles with the Stuart dynasty, invented a phony theory of Magna Carta; Napoleon, as first consul of the French Republic, invoked the image of Caesar Augustus, then discarded it when, in 1804, he threw away the republican mask and crowned himself emperor of the French.

The difficulty with President Obama's reprise of Abraham Lincoln is partly one of style, perhaps of taste. It is one thing to invoke a precedent. It is another thing to trivialize it. In January 2009 Obama paid tribute to Lincoln's memory by coming to the capital for his own inauguration, as Lincoln did for his, on a train. The gesture verged on a gimmick; Obama had, after all, arrived in Washington earlier in the month in the conventional fashion of today's potentates, by jet. (Lincoln himself would not, I think, have given a moment's thought to riding into town on a horse, pretending to be George Washington.) It is said that "Lincoln-inspired foods" were served at the luncheon in the Capitol following the inauguration of the president. Lincoln has already been obscured by a mountain of kitsch. Why add to it?

But there was a deeper oddness in the new president's invocation of his predecessor. Lincoln's principal preoccupation as
a politician was liberty. He ran for president in order to prevent
the extension of slavery into the nation's territories. President
Obama, in his own speeches and writings, has emphasized community rather more than he has liberty. Fair enough: both liberty
and community are essential to a healthy polity. But why, if your
political theme is community, invoke the president whose theme
was freedom?

There is, it is true, a school of thought that holds that Lincoln's solicitude for liberty was a pose; that as a pro-tariff Republican he was hardly a consistent champion of economic freedom;
that his statements about blacks reflected the prejudices of his
age; that he rode roughshod over civil liberties; that if he had
been really committed to freedom he would have let the Con-
federate states secede in the name of national self-determination.
Whatever one thinks of these criticisms, one is probably safe in
supposing that President Obama, if he has not much interest in
the Lincoln-as-Liberty-Lover school of historical interpretation,
has even less in the Lincoln-as-Tyrant school. What, then, does
he see in the man?

Probably it is the Lincoln brand that most deeply interests
him, as well as his own superficial resemblances to the president.
(Lincoln was tall, so is Obama; Lincoln came from Illinois, so does
Obama; Lincoln was a lawyer, so is Obama . . .) It is significant that
the one serious aspect of the Lincoln legacy to which Obama has
laid claim—what the historian Doris Kearns Goodwin has called
Lincoln's "team of rivals" approach to governance—is only half
the story, and arguably the easier half.

That Lincoln sought to conciliate such rivals as William
Henry Seward and Salmon P. Chase by bringing them into his

cabinet was undoubtedly an element of his political mastery. That he refused, in the face of enormous pressure, to conciliate pro-slavery politicians on the question of territorial slavery was another, no less important element. Between Lincoln's election as president in 1860 and the fall of Fort Sumter in the spring of 1861, Seward made several attempts to reach an accommodation with political leaders in the South. In his speech in the Senate on January 12, 1861, he seemed to open the door to a compromise on the question of territorial slavery; in private he went further. Lincoln responded by reiterating his own uncompromising policy on the territorial question and told Seward to stand down. There were limits to his willingness to cooperate with rivals.

Obama's invocation of Lincoln is easy to criticize. But on the whole his fascination with his predecessor is a good thing, for it may serve as a corrective to the too-facile rhetoric of his campaign, in which he suggested that we can have a new conciliatory politics, one that taps the "pragmatic, nonideological attitude of the majority of Americans."

Yes, but: Lincoln's career, like Churchill's, teaches that pragmatic conciliation can take a statesman only so far. Some differences cannot be papered over. The book Obama ought to read (or reread)—the book that counterbalances the conciliatory lessons of Goodwin's *Team of Rivals*—is Churchill's *The Gathering Storm*, one of the best studies ever made of the question when *not* to conciliate a rival.

Lincoln's career teaches something else that President Obama ought to bear in mind. Lincoln presided over a vast expansion of the powers of the federal government. So almost certainly will

President Obama.* Lincoln made clear that his own enlargements of authority were temporary. His "strong measures," he said, would not outlast the emergency: America would no more come to rely on such measures after the crisis passed than a man would "contract so strong an appetite for emetics during temporary illness as to persist in feeding upon them during the remainder of his healthful life."

We can only hope that President Obama takes these words to heart.

---

*I should here explain that this essay was written around the time of President Obama's inauguration in January 2009.

Free to Choose: John McCain's Cult of Teddy Roosevelt versus Sarah Palin's Reprise of Lionel Trilling

*D*uring his 2008 campaign for the White House, John McCain, asked by the *New York Times* to name a conservative model, cited Theodore Roosevelt. Some conservatives were perplexed. Roosevelt has no shortage of virtues; but it is not obvious that conservatism is one of them. A conservative is bound to admire TR's style and gallantry, the charge up San Juan Hill, the rounding up of crooks in the Badlands. His foreign policy was in many respects farsighted, and he was capable of great personal magnanimity—as, for example, when he obtained, for the struggling poet Edwin Arlington Robinson, a place in the customhouse in New York. Roosevelt's record as a domestic reformer is, however, another matter: he advocated a number of questionable reforms, and he ended his career by embracing the dream of a Progressive superstate.

It is true that as a young man Roosevelt resisted the Progressive agenda. In the New York State Assembly he opposed attempts to interfere with the free flow of goods and services, and he voted down a minimum-wage bill that promised to increase unemployment. But he was eager to advance himself, and he soon discovered which way the winds were blowing. As president he proposed the progressive taxation of incomes and estates, to the dismay of classical liberals who argued that laws should not discriminate against particular classes of people, even rich ones. And he supported the Hepburn Act of 1906, which strengthened the Interstate Commerce Commission's authority over the railways, a step that contributed to the deterioration of the railroads and (in time) to the mediocrity of Amtrak.

Roosevelt's dance with the command economy culminated in his "New Nationalism" manifesto. In the John Brown Cemetery in Osawatomie, Kansas, he lamented the "absence of effective state" in America, and he called for a paternalist form of government that would "control the mighty commercial forces" of the republic. Two years later, having failed to wrest the Republican party from Taft, Roosevelt ran for president as the candidate of his own Progressive "Bull Moose" party. Although he outpolled Taft in the general election, he lost to Woodrow Wilson.

Roosevelt and his fellow Progressives were on a wild-goose chase. Roosevelt's tax initiatives were designed to bring the "criminal rich" and "malefactors of great wealth" into line. But wealth per se (which in a free society is merely an account of useful activity) was not the problem. The problem was wealth derived from monopoly. Roosevelt failed to see that the United States lacked an effective anti-monopoly regime. Although the Sherman Act had been on the books since 1890, anti-trust law was in its infancy. Roosevelt's own approach to monopoly was emotional and neurotic. He acted as though he were on safari in Africa, trying to bag big game like the Northern Securities Company for purposes of psychological catharsis. There was nothing in his predatory technique of the coolness and method of Taft, who during a shorter spell of executive power brought nearly twice as many anti-trust suits. Having failed to diagnose accurately the nature of the problem, Roosevelt rashly concluded that the market itself had failed, and that a new gospel of administrative supremacy must prevail.

H. L. Mencken's analysis was astute. The "America that Roosevelt dreamed of," he wrote, "was always a sort of swollen Prussia, truculent without and regimented within. . . . He didn't believe in democracy; he believed simply in government. His remedy for all the great pangs and longings of existence was not a dispersion of authority, but a hard concentration of authority. He was not in favor of unlimited experiment; he was in favor of rigid control from above, a despotism of inspired prophets and policemen. He was not for democracy as his followers understood democracy, and as it actually is and must be; he was for paternalism of the true Bismarckian pattern, almost of the Napoleonic or Ludendorffian pattern—a paternalism concerning itself with all things, from the regulation of coal-mining and meat-packing to the regulation of spelling and marital rights." Teddy's distant cousin, the young Franklin, took note.

Roosevelt became ever more enamored of the social imagination, with its hard and allegedly scientific dogmas; yet his conception of himself became ever more oddly voluptuous. The Roosevelt who strutted and boxed, who exhibited himself bodily and acrobatically on the national stage, is a hothouse growth of the Mauve Decade. He is bathed in the violet glow of the 'nineties. Newspapermen compared his earliest public performances (in the New York State Assembly) to those of Oscar Wilde. The denouement was bound to be painfully fin-de-siècle: the Harvard man who was beguiled by the cowboy, the beast slayer, and the blood sportsman became enchanted with the hero worship of Nietzsche, and he emulated the prancing young Kaiser Wilhelm, that aesthete in jackboots, almost to a fault.*

The patrician became a dancer, and an adorer of muscle tone. TR promised the crowd bread in the form of social progress; but he supplied in his own person the circus. He was lion tamer, certainly—insistently, frenetically masculine; but he was trapeze artist too, with something of the spangled grace and epicene sensitivity of that performer. Where the patrician reformer sings the body electric for the amusement of the crowd, the pathologies of the social state cannot be far off. "Roosevelt is the keenest and ablest living interpreter of what I would call the superficial public sentiment of a given time," Robert La Follette wrote, "and he is spontaneous in his response to it." In the delicacy of his gyrations we find the first dim suggestion of an empathic tenderness that would eventually become obligatory in leaders of the social state.

Roosevelt believed that laissez-faire economics had been superseded by a new, more efficient gospel of administrative supremacy. Edmund Morris, who in *Theodore Rex* was manifestly hypnotized by his hero, argued that "the outdated system of *laissez-faire* . . . was accelerating out of control." So, at any rate, Roosevelt believed.

---

*"Years ago," Mencken wrote in "Roosevelt: An Autopsy," "as an intellectual exercise while confined to hospital, I devised and printed a give-away of the Rooseveltian philosophy in parallel columns—in one column, extracts from *The Strenuous Life* ; in the other, extracts from Nietzsche. The borrowings were numerous and inescapable. Theodore had swallowed Friedrich as a peasant swallows Peruna—bottle, cork, label and testimonials. Worse, the draft whetted his appetite, and soon he was swallowing the Kaiser of the *Garde-Kavallerie* mess and battleship launchings—another somewhat defective Junker. . . . Wilhelm was his model in *Weltpolitik*, and in sociology, exegetics, administration, law, sport and connubial polity no less."

Rather than use the government to promote freer and more competitive markets, he used it to promote government itself. He saw the evils of capitalism, its "gold-ridden, capitalist-bestridden, usurer-mastered" aspects; he had much less sense of its virtues. In the Rooseveltian lexicon, the word "bourgeois" was a pejorative. Yet if Roosevelt was not a capitalist, neither was he deeply or sincerely a Progressive. He was a man of the state.

In disparaging the "timid and short-sighted selfishness" of the "bourgeois type," in cultivating the mystique of the warrior, Roosevelt showed his soul to be tropically rank with the morbid second growth of romanticism which Wagner and Bismarck, Treitschke and Nietzsche, did much to nourish in the latter decades of the nineteenth century. In his 1915 book *Merchants and Heroes*, the German economist Werner Sombart offered an unintentional parody of the philosophy of late romanticism: the heroic aspirations of the Germans were, he maintained, of a higher order than the commercial mores of the English (and by extension the Americans). The coming together of a romantic yearning for the heroic-archaic and a socialist craving for an anti-capitalist utopia (to be administered by a vanguard of technocrats) that Sombart advocated was not a happy one: it led to the cults of blood and bureaucracy that were to doom not only Germany but also Russia, China, and the many smaller countries that followed their examples in the twentieth century. If it would be wrong to implicate Roosevelt in the crimes of the romantic socialists, it would be equally wrong to say that he was wholly uninfluenced by the sort of déclassé romanticism Sombart preached.

~

McCain's admiration of Roosevelt provoked a debate about the nature of American conservatism. His selection of Sarah Palin as his running mate provoked a debate about the virtues of American populism. Ever since her rise to prominence, Palin has elaborated a critique of what she calls elitism. Here, for example, is an exchange between the former Alaska governor and Bill O'Reilly on *The O'Reilly Factor* in November 2009:

> BILL O'REILLY: Do you believe that you are smart enough, incisive enough, intellectual enough to handle the most powerful job in the world?
>
> SARAH PALIN: I believe that I am because I have common sense, and I have, I believe, the values that are reflective of so many other American values. And I believe that what Americans are seeking is not the elitism, the kind of spinelessness, that perhaps is made up for with some kind of elite Ivy League education.

Palin's populism in its narrowest sense is a critique of degree fetish. The criticism is in many ways justified. Degree fetish is, at best, a necessary evil: in a big country it is not always easy to distinguish the wheat from the chaff. We are obliged to rely on things like academic degrees—and on the relative prestige of the institutions that grant them—to a much greater degree than was the case in the past.

This was evident in the comparisons that were drawn between then-senator Obama and then-governor Palin in the summer of 2008. His intelligence was never questioned. Hers was, repeatedly. Undoubtedly his two Ivy League degrees (from Columbia and Harvard) helped him. Her want of prestigious education hurt her: it made it easier for those who disliked her to say she was stupid. This presumption of stupidity was in the air *before* the interviews with Charles Gibson and Katie Couric. Those interviews resembled ambushes, orchestrated by people who had already convinced themselves that she was a moron. Had Obama—who cherishes his teleprompter—been ambushed in this way, his intelligence would have been questioned too.

Degree fetish may be a necessary evil in a big country where there are lots of candidates for jobs and no easy way to rank them. But if in the future the only means of obtaining intellectual credibility in America should be through an accumulation of degrees, the country will almost certainly become stupider. Degree fetish fosters a standardization of the intellect: everyone is obliged to jump over the same hurdles to get his intellectual passports. If standardization has its virtues, particularly in the hard sciences, its promise in the humanities is much less obvious; Edmund Wilson was probably right when he said that *literae humaniores* have suffered under the Ph.D. regency.

There ought to be a place in every civilized polity for the crank, the wild man, the hairy untutored prophet. Teachers must not of course encourage their students to be wild men: it is a vocation reserved for a few, most of whom know who they are. The great evil of degree fetish is its tendency to breed an intellectual arrogance that stifles nonconformity and homespun intelligence. Whitman suffered this condescension. So did Lincoln, and so did Reagan. Emerson, the Harvard man, said that Lincoln was a "clown." Clark Clifford, speaking *ex cathedra* for the Washington establishment, called Reagan an "amiable dunce."

To question degree fetish is not to question the value of learning. A good liberal arts education—an apprenticeship in "the best which has been thought and said in the world"—is a fine thing. But few even Ivy League schools today offer a really Arnoldian education of this sort; and as valuable as a good Arnoldian education is, it is doubtful whether it equips future statesmen to make better choices. Consider the case of Mr. Gladstone. He was consummately learned. At Christ Church, Oxford, he outshone myriads though bright. His activities during the very vacations of the university, duly recorded in his diary, must be the despair of lesser scholars:

> *July 6* [1830] ... —Up after 6. Began my Harmony of Greek Testament. Differential calculus, etc. Mathematics good while, but in a rambling way. Began *Odyssey*. Papers. Walk with Anstice and Hamilton. Turned a little bit of Livy into Greek. Conversation on ethics and metaphysics at night.

> *July 8.*—Greek Testament. Bible with Anstice. Mathematics, long but did little. Translated some *Phædo*. Butler. Construed some Thucydides at night. Making hay, etc., with S., H., and A. Great fun. Shelley.

Yet Mr. Gladstone got two of the most momentous questions of his age wrong. He thought "Jefferson Davis and other leaders of the South" had "made a nation." And he thought Bismarck was a nice guy who, if he defeated France, would usher in a new era of peace under humane German leadership.

~

Palin is right to question the degree fetish that leads us too casually to associate a prestigious education with intelligence and statesmanlike perception, and too readily to suppose that the lack of such an education signifies a want of brainpower. But the larger point of her populist critique of elitism is more important.

Palin's populism is not an expression of the resentment that stupid people sometimes feel toward the more intelligent. Much less is it a form of conventional class warfare or share-the-wealth envy. Her critique of elitism is similar to that of Lionel Trilling, though it is differently phrased. Trilling pointed to the dangers of the ideals of the "educated class," a class which had in a large measure forsaken the habits of what he called the "moral imagination" for those of the social imagination. An educated class that is unacquainted with the habits and discipline of the moral imagination, Trilling suggested, will be incapable of understanding the truth of its own motives; its members will too readily suppose that the rhetoric of social altruism in which they have been schooled reflects the deepest impulses of their hearts.

When Palin argues that elite education in many cases fosters moral "spinelessness" and is at odds with "American values," she is saying something not so very different from Trilling. For both Palin and Trilling, knowledge divorced from the "moral imagination" is dangerous: it is precisely because Faust has severed the desire to know from the obligations of morality that he comes to experience a diabolic horror. The advocates of social reform are in this sense Faustian: they have continuously subverted traditions that feed the moral imagination. Art, Trilling believed, is a crucial instrument in the transmission of moral culture. Literature, because it "is the human activity that takes the fullest and most precise account of variousness, possibility, complexity, and difficulty," illuminates the moral imagination: those who have studied it with care are less inclined to accept a facile and mechanical conception of the mind. Yet schools are ever less faithful to the liberal humanist conviction that the close study of classic texts has a part to play in awakening the moral imagination. The social administrators who exert a large influence over the curriculum of public schools in America naturally look with complacency on the abolition, in the classroom, of the older literary and artistic culture. Trilling himself showed, in *The Liberal Imagination*, that this older artistic culture has long appeared to the social reformer to be an obstacle that stands in the way of his ambition to remake human personality along social lines: the progressive liberal who has embraced the "facile sociological" point of view has, he argued, sacrificed art and its imagination of complexity on the altar of social utility.

Trilling deplored the evaluation of works of art in terms of their creators' social provenance and their sense of "social responsibility," yet what Harold Bloom calls the School of Resentment has carried this critical technique to new and absurd lengths. In the modern university, works of art are too often studied not for the light they throw on the moral imagination but for the degree to which their creators evince a sense of ethnic or racial or sexual grievance.

The social reformers, I suppose, know very well what they are doing. They look upon what Trilling (and Burke) called the moral imagination as an obstacle to their own Pelagian aspirations. The Book of Genesis and the moral traditions that descend from it stand in the way of the secular millennium, the moment when all men "become righteous in one instant" and "the perfection begins." This millennialism is by no means confined to the left; the right too has its style of delusory overreaching. If I have dwelt more on liberal illusions than on conservative ones, it is because it is the liberal element that seems to me bent on eradicating traditions that act, however imperfectly, as a corrective to complacency and pride.

To return to Governor Palin. I have no idea whether she has read Trilling or Dostoevsky, Marlowe's *The Tragical History of Dr. Faustus* or Julien Benda's *La trahison des clercs*: very likely not. But she is not the fool she has been made out to be, and her critique of the infirmities of the elite deserves to be taken more seriously than it has been.

Behind Jefferson's Wall:
The Truth about the Establishment Clause

> Reason's last step is the recognition that
> there are an infinite number of things which
> stand beyond it. It is merely feeble if it does
> not go so far as to realize that.
>
> —Pascal, *Pensées*

*O*pponents of vouchers (which allow parents to send their children to parochial schools) and critics of faith-based initiatives (which permit religious organizations to participate in the distribution of public charity) often argue that the Constitution forbids these programs. They sometimes cite, as authority, a letter that President Jefferson wrote in 1802 to a group of Baptists in Danbury, Connecticut. In the letter Jefferson said that the First Amendment to the Constitution created a "wall of separation between church and state."

Jefferson's Wall became the law of the land when, in 1947, Justice Hugo Black invoked it in *Everson v. Board of Education*. The Wall, Black said, "must be kept high and impregnable. . . .

We could not approve the slightest breach." Under the establishment clause, he said, government cannot "pass laws which aid one
religion" or that "aid all religions."*

Half a century after *Everson*, Justice Black's version of Jefferson's Wall continues to define our understanding of the establishment clause's injunction, "Congress shall make no law respecting
an establishment of religion." There is, however, a difficulty with
this understanding. Black's version of Jefferson's Wall isn't what
Jefferson himself had in mind when he came up with the metaphor
two hundred years ago.

⌐⌐

Historians have recently shed new light on just what Jefferson *did*
have in mind when he wrote to the Connecticut Baptists. In 1998
the chief of the Library of Congress's Manuscript Division, James
H. Hutson, sent Jefferson's rough draft of the letter to the FBI for
examination. Jefferson, Hutson observed, had "heavily edited" the
draft. "Words, phrases, entire lines were inked out," Hutson wrote.
A "marginal note was added to explain a section that was circled
for deletion."

Graphologists in the FBI lab restored Jefferson's ink-stained
words. The president, it appeared, had originally intended his letter to be a detailed statement of his administration's policy on religious matters. Jefferson was sensitive on the score of religion: some
of his enemies in the Federalist party accused him of being secretly
an atheist. Why, they asked, did President Jefferson refuse to pro-

---

*In *Everson* Black also for the first time applied the establishment clause to state governments by "incorporating" its provisions in the due process clause of the Fourteenth
Amendment.

claim national feast days and days of mortification, as President Washington and President Adams had done? The opportunity to reply to the Baptists, Jefferson told his attorney general, Levi Lincoln, "furnishes an occasion too, which I have long wished to find, of saying why I do not proclaim fastings & thanksgivings, as my predecessors did."

In his draft Jefferson said that he had "refrained from prescribing even those occasional performances of devotion"—such as Thanksgiving feasts—that were, in his opinion, "religious exercises." The "duties of my own station," the president said, "are merely temporal." Jefferson showed the draft to Lincoln, who advised him to omit the references to fasting and feasting. The attorney general said that the letter, as drafted, would only provoke anger in New England, even among the president's friends. "The people of the five N England governments," Lincoln wrote, "have always been in the habit of observing fasts and thanksgivings in pursuance of proclamations of their respective executives." The custom, he said, was "venerable, being handed down from our ancestors."

Jefferson acted on his attorney general's advice; he circled the relevant language for deletion. In a marginal note he explained that the "paragraph was omitted on the suggestion that it might give uneasiness to some of our republican friends in the eastern states where the proclamation of thanksgivings etc. by their Executives is an antient habit & is respected." Jefferson also crossed out the assertion that the duties of his office were "merely temporal." The result was a letter aimed at assuaging the feelings of friends of the administration who disliked established clergies without offending allies who rejoiced in Thanksgiving feasts.

But the letter to the Baptists was not a purely political exercise; it was also an effort to contribute to an ongoing debate about how to do justice, in the modern world, to both man's secular and his spiritual impulses. Two recent books, Daniel L. Dreisbach's *Thomas Jefferson and the Wall of Separation between Church and State* and Philip Hamburger's *Separation of Church and State*, describe the double nature of the debate. The strand most familiar to us today was the work of Enlightened secularists who wished to erect a barrier between church and state in order to protect secular life from the aggrandizing power of religion. Voltaire and Thomas Paine believed that, where clerics got hold of the machinery of government, they invariably sought to monopolize truth and prevent the diffusion of knowledge that threatened their supremacy. Yet in developing these arguments the Enlightened secularists were themselves influenced by Protestant sages (such as Martin Luther and Richard Hooker) who sought to erect a barrier to protect churches from the state, which might be tempted to commit the Erastian sin of subordinating spiritual institutions to temporal authority.

Jefferson is usually identified as one of the Enlightened secularists who, in the tradition of Voltaire, sought to protect a secular vision of life from the tyranny of the churches. But Dreisbach and Hamburger show that such a view is too simple: in building his Wall, Jefferson wanted both to protect man's secular life from religious authority and to shelter his spiritual life from secular forces that might otherwise overpower it. Jefferson was more sensitive to the value of religious devotion than is often supposed, and what are often taken as expressions of Jeffersonian hostility toward religion in general prove, on closer examination, to be expressions

of Jeffersonian impatience with those whom he accused of trying to impose their own religious beliefs on others. In his book
The Culture of Disbelief, Yale Law School professor Stephen L.
Carter says that it "is likely that at the time of the founding Jefferson shared the general view that government support for religion
was not in itself an evil, but that the state had to be prevented from
exercising coercive authority over the [nation's] religions."

Jefferson, for his part, thought religion essential to good government. "No nation," he was quoted as saying, "has ever yet
existed or been governed without religion. Nor can be." Contrary to the holding of *Everson,* Jefferson believed that government can aid religious institutions. Justice Black's assertion that
Jefferson's Wall requires government to forswear any role in the
spiritual life of the nation cannot be reconciled with Jefferson's
own thoughts and acts.

⌒

Consider, for example, the University of Virginia, the work of
Jefferson's winter years. The university was, and is, an institution
aided by the government. But the university was not, when Jefferson conceived it, neutral on the question of religion. Jefferson
did not, as some have asserted, "prohibit the teaching of theology
altogether" in the university. In his *Report of the Commissioners for
the University of Virginia,* Jefferson wrote:

> In conformity with the principles of our Constitution, which
> places all sects of religion on an equal footing, with the jealousies
> of the different sects in guarding that equality from encroachment
> and surprise, and with the sentiments of the Legislature in favor
> of freedom of religion, manifested on former occasions, we have

proposed no professor of divinity; and the rather as the proofs of the being of a God, the creator, preserver, and supreme ruler of the universe, the author of all the relations of morality, and of the laws and obligations these infer, will be within the province of the professor of ethics; to which adding the developments of these moral obligations, of those in which all sects agree, with a knowledge of the languages, Hebrew, Greek, and Latin, a basis will be formed common to all sects. Proceeding thus far without offence to the Constitution, we have thought it proper at this point to leave every sect to provide, as they think fittest, the means of further instruction in their own peculiar tenets.

Government, Jefferson argued, *can* aid religion—by, among other things, establishing a university that teaches "the proofs of the being of a God, the creator, preserver, and supreme ruler of the universe, the author of all the relations of morality, and of the laws and obligations these infer." But government can proffer this aid, Jefferson believed, only in such a way as to maintain "all sects of religion on an equal footing." For Jefferson, the "equal footing" principle permitted a state-subsidized professor of ethics to teach so much of theology and divinely sanctioned morality as "all the sects agree" on. The professor of ethics could legitimately provide a "basis" of religious and ethical instruction. Students who sought "further instruction" would have to apply to the "sect" of their choosing.

Some object that since Jefferson limited these observations to the practice of the state government of Virginia, under its *state* constitution, they do not necessarily reflect his views on the powers and duties of the *federal* government. Yale law professor Akhil Reed Amar, for example, maintains that, while Jefferson the Virginian was "willing to flirt with governmental endorsements of religion at the state level," Jefferson the American "argued for an

absolutist interpretation of the First Amendment" and believed
that "the federal government should have nothing to do with religion in the states."

Professor Amar notes that "while President Jefferson in 1802
refused to proclaim a day of religious Thanksgiving, he had done
just that as Governor Jefferson some twenty years before." But Jefferson could hardly have founded his opposition to *presidential*
proclamations of Thanksgiving feasts on the language of the First
Amendment: the establishment clause, in stating that "*Congress*
shall make no *law* respecting an establishment of religion," in no
way limits the proclamatory powers of the president. True, Jefferson also cited the Tenth Amendment ("powers not delegated to
the United States by the Constitution ... are reserved to the States
respectively, or to the people") to explain why he believed that
the president as well as Congress was "interdicted by the Constitution from intermeddling with religious institutions, their doctrines, discipline, or exercises." But not even the invocation of the
First and Tenth Amendments together adds up to the "absolutist"
position that Professor Amar detects in Jefferson's thinking about
the federal government's relation to religion.

As president, Jefferson authorized or condoned a variety of
federal aids to religion. At the same time he groped his way toward
the "equal footing" theory of his University of Virginia commissioners' report. In January 1802 he attended a service of Christian
worship in the House of Representatives. During the remainder
of his term he "was a most regular attendant" at these services;
the seat he first chose was "ever afterwards by the courtesy of the
congregation, left for him." He permitted, too, religious services,
including the Christian communion service, to be held at the
War Office and the Treasury. James Hutson has documented the
"nondiscriminatory" nature of the devotional practices Jefferson

sanctioned: clergymen from various denominations officiated, on a rotating basis, at the services he attended in the House, and a variety of sects received permission to offer up their liturgies in the other federal office buildings.

It might be objected that Jefferson's policy was not a national but a narrowly federal one, one that touched only the life of the District of Columbia. However plausible the argument, it is not true to the realities of presidential power. Jefferson understood, as all presidents do, the power of the symbolic act. When he attended religious services in the Capitol, or when he permitted devotional exercises on federal property, he knew that the reverberations would be felt beyond the perimeters of the federal city. He meant his policy to move the nation as a whole.

My argument so far has been a merely technical one, one that is no more likely than any other merely technical exercise to persuade others to reconsider the meaning of Jefferson's Wall. But Jefferson's "equal footing" theory of establishment-clause jurisprudence is rooted in something deeper than the intellect. If we can recover not only the theoretical and analytic but also the spiritual tints that colored Jefferson's conception of the proper relationship between God and man, church and state, we must look a little harder at Jefferson himself.

In doing so we find that his reputation as a man who upheld what Kant called a "religion within the limits of reason alone" is in many ways undeserved. It is true that Jefferson professed himself a man of common sense; certainly he was skeptical of the sort of claims Aristophanes classified under the heading "speaking ingeniously concerning smoke." He was devoted to the rational interpretation of empirical facts. But his yearnings outstripped his philosophy.

Consider his liberty tree. "The tree of liberty," he wrote in 1787, "must be refreshed from time to time with the blood of patriots and tyrants. It is its natural manure." The neoclassical sages of the eighteenth century tended to sentimentalize the poetry of the ancients: they found in it so much "sweetness and light." But Jefferson's liberty tree was not in the least a sentimental growth; it has its origins in the bloody fertility rituals of Attis and Adonis.* The liberty-tree letter was provoked by Shays's Rebellion in Massachusetts and by the question of whether the United States should adopt a new constitution, but the significance of its imagery seems to lie deeper, in the violence through which Jefferson himself had lived during the Revolution. In the struggle to vindicate American liberty, men had died and corpses had piled up. Jefferson had himself been hunted by British dragoons. When Benedict Arnold sacked Richmond, Jefferson, then governor of Virginia, fled for his life. Some said that he spent a night in January 1781 cowering in a barn: he himself was always silent on the matter. Later Lord Cornwallis dispatched a raiding party to Monticello to seize the governor. Jefferson, warned in time, booted and saddled for an escape. But a man who has once been hunted does not easily forget the experience.

Jefferson developed various theories to explain the place of violence in the world. The "pugnacious humor of mankind," he

*Jefferson invoked the "tree of liberty" in a 1787 letter to John Adams's son-in-law, William Stephens Smith. Five years later, during the French Revolution, Bertrand Barère concluded an address to the French Convention by declaring that the "tree of liberty, as an ancient author remarks, flourishes when it is watered with the blood of all classes of tyrants." It is most unlikely that Barère knew of Jefferson's letter, which for many years remained unpublished. The more plausible explanation is that both Jefferson and Barère drew on an anterior source, but it has never yet to my knowledge been identified.

told John Adams, "seems to be the law of his nature, one of the obstacles to too great multiplication provided in the mechanism of the Universe. The cocks of the henyard kill one another up. Boars, bulls, rams do the same. And the horse, in his wild state, kills all the young males, until worn down with age and war, some vigorous youth kills him, and takes to himself the Haram of females."

But Jefferson's theory of a "mechanism" for population control in the universe was a little too neat to do justice to the savagery he had seen and felt. Neither did his clockwork explanations illuminate the mysteries of death and grief. "I have often wondered for what good end the sensations of Grief could be intended," he confessed to John Adams. He was an old man when he wrote these words; he had watched his wife and five of his six children precede him to the grave. But on the threshold of great age he was no nearer an answer.

⌖

Jefferson's notion of the clocklike "mechanism" of the universe grew out of the scientific theories of his age and the discoveries of Newton and Kepler: it has led some to conclude that he was, in conviction and sensibility, a Deist. He believed, Cardinal Dulles observed, "in one God, in divine providence, in the divine moral law." He did not believe that the Bible contains the revealed word of God, that Jesus is divine, or that the doctrines of the Trinity and the Atonement are true. He doubted whether the deity was in the habit of suspending the ordinary laws of nature in order to perform miracles, and he abhorred what he called "priestcraft" and "monkish superstition and ignorance."

Yet Jefferson seems never to have called himself a Deist. He once described himself as forming a "sect by myself." At other times he professed himself a Christian. "To the corruptions of Christianity I am, indeed, opposed," he wrote to Benjamin Rush in 1803, "but not to the genuine precepts of Jesus himself." "I am a Christian," he said, "in the only sense in which he [Jesus] wished any one to be; sincerely attached to his doctrines, in preference to all others; ascribing to himself every *human* excellence; and believing he never claimed any other." In an 1816 letter to Mrs. M. Harrison Smith, Jefferson said that

> the priests indeed have heretofore thought proper to ascribe to me religious, or rather anti-religious sentiments, of their own fabric, but such as soothed their resentments against the act of Virginia for establishing religious freedom. They wished him to be thought atheist, deist, or devil, who could advocate freedom from their religious dictations. But I have ever thought religion a concern purely between our God and our consciences, for which we were accountable to Him, and not to the priests. I never told my own religion, nor scrutinized that of another.

In at least one respect Jefferson parted company with the Deists, or with some of them at any rate. A number of Deists believed that there was nothing which could not, in theory, be understood by human reason; anything that was impervious to human reason was, they supposed, inherently irrational.* True, many things are at present incomprehensible to human reason; but they are ultimately explainable by it. Jefferson's view was different. There

---

*In his 1696 pamphlet *An account of the growth of Deism in England*, the clergyman William Stephens attributed to those who have been influenced by Deism a conviction that that which is "above Reason must be above a rational Belief," and that to believe in something above a "rational Belief" is to embrace an "irrational Belief." Pascal had a different conception of the explanatory power of human reason. That which lay beyond it was not necessarily irrational; it might instead embody a different, and perhaps a higher, reason: "*Le cœur a ses raisons*," he said in the *Pensées*, "*que le raison ne connâit point*." "The heart has it reasons, of which the reason knows nothing."

were, he believed, things "hid and barr'd from common sense" and rational intelligence; there were mysteries which the human mind could not penetrate. In an 1801 letter to the Reverend Isaac Story, he alluded to Montaigne's panegyric on ignorance* and suggested that, for reasons unknown to us, we are meant to be in certain directions stupid. "The laws of nature," Jefferson told Story,

> have withheld from us the means of physical knowledge of the country of spirits, and revelation has, for reasons unknown to us, chosen to leave us in the dark as we [misprint for "it"?] were. When I was young I was fond of the speculations which seemed to promise some insight into that hidden country, but observing at length that they left me in the same ignorance in which they had found me, I have for very many years ceased to read or think concerning them, and have reposed my head on that pillow of ignorance which a benevolent Creator has made so soft for us, knowing how much we should be forced to use it. I have thought it better, by nourishing the good passions and controlling the bad, to merit an inheritance in a state of being of which I can know so little, and to trust for the future to Him who has been so good for the past.

Jefferson dwelt again on the limits of human understanding in a March 1820 letter to John Adams. "When I meet with a proposition beyond finite comprehension," he wrote, "I abandon it as I do a weight which human strength cannot lift: and I think ignorance, in these cases, is truly the softest pillow on which I can lay my head." At other times Jefferson seemed, it is true, to profess a more thorough materialism: "When once we quit the basis of

---

*"Oh what a soft, easy and wholesome Pillow is Ignorance and Incuriosity, whereon to repose a well contriv'd Head." Montaigne, "Of Experience," in *Essays of Michael Seigneur de Montaigne*, trans. Charles Cotton (three vols., London: Brown, Nicholson, *et alia*, 1711), III, 403.

sensation," he wrote to Adams in August 1820, "all is in the wind. To talk of *immaterial* existences is to talk of *nothings*." It is not, however, clear from the letter whether Jefferson means to say that there is no such thing as a spiritual reality, or whether he means to say that, although there may indeed be such a reality, our senses cannot perceive it, and therefore to talk of its characteristics is to talk of nothings.

In his book *Axel's Castle*, Edmund Wilson observed that the theories of Newton and Descartes led the thinkers of the Enlightenment "to regard the universe as a machine, obeying logical laws and susceptible of rational explanation: God figured merely as the clockmaker who must have existed to make the clock." Yet even as the novel theories seemed to explain the universe, many thinkers whom we associate with the Enlightenment were conscious of all that the theories did *not* explain. Newton himself was one of these. "I do not know what I may appear to the world," he said, "but as to myself, I seem to have been only like a boy playing on the seashore, and diverting myself in now and then finding a smoother pebble or a prettier shell than ordinary, whilst the great ocean of truth lay all undiscovered before me."

It is an error to suppose that because a man holds a particular theory he is necessarily oblivious to all that the theory cannot explain. Jefferson was conscious of the inadequacy of his philosophy before what T. S. Eliot called the "awful mystery" of life, and he resorted on occasion to motifs with mysticism and truer to the strangeness.*

*David Hume was another Enlightened sage who, like Jefferson, was conscious of the mystery of life. The more he thought about it, the stranger the universe and his own existence seemed to him, and in his *Treatise of Human Nature* he left a memorable account of the "melancholy" and "despair" into which his thinking led him: "Where am I, or what? From what causes do I derive my existence, and to what condition shall I return? Whose favour shall I court, and whose anger must I dread? What beings

It is sometimes said that men like Jefferson turned to the art of the Greeks and Romans because they found in the classical civilizations an aesthetic vocabulary consistent with the severe and rational geometry of their Enlightened ideals. Jefferson, however, turned to the classical motifs precisely when his Enlightened oracles failed him. Certainly it was a motive deeper than reason that led him to preserve, in the idiosyncratic classicism of Monticello, the emblems of a darker revelation. Over the years he made his house a place in which every column and every cornice embodied, and nourished, some part of his imagination, the dark places as well as the light. If you doubt it, look again at the interior friezes, with their griffins and demon spirits, their knives and axes and ambrosial bowls. The house is filled with images of the primitive blood-sacrifice, and the bulls' skulls are fatally garlanded.

One might of course dismiss Jefferson as merely another philosophic pagan, one who amused himself with antiquarian arcana in the manner of such eighteenth-century dilettantes as Sir Francis Dashwood and Richard Payne Knight. But the dilettanti were frivolous men, and Jefferson, whatever else he might have been, was not frivolous. Still less was he actually a pagan, one who, like Julian the Apostate, sought to efface the mark of Christian baptism in the ritual bath of hot bull's blood. (Such a bath alone, it was believed, could purify a soul that had consumed the body and blood of Christ: see the curious remarks of Gibbon in the twenty-

surround me? and on whom have I any influence, or who have any influence on me? I am confounded with all these questions, and begin to imagine myself in the most deplorable condition imaginable, inviron'd with deepest darkness, and utterly depriv'd of the use of every member and faculty." Hume did not, however, seek consolation in mysticism or religious faith; he sought to be faithful instead to a philosophy of what he called "natural and agreeable" folly.

third chapter of the *Decline and Fall*.) Julian was sincerely a poly-
theist, something that cannot be said of Jefferson. The author
of the Declaration of Independence was, I think, searching for a
mysticism that could replace the one in which he had bred but
in which he could no longer believe. Monticello, if it is a temple
of reason, is also a mystic shrine: its maker counterbalanced the
rational and Enlightened ideals of its salons with an art, or more
precisely a symbolism, that acknowledged all those mysteries that
a purely rational intelligence can never comprehend.*

Coleridge would later observe how difficult it is for a man to
live wholly in "the faith of reason":

> But still the heart doth need a language, still
> Doth the old instinct bring back the old names . . .

Jefferson, in his painstaking labors to endow Monticello with its
curious and unsettling imagery, appeared to recognize that the
heart does indeed require a language beyond that of reason. When
the axes fell, and the blood flowed, the drippings fed a soil that
reason and Enlightenment could not refresh.†

<hr />

Jefferson pondered other mysteries that lay outside the domain
of his Enlightened theories. The old Western vocabularies of
benevolence and compassion (*caritas*, *agape*) stirred him deeply.
"Pity and help any thing you see in distress," Jefferson advised his

---

*"A Symbol," says Coleridge, "is characterized by a translucence of the Eternal through
and in the Temporal."
†The evidence of Monticello suggests that Jefferson would have sympathized with the
lament of Diderot, who said that he was "furious at being caught up in a damnable philosophy [that of the Enlightenment] that my mind cannot help but believe, and my heart
cannot help but deny."

grandchildren. He tried, with mixed results, to honor the advice in his own life.

Doubtless some of his ideas on this subject derived from the old Greek notion that love is the repairer of souls; but as a young man he absorbed, as well, the sentimental faith of the eighteenth century, those ideas of benevolence, humanity, and sympathy that fill the pages of the Scottish philosophers. Without the "feelings of sympathy, of benevolence, of gratitude, of justice, of love, of friendship," Jefferson told Maria Cosway in 1786, men would lapse into a narrow and savage solipsism. But the core of this philosophy was much older than the philosophy of David Hume, Adam Smith, and Francis Hutcheson. With words like "compassion," "sympathy," and "humanity," the Scots were reaching for a more familiar word: "love." Theirs was a secular version of the medieval language of love. They could not believe, as Dante did, in a love that could gather up the scattered pages of the universe and bind them together, as though in one book. But they retained as much of the older faith as they believed they reasonably could.*

Jefferson sensed the deficiency and went back to the "master workman," as he called him, who said, "These things I command you, that ye love one another." Scholars such as Dickinson Adams, Paul K. Conkin, Edwin S. Gaustad, and Jean M. Yarbrough have in recent years illuminated the mature Jefferson's

---

*The Scottish sages sought to reconcile the Christian ideal of love with the modern commercial ethos of acquisitive self-interest. They championed the virtues of the market, yet they were conscious always of its vices. There was, they believed, a spiritual usury in the market which, if unresisted, would deplete the reserves of human nobility; Smith observed that the ever more specialized forms of behavior the market encouraged had already begun to disfigure human character. The highest ambition of the Scottish thinkers was to unite the rose and the cash register, but their effort to transform the tradition of *amor* and *caritas* into a secular ideal, one that could take the place of the divine one, seems to me to have been a failure. Their concept of sympathy was too anemic to take strong root in the imagination, or to be the cause of much practical good (in the way, for example, that the medieval notion of courtesy was).

fascination with Christianity's vision of love's place in the order-
ing of human life. Jefferson never accepted the divinity of Christ,
but as president he assembled a "digest" of Christ's teachings,
which he believed showed that Jesus' "system of morality was
the most benevolent & sublime probably that has been ever
taught." The "moral doctrines" of Jesus were, he said, "more
pure & perfect than those of the most correct of the philosophers." Christ "went far beyond" those philosophers in "incul-
cating universal philanthropy, not only to kindred and friends,
to neighbors and countrymen, but to all mankind, gathering all
into one family, under the bonds of love, charity, peace, common wants and common aids." Jefferson called his digest the
Philosophy of Jesus, and he believed that it evinced the "peculiar
superiority of the system of Jesus over all others."

Critics have dismissed these exercises as so much Tartuffery.
There is of course no way to know the quality of another man's
heart; but whatever might have been his motives in searching the
Gospels, Jefferson was, during much of his career, quite honestly
and demonstrably concerned with understanding the place of
benevolence in a commercial republic. Historians have long been
sensitive to his desire, expressed in his idea of the Wall, to prevent
the power of the churches from overmastering civil authority; but
they have been less alive to this ambition of his to protect, from
the expanding energies of commerce, certain kinds of encounters
between human beings. Those spiritual disciplines, like the Christian ideal of *caritas*, that lift human relationships out of the realm
of the utilitarian seemed to Jefferson to have little place in the new
world that commerce was bringing into being.*

---

*Not, of course, that they had an altogether secure reign in the georgic world of Monti-
cello, where Jefferson presided over a slave-driven economy.

The fears he harbored became commonplace during the nineteenth century, but his approach to the problems posed by commercial growth was in its own way original, for unlike many later critics he never surrendered his Whig faith in personal freedom or in liberty of trade (if one excepts the 1807 Embargo Act). And yet even as he championed liberty, Jefferson worried that Americans would fail to do justice to the full possibilities of their freedom. If his public career was dedicated to the vindication of Whig liberty, the work of his private life and retirement was devoted to the construction of little pavilions of compassion. He labored to show how traditions of benevolence could be made to flourish, in a small way, in the great Whig republic that he had, in his younger days, done so much to create. He became the explicator of the little community, the miniature *polis*, the well-wrought agora, those minor forms of moral and spiritual order that spring from pools of affection deeper than self-love. His contributions in these closed kingdoms, though less celebrated, are quite as valuable as his exercises in the realm of politics. If his public work was made up of large, state-shaking endeavors, his private œuvre was a concise little collection of gems, each of them bright and sharply cut.

Monticello was one of these. The University of Virginia was another. In designing his "academical village," Jefferson carefully thought out the elements that make for vitality in a little platoon. A naked and open daylight, he knew, was not enough; there must be masques and mummeries as well. The artist in him understood the role that a civilizing mysticism plays in the creation of desirable patterns of order. Once more he incorporated little mystical touches in the architecture. Ox skulls and demon spirits grace the porticos of the pavilions; the rotunda at the top of the Lawn, built in the style of Emperor Hadrian's pantheon in Rome, was a library that promoted the love of scholarship and the care of books.

If we study Jefferson's idea of the nature and purpose of the sheltering pavilion in the modern world—the pillared place consecrated to *caritas* and marked off from life's violence and its unavoidable but too often hurtful competitions—we will, I think, deepen our understanding of what is called "civil society." We will see that this phrase is too drab to do justice to the elements that make these sanctuaries vital, the traditions, rites, and mysteries that give an institution (a school, a family, a neighborhood, a town square) a claim not only on our minds but also on our hearts. These things are, for us, all that the public faith of the *polis* was to the ancient Greek: they are our agoras, the focus of our desire for community and civic cohesion. The Greek could invest his love in his city, for it was not too big for his heart; our cities *are* too big, and we must exercise our compassion in smaller arenas. A man who lives in the modern city must, Leopardi said, "build himself a little city within the great one."

Jefferson understood that communities like the University of Virginia are, or rightly understood can be, the moral *palestrae* of the modern (Whig) civilization, places in which people are free to develop qualities of soul which, though they have no measurable value in the Whig marketplace, are nevertheless essential to civilized life.

~

The state has an obligation to help in this civilizing work. The "equal footing" doctrine—the theory that most closely approximates Jefferson's understanding of the purposes of the Wall erected by the First Amendment—teaches us that government *can* aid religion and religious associations that perpetuate moral and spiritual ideals, provided that it finds ways to do so (voucher programs, for example) which do not favor particular creeds. (Under a voucher program, the recipient of a voucher for public assistance would decide for himself whether to use it to seek help from a secular organization or from a religious one.)

Justice Black's reading of the First Amendment, by contrast, requires the state to impose in many areas of public life the imaginatively sterile and spiritually impoverished religion of dogmatic secularism. Stephen Carter, in *The Culture of Disbelief*, raises the possibility that the secularist jurisprudence of Black and his epigoni may represent yet "another effort to ensure that intermediate institutions, such as religions, do not get in the way of the government's will." He argues that the Supreme Court's establishment-clause jurisprudence may be

> a way of ensuring that only one vision of the meaning of reality—that of the powerful group of individuals called the state—is allowed a political role. Back in Tocqueville's day, this was called tyranny. Nowadays, all too often, but quite mistakenly, it is called the separation of church and state.

Neither Jefferson nor the other Founders would have countenanced Justice Black's reading of the establishment clause, and they almost certainly would have raised their eyebrows over his method of construing constitutional texts. Consider again the language of the establishment clause: "Congress shall make no law respecting an establishment of religion . . ." To "establish" a religion, according to the Oxford English Dictionary, is "to place (a church or a religious body) in the position of a national or state church." Justice Black maintained that the establishment clause requires the state to be "neutral in its relations with groups of religious believers and unbelievers." Yet the clause says nothing about an obligation of neutrality; it says nothing about forbidding the state to make use of religious and spiritual resources in its work; it says only that the state shall make no law respecting an "establishment of religion."* The state shall not, that is, create a state or national religion (such as those in England and Germany) with a clergy and houses of worship maintained at taxpayer expense.†

Justice Black claimed to construe the Constitution strictly; but he was notoriously a judicial activist in the New Deal tradition, and he did not shrink, on occasion, from making the Constitution say what he wished it to say. Tony Freyer, in his study *Hugo L. Black and the Dilemma of American Liberalism*, shows that Black was deeply committed to the cause of the social state. He had, moreover, been influenced by the jurisprudential philosophy that New Deal lawyers devised to remodel the Constitution in order that its text might accommodate the institutions and methods of the social imagination. The founders of the school of "legal realism" which flourished at Yale Law School in the 1920s and 1930s disparaged traditional principles of legal interpretation: they encouraged judges to decide cases in a manner consistent with contemporary social ideals. Through the work of judges like Black, the "realist"

---

*Were the country to abandon the establishment-clause jurisprudence of Justice Black, citizens of particular communities would of course be free to promulgate in their own jurisdictions Black's code of a state secularism, provided that such a code did not prohibit the "free exercise" of religion. The point is that many of the decisions that now fall within the arbitrary prerogative of the *noblesse de la robe* ought to be left to the discretion of citizens acting through their democratic institutions.

†The other purpose of the establishment clause was to prevent the federal government from *disestablishing* the state religious establishments of the early republic. The law establishing Connecticut's state church, for example, remained on the books until the adoption of the state's constitution of 1818.

theory has become entrenched in the legal profession, and today many cultural decisions once left to the discretion of particular communities fall within the arbitrary power of jurists who act less as interpreters of the law than as arbiters of social policy.

Whittaker Chambers once said that "man without mysticism is a monster." Having lived for several decades under a jurisprudence that imposes on American communities the anti-mysticism of the social state, Americans may at last be ready to return to a truly Jeffersonian understanding of the meaning and purpose of the establishment clause.

Revenge of the Castle People:
Reflections on the Death of the Agora

*R*elations between the aristocrat and the common man have never been easy. The antipathy between castle people, who dwell in the manor house, and agora people, children of the marketplace, runs like a fault line through the moral landscape of the West. The chasm is evident already in the *Iliad*, in the thrashing Odysseus gives Thersites; Proust, in the twentieth century, was as conscious of the gulf when he insisted that the "misunderstanding" between the upper castes and their bourgeois inferiors was "complete."

The marketplace came out on top. Democracy vanquished feudalism. Or so we like to pretend. There are suburbs of New York and Philadelphia in which you might, with only a slight exertion of imagination, fancy yourself in the world of the crusader dukes. The persistence of castle culture is one of the curiosities of the country's social archaeology, another of the cultural contradictions of capitalism, if not of democracy itself. The Gilded Age robber barons, living in fear of the industrialized masses, built neo-Romanesque castles like the Hay-Adams houses (since demolished) on Washington's Lafayette Square. The thicker the masonry, the more likely the fortress would withstand the anticipated *Jacquerie*. Later, a more confident generation of castle people found inspiration in the vanilla-ice-cream neoclassicism of Cass Gilbert and John Russell Pope. The 1980s brought the first prefabricated McMansions.

Just now a fresh breed of castle builders is spawning, ready to replace the fallen castellans who earned their turrets on Wall Street and built their McCastles during the credit bubble, but whose ideal of the financier-sage has, in the light of the crash, come to seem dubious. Robert Rubin and Hank Paulson, dragon slayers of this now-defunct castle romance, are giving way to a different species of aristocrat, the administrative "tsars" who are today rising to power in Washington and London.

The newly ascendant castle people are closer in their politics to the New Deal mandarins of the 1930s than they are to the financial wizards of the last two decades. But however egalitarian their rhetoric, the new castle elites, like their predecessors, will almost certainly conform to the proprieties of castledom. They will set themselves up in gaudy châteaus in prosperous suburbs, will send their children to private schools done up in revived Gothic, will not probably refuse invitations to appear in America's stud book, the *Social Register*. President Obama sends his daughters to Sidwell Friends, the most exclusive school in the capital, while Michelle Obama, who was rumored to look coldly on Britain on account of the empire, has become a pal of Queen Elizabeth. Not far from the palace, a host of Labour MPs, who in theory at any rate carry on the tradition of Jack Cade and Wat Tyler, have fudged their expense accounts in pursuit of chauffeur-driven cars, Farrow & Ball wallpaper, and insurance for antiques.

That those who rhetorically oppose the privileges of the castle should covet its little vanities is on the whole good. Such hypocrisy preserves the equilibrium of society. It is not pleasant to see empty beer cans lying on the roadside, but the prospect brightens when you find that many of them today are brands of *light* beer. The good old boy, unashamed to toss his empties out of the pickup, frets over his beer belly, with its low-caste bulge. He covertly aspires to the slenderness of the underfed, tofu-chewing upper crust. By a similar paradox the most hardened progressive will join a fancy club, sail his yacht in regattas, and even go out for polo, as Ted Kennedy did before old Joe shook his head. Humble or great, each of us cherishes his little theory of distinction. The stability of society depends on this weakness in our natures—on people who, however populist their sentiments, have a little place in their souls where Jay Gatsby spits in the democratic well from which he drinks.

For a complete overthrow of the aristocratic element in society would be a catastrophe. The castle was born in crude strength and was at first merely an instrument of power, and perhaps a kind of wooing plumage. But over time it became a civilizing force. Castle people refine life's pleasures. Evelyn Waugh's portrait of Hooper, the uncultured plebeian in *Brideshead Revisited*, is manifestly unfair; yet just about everyone who reads the book sympathizes not with Hooper the Everyman but with the Flyte-Marchmains, the aristocratic exceptions, the sensuous vanquishers of drabness. In vain did Edmund Wilson argue that "Waugh's snobbery, hitherto held in check by his satirical point of view, has here emerged shameless and rampant." Hooper is dull; the Marchmains are not.

Certainly there is evil in the castle, as there is in any tradition of human culture. But there is also much in it that is good. The arrogance never entirely disappeared. It came in time however to be tempered by ideals of courtesy and chivalry, of magnanimity and honor. The mind of the nobleman was opened, his sentiments refined and exalted: he learned, in the phrase of Aristotle, to "take possession of the beautiful."*

~~~

The problem is not that castle culture thrives in a democratic soil. It is that it has obtained a monopoly. Its growth, Dickens showed, has come at the expense of another, no less valuable plant. Dickens was struck by the way common folk in his day, whose heritage was the village and the market square, should so often set up in suburban plots as squires and knights errant. In *Great Expectations* he depicts Wemmick, a clerk, getting up his cottage as a castle, complete with turret, drawbridge, and Gothic windows. This castle culture was very different from that of the village in which Pip, the book's hero, grows up, with its civic and communal atmosphere. But communities like Pip's, Dickens saw, were fast disappearing. Where the communal cords have snapped, where the market square has become a strange and bewildering place, where one no longer knows or trusts one's neighbor, one will prefer, as Wemmick does, the security of the suburban keep. And not merely its physical security. In the vast impersonal metropolis, the exclusive house, the exclusive school, the exclusive club offer spiritual security, a means of distinguishing oneself from the crowd.

What was in danger of being lost, Dickens believed, was the common culture of the market square, a species of cultural organism that descends from the agora of the Greeks. If the castle has

---

*"The history of Greek culture," Werner Jaeger wrote in *Paideia*, "actually begins in the aristocratic world of early Greece, with the creation of a definite ideal of human perfection, an ideal towards which the élite of the race was constantly trained. . . . All later culture, however high an intellectual level it may reach, and however greatly it may change, still bears the imprint of its aristocratic origin. Culture is simply the aristocratic ideal of a nation, increasingly intellectualized."

from time out of mind been the seat of aristocratic culture, the marketplace was once the crucible of a no less vital culture of the common man. The standard was pretty high. If the aristocrats had the heroic poetry of their epic bards, the agora people had their tragic poets, whose dramas were initially staged in the Athenian agora and more recently in Shakespeare's Globe in Southwark. The Greek marketplace that inspired the *Oresteia* was succeeded by a Gothic one that midwifed Chartres and *The Divine Comedy*; the medieval marketplace, in turn, gave way to a Renaissance one, the agora-piazza of Michelangelo and Leonardo.

Unlike castle culture, agora culture is inclusive. No one is turned away. The Athenians called the late morning and noontide the time of the "full agora" (*agora plethousa*), a time when citizens are "in good agora form." The expression comes from the Greek verb *agorazein*, a word "not to be translated by one word of any other language," the historian Jacob Burckhardt wrote. "Dictionaries give *to traffic in the market place*, to *buy*, to *talk*, to *deliberate*, etc., but cannot reproduce the combination of business and conversation mingled with delightful loafing and standing around together" that the Greek word conveys. In the Gothic marketplace, Erwin Panofsky said, "the priest and the layman, the poet and the lawyer, the scholar and the artisan could get together on terms of near-equality." In the Renaissance piazza, Walter Pater wrote, artists, philosophers, and men of action "do not live in isolation, but breathe a common air, and catch light and heat from each other's thoughts."

Much of what is democratic in the culture of the West is closely connected to the life of these civic focal points. Go to the Place de la Maison Carrée in Nîmes, or the Piazza del Campo in Siena, or the Place de la Comédie in Montpellier, or to any of a thousand lesser forums, and you find, in the buildings, the statues, the paintings, a sort of civic jewel box. And this plastic art is but the remnant of a more comprehensive artistry: it is a skeleton which, in its prime, was clothed by music and poetry. The rhythms and harmonies of the plastic art of the agora were reinforced by those of its festivals and liturgies, its choral hymnody and dramatic verse, its folk ballads and folk dances. The urge to "roam the town and sing out carnival" brought the civic space to life, as did the poetic initiation rites of the grammar and Latin schools that had once an important place in the market square.

No civilization, even the most bovine, can entirely do without this cathartic machinery. Aristotle credited the poetry of the agora with forming the character of citizens and easing the psychic burdens of common life. The "instinct for harmony and rhythm," he said, "lies deep in our nature." "There seems to be in us a sort of affinity to musical modes and rhythms, which makes some philosophers say that the soul is a tuning, others, that it possesses tuning." Plato, in the *Laws*, maintains that the agora arts of rhythm and harmony are innate.*

Science may at last be vindicating the belief of the ancient philosophers that agora art touches what Frederick Turner calls our "neural lyre." Scientists suppose that gossip, rhythm, music, and

*"The gods, in their compassion for the hardships incident to our human lot, have appointed the cycle of their festivals to provide relief from this fatigue, besides giving us the Muses, their leader Apollo, and Dionysus to share these festivals with us and keep them right, with all the spiritual sustenance these deities bring to the feast." The capacity to enjoy rhythm and melody, Plato says is innate, and poetry constitutes our earliest education: "No young creature whatsoever, as we may fairly assert, can keep its body or its voice still; all are perpetually trying to make movements and noises. They leap and bound, they dance and frolic, as it were with glee, and again, they utter cries of all sorts. Now animals at large have no perception of order or disorder in these motions, no sense of what we call rhythm or melody. But in our case, the gods of whom we spoke as given companions in our revels have likewise given us the power to perceive and enjoy rhythm and melody. Through this they stir us to movements and become our choir leaders. . . . Now may we begin by taking this point as settled? May we assume that our earliest education comes through the Muses and Apollo, or not?" *Laws*, 653c–654a.

poetry—the germ of agora life—developed in primitive human groups to satisfy a human need. Over time these grooming techniques became ever more refined, subtle, and artistic. Gossip and storytelling, poetry and music, gave rise to explanatory myth, to dramatic narrative, to liturgical art, grooming techniques that were at once pastoral tools that knitted the flock together and educational devices that prepared the young for the obligations of civil life.

Consider, for example, the springtime songs of the primitive peasantry of old Greece. These songs had originally a magical intention: they were bound up with the desire of the farmers to propitiate the spirits that brought the earth to life again in the spring. Much of this springtime music was associated with Dionysus, the dying and reviving god who symbolized the annual decay of the vegetation and its subsequent regeneration. Civilization advanced, but the old songs did not die. In Athens civic choruses competed, in the spring, in the singing of *dithyramboi* (dithyrambs), choral lyrics sacred to Dionysus. Gilbert Murray, in an essay in Jane Ellen Harrison's 1912 book *Themis*, speculated that tragic drama—the greatest of the agora's grooming tools—evolved from annual rituals celebrating the advent of Dionysus and the coming of the spring.*

**Tragoidia means "goat song" (Dionysus often took the form of a goat); the dramatic contests at Athens were staged in March. To sponsor the drama was an act of civic virtue at Athens: the office of *choregos*, or chorus leader, was undertaken by a prominent citizen (at his own expense) as a civic liturgy—a *leitourgia* or "people-working." Scholars are divided on the question of whether Murray's theory of the birth of tragedy is plausible, but even those who dispute his thesis most sharply concede that tragedy is in some way or other a by-product of the old Dionysian music. A. W. Pickard-Cambridge, for example, argued that tragedy arose not from Dionysian ritual in the way Murray proposed but from other vestiges of the Dionysian tradition. Tragedy began, he said, when "village drama met and mingled in Athens with another outcome of the solemn side of Dionysiac ritual, the lyrics which were composed to music in the *tragikos tropos* invented by Arion." Long before Murray and his fellow Cambridge Ritualists elaborated their theories, Aristotle speculated that the germ of Athenian tragedy was to be found in the dithyramb. This Dionysian music, Aristotle said, gradually became civic music. The early tragic

If there is any truth in these speculations, it follows that such basic cultural tools as music, poetry, and storytelling lose something vital when they are detached from the comparatively small circles in which they originally developed. It follows, too, that the marketplace itself will suffer when such artistic and cultural work is no longer carried on there: it will no longer possess the grooming tools that bring a community together. It follows, finally, that smallness of scale is an essential element of civic culture. In the *Politics*, Aristotle said of the agora community of the *polis* that it ought not to extend beyond the range of the herald's—the town crier's—voice. The citizens must "know each other's characters." Dr. Robin Dunbar maintains that "there is a cognitive limit to the number of individuals with whom any one person can maintain stable relationships." This cognitive limit, according to Dunbar, is "a direct function" of the size of the neocortex. "Dunbar's Number" is commonly said to be 150, the "cognitive limit to the number of individuals with whom any one person can maintain stable social relationships . . . the kind of relationships that go with knowing who each person is and how each person relates socially to every other person."

⌒

The agora was the university of the common man: Socrates and Shakespeare are among its alumni. It was also the common man's club. Its art was his poetry. Theognis said of the common people, "They have no tradition." He was wrong. They have the agora, the

---

poets, he said, made "their characters speak the language of civic life." Even after the language changed, tragedy continued to serve a civic purpose. It purged the community, Aristotle said, of its pent-up emotions: "all are in a manner purged and their souls lightened and delighted." The primitive music had become the grooming instrument of a highly developed agora culture.

historic core and center of the civic life of Western communities and the reliquary of their ancient culture. But by the nineteenth century agora culture was in decline. When Nietzsche has Zarathustra revile the marketplace as the province of "solemn jesters" and "poisonous flies," it is evident how far the old market squares had fallen. The agora was not for Nietzsche a civilizing institution; the refinements of culture, he believed, came for the most part from the castle, and were the by-product of "a closed aristocracy."

The agora was deteriorating even as the democratic man its culture nurtured gained his victories over feudal aristocracy. The poetry that brought coherence to the market square—a poetry that had its place both in the market square's grammar school and in its dramatic and liturgical art—no longer animates the West's public spaces. It is not easy to say why this was so. The decay of the market square, like its growth, has been little studied; if we possessed a more extensive knowledge of its history we should know better the reasons for its fall. We should see how a rapid growth in population and a vast expansion of commerce overwhelmed the old centers. We should understand how the nation-state and its metropolitan elites created new aspirations; how young people fled the provincial market squares to pursue the glittering prizes of the capital; how the provinces, in the words of Tocqueville, came "under the thrall of the metropolis, which attracted to itself all that was most vital in the nation." We should have a better understanding of why the metropolitan marketplaces were overwhelmed and why the provincial ones were deserted: we should know how the tradition of the agora ceased to be a living one.

At the same time we would have a deeper insight into the changing allegiances of the traditional patrons of agora culture, the merchant princes who were once proud of their market squares but who abandoned them to ape the gentry. Toward the end of the

Renaissance, the man of business seems to have lost the faith of the stout old burghers from whom he was descended. He found it infra dig to live near his shop; he built himself a mansion in a fashionable aristocratic district.

The agora, if it was to survive as a civilizing force, needed to be reinvented. But rather than reinvent it, the social reformers believed they could do better. They saw that the great expansion of commerce and industry, if it had created much new wealth, had created much new disorder. But instead of refashioning agora institutions to meet the needs of an altered world, the reformers devised an entirely new system of remedial machinery, one in which the agora principle had no place. To social experts whose philosophy was shaped by Comte and his disciples, the civic artistry of the old marketplace seemed quaint and even irrational. The modern planners who condemned the old market squares failed to see, beneath a surface of heterogeneous activity, the unity of a civic whole. They were contemptuous of a space in which people ate and drank, shopped and prayed, worked and played in the shadow of a unifying art; such a forum was not, for them, an instance of coherent poetic form but "an amateurish combination of simple undifferentiated space and functions." The school of Phidias and Michelangelo gave way to that of Le Corbusier and Robert Moses.

The experts had still less patience with the artistic ornamentation of the old marketplaces, the carved entablatures, the sculpted pediments, the crafted portals. Already in the nineteenth century Nietzsche noted a growing insensitivity to the power of architecture's idioms, an indifference to the "symbolism" of its "lines and figures." We "no longer imbibe this kind of cultural mother's milk," he wrote, "from the first moment of our lives." Social planners and modernist designers condemned what they did not understand, much as a tone-deaf critic might question the value of the similes in

Vergil or Proust. "The evolution of culture," the Viennese architect Adolf Loos wrote, "is synonymous with the removal of ornament from utilitarian objects." Buildings were in Loos's view "utilitarian objects," and ornament a form of excrement. "A country's culture," he said, "can be assessed by the extent to which its lavatory walls are smeared. In the child this is a natural phenomenon. ... But what is natural to the Papuan and the child is a symptom of degeneracy in the modern adult."

There is another element of agora culture, now for the most part lost, which must also be taken into account. Anyone who studies the traditional marketplace will be struck by how much of its art was devoted to the image of the shepherd. The shepherd was for the agora poets the classic expression of the pastoral care of things. Good shepherds figure in the earliest agora myths and dramas as nurturers of the weak: Telephus and Lycastus, Oedipus and Aegisthus, Asclepius and Parthenopaeus, Daphnis and Chloe, are all cared for, as infants, by kindly herdsmen. The same human type figures in the West's last agora-inspired art, in the tales of the nineteenth-century novelists who composed the epitaph of the old marketplace. Monseigneur Myriel, the Bishop of Digne, in Hugo's *Les Misérables*, Alyosha in Dostoevsky's *The Brothers Karamazov*, Josiah Crawley in Trollope's *The Last Chronicle of Barset*, are the successors of the good shepherds who figure in the town-square art of Sophocles and Euripides. These pastoral characters, kindly and sensible, ministered to young people, as Alyosha ministers to Ilyusha in Dostoevsky's book, and they helped strayed souls, as Monseigneur Myriel helps Jean Valjean in Hugo's novel.

The town square became the focus of this pastoral light: the civic focal point was the crucible in which the community was forged and the inward culture of the citizen molded.* The pastoral art of grooming the flock became a metaphor for the civic art of grooming the citizen. Plato, in the *Statesman*, has one of his characters say that the art of the *polis* is the art of "rearing a particular kind of flock." If the herdsman is "the master of the music best suited to his herd," so the *polis* perfected the music best suited to the human flock that constitutes the community.

That agora culture fostered pastoral care was self-evident to Dante, who far more than his fellow Florentine, Machiavelli, was his city's most astute interpreter of the civic ideal. In *Paradiso*, Dante calls Florence a "fair sheepfold" (*bello ovile*). Before his exile he slept there like a lamb (*agnello*), for the city is a place where citizens (*cittadini*) live beautifully, in true community (*fida cittadinanza*). Quite as much as Plato, Dante saw at the heart of pastoral care a quality of inspired perception akin to that of the poet and the maker of music, whose "divine madness" is the source of his deeper apprehension. The shepherd is both archetypal pastor and archetypal poet: he apprehends the needs of his flock and tunes his song accordingly. The most virtuous citizens of the "sheepfold" of Florence, Dante says, possess the same gift of insight: in the *Vita Nuova* he speaks of those Florentines who possess the "*intelletto d'amore*"—the "understanding of love"—which makes

---

*The idea of culture itself has its origins in pastoral-agrarian notions of grooming and cultivation. The primary meaning of the Latin *cultura* is the husbandry of the soil: it came figuratively to mean *cultura animi*, the husbandry of the soul. The Italian *cultura*, the English and French *culture*, and the German *Kultur* all have to do with the bestowing, on the soul, of the same labor and attention that the farmer bestows on the soil and the shepherd on the flock. Hugo has fixed the identity of the cultivation of the soil and the culture of the spirit in his portrait of the Bishop of Digne: "he dug his garden or read and wrote, and for him both kinds of work bore the same name; both he called gardening. 'The spirit is a garden,' he said."

pastoral comprehension possible. The *"intelletto d'amore"* was originally cultivated in the castle: it was a kind of compassionate seeing, one which the troubadours associated with courtly love. Dante, the citizen of Florence and the inheritor of its agora traditions, made the castle romance of the trouvères democratic. He converted castle poetry into civic poetry (as well as into spiritual poetry, as St. Francis did also). In the *Vita Nuova*, Dante finds the *"intelletto d'amore"* not in aristocratic courts but in the streets of Florence, in which he delighted to wander.

The Bishop of Digne in *Les Misérables* is a civic-pastoral character in this old Western line: "the Bishop," Hugo writes, "overflowed with love." His crozier is really a shepherd's crook, and it is in his capacity as a shepherd that he welcomes Jean Valjean into his house in the town square. Dostoevsky was being melodramatic when he described, in *The Brothers Karamazov*, the pastoral perception that penetrates the soul of another at a glance. But he was getting at a truth, the truth that pastoral perception is deeper than that of ordinary sight. Agora people cultivated the pastoral ideal and inculcated it in their poetry, from practical and prudential as well as from moral and ethical considerations: the pastoral arts were for them a grooming tool, one that helped them gather in the civic flock. Dante, in Florence, was grateful to have been the object of this kind of compassionate perception. For it is bothersome to be seen wrongly or stupidly, just as it is annoying to be trivially judged. Thus George Orwell speaks of "the peculiar relief" that comes "from *being understood.*"

⌇

Already in the nineteenth century the pastoral sages began to seem archaic. So did the grooming tools they used. Liturgies were revised and degraded; the poetic initiation rites of the grammar school were abolished. The guardians of civic life looked to the social sciences to make up for the loss of this pastoral tuition. When Bismarck and Roosevelt established their social welfare regimes, their lieutenants drew on the new social techniques to minister to their post-agora charges, much as their successors would draw on the planning ideals of such artists as Le Corbusier. Whatever the virtues of these methods, they were easily abused. In *The Human Condition*, her 1958 defense of agora culture, Hannah Arendt argued that, as a result of the replacement of agora methods by those of sociologists, psychologists, and planners, man's civic capacities were being diminished; the new "behavioral sciences," she concluded, were subtly authoritarian. In socializing away man's "anti-social" tendencies, the masters of the new social mystique nurtured not independent citizens but passive conformists who would more easily acquiesce in the social-planning mandate.

As the agora shepherd gives way to the postagora social worker and guidance counselor, as the civic focal point ceases to transmit civic culture, the cruder democratic personality that Waugh associated with Hooper comes to the fore, and the castle once again becomes a threat to the community. For where agora culture has disintegrated, there is very little to prevent the castle elites from having their way. The safeguards of laws and constitutions are themselves scarcely more than parchment barriers where the mass of the people have not infused them with their own will and spirit. The citizen who, as a result of the paternal policy of the social state, is more acted upon than acting inclines to a fatal passivity. When people are accustomed to think that the problems their community confronts are so intricate that they can only be solved by social experts, when they come reflexively to suppose that the state will either improve their lot for then, or has placed so many legal and regulatory obstacles in the way of a reformation of their condition as to make their own exertions vain, they almost necessarily succumb to an apathy that saps the deeper vitals of the will. Kafka's *The Castle* is, among other things, a meditation on how a renovated castle culture, with all the resources of modern bureaucracy at the disposal of its "Control Authorities," humbles and demoralizes the common people of the village. The villagers come to worship the castle people much as the landlady in Kafka's book adores the castle functionary Klamm.

The social expert has, to be sure, learned to justify his castle power in accents softer than those of the castle people of old. In their book *Nudge*, Richard H. Thaler and Cass R. Sunstein of the University of Chicago "show that by knowing how people think, we [i.e., the social experts] can design choice environments that make it easier for people to choose what is best for themselves, their families, and their society." Professors Thaler and Sunstein do not propose to go so far as to push us into doing what is good for us: they propose only to nudge us, to manipulate our "choice environments." Stripped of its gentle phrasing, *Nudge* is a brief for a less free and ultimately a more stupid world.* It is an apology for enlarging the castle authority of the social expert and giving him new power to shape our "choice environments." It is still the school of Pavlov: Herr Klamm has merely learned to appear empathetic. The cover of *Nudge* is revealing: it shows a mommy elephant nudging a baby elephant. The citizen, in other words, is a child. The social expert, armed with the power of the state, is his benevolent mother.

*The authors of *Nudge* seem not to understand that the welfare of a people depends in part on their being free to choose badly. Advances in civilization are very often the result of people failing to choose what seemed (by the lights of the moment) to be good for them. Their errors led them fortuitously into a better path, or brought them so low that they were forced to find a new and previously unsuspected road. Probably most people, in reflecting on their own lives, can point to experiences when their mistakes proved fruitful. It is in many cases only by doing something really dumb that we are able to get to a place that is actually better. Should we gradually foreclose the freedom to be stupid, we will almost certainly end by being less intelligent.

~~~

"Do you understand, sir," Dostoevsky's Marmeladov asks Raskolnikov in *Crime and Punishment*, "do you understand what it means when you have absolutely nowhere to turn?" The tragic characters of nineteenth-century fiction—Dostoevsky's Marmeladov and his Snegiryov, George Eliot's Tertius Lydgate in *Middlemarch*, the harried fathers in Dickens—have nowhere to turn. As town-square culture waned the old civic-pastoral institutions deteriorated, or were without resources to address the problems created by the great expansion of commerce, industry, and population. Others fell victim to the social state. In France, under the ministry of Émile Combes at the beginning of the last century, the "religious orders, men's and women's alike, contemplative as well as teaching orders, were dissolved, all except five which were allowed to remain under strict state surveillance." Yet one has only to consider Hugo's Bishop of Digne, who was modeled on an actual prelate,* or Trollope's Josiah Crawley, the curate of Hogglestock, to see that the civic-pastoral impulse was not wholly dead. Even in the smoky depths of Lawrence's "The Bottoms," in the coal-hell of the English Midlands, the civic-pastoral system functioned. When Morel is too sick to work, the money nevertheless comes in. The family

> had seventeen shillings a week from the clubs, and every Friday Barker and the other butty put a portion of the stall's profits for Morel's wife. And the neighbours made broths, and gave eggs, and such invalids' trifles. If they had not helped her so generously in these times, Mrs. Morel would never have pulled through, without incurring debts that would have dragged her down.

---

*Monseigneur François-Melchior-Charles-Bienvenu de Miollis, the Bishop of Digne from 1806 to 1838.

The embers that were still glowing might yet have been fanned into flame. The social reformers, however, disdained the cumulative wisdom inherent in the institutions of the agora. It was in part because the reformers declined to avail themselves of this stock of moral know-how that the remedies they devised either failed to alleviate the distress they found around them, or did so only by creating problems no less vexatious than those they hoped to solve.

A recital of the mere outward facts of the social revolution that gave the coup de grâce to town-square culture cannot convey the deeper loss. The castle, like all institutions concerned with the maintenance of power, is at times a pompous and oppressive place; that is why Sir John Falstaff and Prince Hal go down to Eastcheap, to the agora world of the Boar's Head Tavern. The old marketplace was, finally, a playground. The historian Johan Huizinga, in his book *Homo Ludens: A Study of the Play Element in Culture*, observed that the nineteenth-century progressive philosophies, both liberal and socialist, which gave birth to the social imagination were "inimical to the play-factor" in life. Their bureaucracies crushed the spirit of flexibility and improvisation, of imagination and poetry, which is essential to the health of the agora.* "Our point of departure," Huizinga wrote,

> must be the conception of an almost child-like play sense expressing itself in various play-forms, some serious, some playful, but

*Compare John Stuart Mill: "spontaneity forms no part of the ideal of the majority of moral and social reformers, but is rather looked on with jealousy, as a troublesome and perhaps rebellious obstruction to the general acceptance of what these reformers, in their own judgment, think would be best for mankind."

all rooted in ritual and productive culture by allowing the innate human need of rhythm, harmony, change, alternation, contrast and climax, etc., to unfold in full richness.

Much of what Huizinga called the "play-element" in culture was once concentrated in the life of the marketplace. Quite as much as his "play-sphere," the agora is the "sphere of the festival," of the "sacred performance and the festal contest," of "liturgical and the-atrical representations," of dancing and rhythmical movement. It is the place where young people leap and know the "choral joy" that Electra, in her sorrow, could not know.

> I am too sad, I cannot stand
> in choral joy with the maidens
> and beat the time with my whirling foot.

Nothing is so dispiriting in Lawrence's agora-less coal towns as this absence of beautiful play. Lady Chatterley, driving out in her chauffeured car from Wragby, finds in the black slate roofs and the mud black with coal dust the "utter negation of natural beauty, the utter negation of the gladness of life, the utter absence of the instinct for shapely beauty which every bird and beast has, the utter death of the human intuitive faculty." "The vast plumes of smoke and vapour rose from the new works up above, and this was now Stacks Gate: no chapel, no pubs, even no shops." It is not merely that the institutions of the market square—the pubs, the shops, the churches—have failed, so too has the music:

> Standard Five* girls were having a singing lesson, just finishing
> the la-me-do-la exercises and beginning a "sweet children's song."

---

*"Standard Five" refers to one of the standards promulgated by the Elementary Education Act of 1870. It was roughly comparable to a grade in an American school.

Anything more unlike song, spontaneous song, would be impossible to imagine: a strange bawling yell that followed the outlines of a tune. It was not like savages: savages have subtle rhythms. . . . It was like nothing on earth, and it was called singing.

Huizinga believed that "the more highly organized forms of society" inevitably "lose touch with play." Max Weber spoke of the peculiarly modern form of darkness that came with the "disenchantment" or "demagification" of the world. Whatever the cause of this failure of light, it is now pretty clear that the remedies of the social reformers have only deepened the darkness.

Ronald Reagan and Margaret Thatcher restored the marketplace as an economic ideal. They did not revive its historic culture. Liberals have done no better. Although he exalts community, the modern liberal is skeptical of the agora; he is suspicious of association that lessens the individual's reliance on the state. In his 1953 book *The Quest for Community*, Robert Nisbet showed how "intermediate associations" such as families, neighborhoods, and places of worship—prime constituents of agora culture—have been gradually undermined by progressive statism and the intrusive regulatory machinery of ever nosier elites. No less crippling are the liberal's artistic inclinations. Being a child of Rousseau, the liberal believes, deep down, that progress can be made only after the old artistic forms—the corrupt and archaic poetries of the past—are overthrown. He wants to make a community from moral and aesthetic scratch.

Can conservatives do better? The only hope of regeneration, it seems to me, lies in experiments in civic artistry undertaken by philanthropists eager to refurbish the culture of the marketplace. One thinks of Poundbury, the little city, rich in civic focal points, that the Prince of Wales commissioned the architect Léon Krier to build in Dorset. Poundbury has attracted a good deal of attention, and it and the model towns of such "new urbanist" architects as Andrés Duany and Elizabeth Plater-Zyberk might conceivably inspire a broader civic movement, much as Thoreau's experiment at Walden Pond inspired the environmental movement. Most people today recognize the importance of conserving natural resources, though naturally they differ concerning the means. A time may come when people will insist as passionately on the necessity of conserving cultural resources.

They must, however, first be persuaded that the agora can give them satisfactions they now associate with the castle. At present the castle has a monopoly of culture: it is the only instance of a higher manner, a more generous standard of cultivation, conveniently to hand. From the fake Gothic parapets of Princeton to the fake castellated towers of Yale, from the prep school to the summer resort, castle spirit monopolizes much of what is attractive in the culture. It has become the main source not merely of tone and breeding but of that urbanity that comes with large perspectives and knowledge of the world. Liberal arts colleges come to resemble finishing schools, imparting just enough of the old aristocratic culture to make their charges clubbable. Newcomers to America find an ideal in the castle fantasy of Gatsby: his castle tragedy becomes their castle dream. Fourteen-year-old Jinzhao Wang, "who immigrated two years ago from China, has never seen anything like the huge mansions that loomed over Long Island Sound in glamorous 1920s New York," Sara Rimer writes in the *New York Times*. "But F. Scott Fitzgerald's 1925 novel, *The Great Gatsby*, with its themes of possibility and aspiration, speaks to her." The pursuit of the American dream comes to be identical with the pursuit of the American castle—so much so that even those who have no interest themselves in the character-molding conventions of castle culture wonder whether they will not smooth a path for their children.

Yet it is precisely because the castle has become, in many parts of the West, not only the primary but even the sole path to culture that it has become an ever less reliable one. Cultural enterprises quite as much as economic ones suffer from the lack of competition. With its victories over the town square, the castle has grown ever more flabby and superficial, the mere gross multiplication of money and power. It was once the boast of the castle person that through his culture he could "beget in the beautiful." He is now content with the charmless and the second rate. From Montaigne in his tower to the private equity man in his McMansion is a steep descent.

Flaubert's diagnosis of the problem is as cogent as ever. His homage, in *Salammbô*, to the agora culture of Carthage, with its domes, its obelisks, its voluptuous mysticisms, is overdrawn, but for all that, the city is alive in a way that Yonville-l'Abbaye, the marketplace in *Madame Bovary*, is not. We succumb to castle fever, Flaubert suggests, in part because the alternative agora tradition is dead, and we cannot bring ourselves to believe that it ever lived. "Civic" is for us a synonym for "dull." The "mirth, high cheer, and wine" of life seem to us to be concentrated in the castle. Emma Bovary dreams of Scottish lords and Parisian duchesses. She falls in love with a landowner whose hair curls like Lord Byron's. Yet Emma is not a fool. "Madame Bovary," Flaubert said, "*c'est moi.*" Both he and his most famous character would have fared better, he implied, had there been in their time another path to culture and pleasure.

It is just possible that experiments in the Poundbury line will convince people that a renovated agora can be the other path. Such experiments would, to be sure, have to go beyond Poundbury in recreating not merely a style of civic design but the pastoral grooming culture Aristotle thought essential to civic life. Conservatives ought in principle to be sympathetic to such a quest. There is in the autonomous character, commercial vibrancy, and Burkean artistry of the traditional marketplace a good deal to attract them.

To infuse new life into the agora conservatives will need to enlist the energies of people they long ago stopped talking to, but who will be necessary to any effort to revive the poetic-grooming side of the market square. There is a certain kind of person who, like Jude Fawley in Hardy's *Jude the Obscure*, fulfills his nature in the adornment of a community. If the agora has since degenerated, as a species of cultural organism, into the cruder plasma of the shopping mall, the food court, and the community center, it has done so in part because of the misallocation of creative power that has occurred as a result of the decline of agora culture. The civic ingenue today cannot chisel stone for the agora, as Jude Fawley does, or carve wood for it, as Lawrence's Will Brangwen does. He must, like one of Balzac's heroes, make his fortune in the metropolis and push his way in those overcrowded forums. Much of the talent and artistry that, rightly directed, could be the ornament of a smaller space is now destined to expire fruitlessly in an urban garret. Those spirits which, in another age, might have molded the saints that smile in the niches of the Gothic cathedral, or fashioned the figures that grace the pediments of the classical temple, have little choice today but to join the artistic rabble of Tribeca.* As a

---

*The efforts of the social state to solve the problem have merely exacerbated it. The National Endowment for the Arts, a symbol of the cultural aspirations of the social state, has failed to address the underlying crisis of art, the inability of communities

result, art has ceased to be a characteristic feature of the local market square. It is either a thing shut up in a mausoleum (museums being a symptom, not of cultural vitality but of cultural morbidity) or else it is the costly plaything of the metropolitan tycoon.

When the civic focal point thrived, artists had a place in the community and a means of getting bread. They carved the stone, frescoed the walls, painted the ceilings, gilded the domes, composed the masques and harlequinades. But the agora in which they might once have become absorbed is gone. They are today rebels without a cause, misfits who dine off grant money and alienation from the marketplace, and create art that is generally faith-

---

today to produce the kinds of art that the agora people of the West once produced spontaneously, joyously, almost as a matter of course. The NEA, in "bringing," as it professes to do, "great art to all fifty states, including rural areas, inner cities, and military bases," exports art from places where it is made to places where it is not made. This is a palliative. The NEA's import-export approach to the arts derives from its flawed Romantic model of creativity. In the Romantic model the artist is an alienated figure. He lives in a kind of artistic industrial zone, typically a bohemian neighborhood in a great city, and he mingles, for the most part, with other artists. He is not part of a larger community in the way Aeschylus and Sophocles were part of Athens or in the way Dante was part of Florence; instead the artist has, ever since the downfall of agora culture, been estranged from civic life, his existence a kind of protest. By trucking artists from their lofts in Tribeca or their garrets in San Francisco—a disproportionate amount of federal arts money goes to California and New York—into "rural areas, inner cities, and military bases," the NEA perpetuates the Romantic stereotype of the artist as alien, a circus performer who has only the slenderest relation to the nonartistic natives. It is of course to be expected that the artist will in some measure be a misfit: his weirdness is a source of his creativity. But when the artist lives not in an artistic ghetto but in an ordinary community, he finds a greater fund of material and inspiration: he need not feed on his own disaffection. The spectacle of the petulant poet or painter dramatizing his revolt against the world through a kind of idolatry of the grotesque no longer has the power it did when Byron composed *Manfred*. The bohemian pose of alienation is now used by entrepreneurs to sell coffee to lawyers. Nor is it the merchant class alone that has bought, tamed, and trivialized Romanticism's tropes of decadence and revolt. It is all but impossible to take seriously an art of rebellion crafted by pensioners of the state. The revival of the civic focal point—the recovery of a Parthenon-Chartres model of agora creativity—would not only encourage the kind of art that makes federal subsidies unnecessary, it would do something to relieve the creative frustration that is so remarkable a feature of modern life.

ful to the solipsistic bleakness of their situation. A revived agora could renew their *virtù* and give them the transfiguring work they need. Successful civic movements begin not in the social tinkering of castle people but in the mobilization of creative personality. Athens, Venice, and Florence exist because the requisite passions were there employed in the refinement of the civic focal point.

Plato said that we are strung together by God "on a thread of song and dance." Life "must be lived as play, playing certain games, making sacrifices, singing and dancing: then will a man be able to gain heaven's grace, and defend himself against his enemies, and win the contest."* Modern science has begun to illuminate the insight, yet it seems still, to the modern mind, a little fuzzy and fantastic—a primitivist whimsy, of a piece with the quaintness the sentimental tourist is apt to discover in less-developed regions.† The emphasis the agora prophets lay on the virtues of poetry, too, is likely to be suspect in modern eyes, poetry having become for us a vessel into which we pour a quantity of superfine but essentially vague and inchoate aspiration.

---

*"I say that a man must be serious with the serious. God alone is worthy of supreme seriousness, but man is God's plaything, and that is the best part of him. All of us, then, men and women alike, must fall in with our role and spend our life in making our *play* as perfect as possible." Plato, *Laws*, 803c–e.

†Compare D. H. Lawrence on the Bavarian highlander: "Yet they are convivial, they are almost the only race with the souls of artists. Still they act the mystery plays with instinctive fulness of interpretation, they sing strangely in the mountain fields, they love make-belief and mummery, their processions and religious festivals are profoundly impressive, solemn, and rapt. It is a race that moves on the poles of mystic sensual delight. Every gesture is a gesture from the blood, every expression is a symbolic utterance. For learning there is sensuous experience, for thought there is myth and drama and dancing and singing."

In the nineteenth century the agora got more credit: perceptive spirits were in those days still near enough to the old market square to feel the truth of Plato's words, and yet far enough away from it to be conscious of the loss. The difficulty with the nineteenth-century apostles of the agora is that each of them pleaded for a mere piece of the tradition, a particular heirloom. Ruskin pled the masonry, Pater the masques and the plastic arts, Scott the balladry and minstrelsy, Newman the ritual and liturgy, Morris the craftsmanship. Fustel de Coulanges described the civic imagination of the Greek cities, out of which rose the classical temple; Viollet le Duc analyzed the civic spirit of the medieval communes, which created the Gothic cathedral. If none of these sages saw the agora steadily or saw it whole, each showed how a certain facet of it was faithful to the complexities of the human heart and to the wants of particular communities.

Valuable as the nineteenth-century apostolate was, it bore little fruit, and some of that rotten, like Revived Gothic. Twentieth-century thinkers were less successful still. The twentieth century was in many respects a castle age. The crucial philosophical development of the period was the marriage of Marx and Nietzsche—the will to the castle, disguised as a struggle to recover the vitality of the heroic man or the sociability of the common man. Georges Sorel and Carl Schmitt, Charles Maurras and Maurice Barrès, Lenin and Mussolini, openly advocated force and violence. George Bernard Shaw and Jean-Paul Sartre worshiped power. A succession of strongmen and warlords emerged: Stalin and Hitler, Mao and Pot, Franco and Pinochet, Castro and Kim. The Bolsheviks attained their castle end: they moved into the Kremlin. Hitler built himself a vast keep in the Wilhelmstrasse. The castle people of the nineteenth century had been hedged by law and custom, were gentle in aspiration if not always in fact; the twentieth-century castle, with its barbed wire and reinforced concrete, its bunkers and its dungeons, was a cruder assertion of *auctoritas*.* Constitutional states on the English model fared better than most of the rest of the world, and in America anti-monopoly legislation ended the reign of the robber baron. But no sooner was the Gilded Age castle reduced than new structures of castle authority began to be built up bureaucratically, under altruistic pretenses.

The great expansion of material power that has taken place since the eighteenth century disrupted older patterns of life in the West: the remedies that were devised to repair the breaches proved in many cases more damaging than the initial ruptures. What is needed today is a recovery of the wisdom that was lost during the upheaval.† The overlooking of the agora principle in human affairs has been one of the signal failures of the cultural philosophy, both liberal and conservative, of the last hundred years. Liberals have

*The power of the old castle elites was hedged, too, by religious sentiment, which acted as a real, though of course far from perfect, restraint on their authority. Modern castle elites have largely done away with this check by marginalizing religious sentiment: they have sought, in the words of the Roman Catholic scholar George Weigel, "to exclude transcendent reference points from cultural, social, and political life." The laicism of the new castle people has played a part in their suppression of traditional marketplace culture, for the agora, in its prime, was consecrated not merely to the civic virtues, and to an ideal of individual excellence, but also to the transcendent and the divine.

†The conservative will always feel an alarm when he sees an ancient tradition of culture, one that has been evolved slowly over the course of many centuries, done away with abruptly, in a comparatively short period of time. Absent a convincing showing that a tradition is inherently vicious, or that it has become so over time, the tradition has, in the conservative's eyes, a prescriptive right to toleration, indeed to veneration. Its very endurance is a presumptive evidence of its value and suggests that while it flourished it did more good than we can perhaps rationally account for. The tradition might need to be reformed; it should not be abolished. Its hasty destruction is likely to involve us in a host of deleterious consequences we cannot possibly foresee. A tradition is the repository of the wisdom of ages, and while this wisdom is by no means infallible, neither is the much smaller stock of wisdom we generally possess in ourselves at any given moment in time. "When ancient opinions and rules of life are taken away," Burke says, "the loss cannot possibly be estimated. From that moment we have no compass to govern us; nor can we know distinctly to what port we steer."

yet to realize that something has gone wrong: they continue to hawk a watered-down social wine. The conservatives who have most effectually deplored the progress of the social imagination have themselves failed to do justice to the thing it helped destroy. Ortega y Gasset, Giuseppe Lampedusa, and Evelyn Waugh found refuge in a nostalgia for the old castle: they had little interest in a renovation of the old market square. Faulkner too: he deplored the ascendancy of the plebeian Snopeses (his anagrammatic *peones*) over the aristocratic Sartorises (*aristoi*). T. S. Eliot made a plea for royalism in politics (though he also sought to revive the poetic drama, the touchstone of agora art). Other conservatives have either settled for mere opposition to the social trends or have, like Nixon, actually embraced them.

One of the tasks of the conservative today, it seems to me, must be to try to revive the habits of civic-pastoral culture. If the conservative does not do this, it is not likely that anyone else will. If there is no renewal of the older culture, it is quite possible that our modern democratic civilization will realize Tocqueville's prophecy of the last democratic man, shut up "in the solitude of his own heart." In his novel *Inconnus dans la Maison*, Georges Simenon describes the return to the market square of the lawyer-recluse Hector Loursat. Loursat's family had long been involved in the civic life of Moulins, in Bourbonnais; his grandfather had been mayor of the town, and Loursat himself was an advocate of distinction. But after suffering hurt and humiliation, he turned his back on the community and withdrew to his library and his burgundy. In the end, however, he is drawn back: he leaves his house and goes "running all over" the town. Moulins, he discovers, is no mean city. There are

people, sounds, smells, stores, lights, feelings, a swarming world that had no relation to classical tragedies [actually it probably

did, but that is not the point], a world that was full of those mysterious and generally trivial details you don't find in books, a gust
of wind in a dirty back alley, a loiterer on a street corner, a store
still open, God knows why, long after all the others had closed,
an impatient, highly strung boy waiting all keyed up outside a
watchmaker's for the friend who was going to lead him into a new
and unknown future.

It is an appealing story. Might it yet become the expression of a
living truth?

Acknowledgments

EARLIER VERSIONS of most of the writings in this book appeared either in *City Journal* or in *National Review*. I am grateful to the editors of those periodicals—Paul Beston, Steven Malanga, Karen Marston, Ben Plotinsky, and Sol Stern at *City Journal*; Linda Bridges, Rick Brookhiser, Edward John Craig, Kathryn Jean Lopez, Rich Lowry, Jay Nordlinger, Michael Potemra, Fred Schwarz, Jason Steorts, and Robert VerBruggen at *National Review*—for their help, encouragement, and support. I am grateful too to Michael Carlisle for his advice and counsel.

I owe special debts of gratitude to Brian Anderson, the present editor of *City Journal*, to Myron Magnet, the former editor, and to Ivan Dee for their help in connection with this book. I must finally thank the members of my family who have been so generous to me and so indulgent of my failings.

M. K. B.

South Salem, New York
May 2010

Index

A NOTE ON THE AUTHOR

Michael Knox Beran is a lawyer and writer. His previous books include *Forge of Empires 1861–1871* and *The Last Patrician*, a *New York Times* Notable Book of 1998. His writing has appeared in a number of publications, among them the *National Review*, the *New Yorker*, the *Wall Street Journal*, and *City Journal*, where he is a contributing editor. Born in Dallas, Texas, he was educated at Columbia, Cambridge, and Yale Law School. He lives in Westchester County, New York, with his wife and daughters.